SECOND EDITION

CANADIAN
Business & Society

The Business, Government and Civil Society Mosaic

David H. J. Delcorde

Kendall Hunt
publishing company

Cover image © Shutterstock, Inc.

Kendall Hunt
publishing company

www.kendallhunt.com
Send all inquiries to:
4050 Westmark Drive
Dubuque, IA 52004-1840

To my mother Donna Fraser, and the memory of my father Harold – with gratitude for everything, and appreciating with age!

CONTENTS

Chapter 2

Chapter 3

Chapter 4

Chapter 5

Chapter 6

Chapter 7

Chapter 8

Chapter 9

FIGURES

TABLES

ABOUT THE AUTHOR

Dr. David H.J. Delcorde is the Director of Undergraduate Programs at the Telfer School of Management, University of Ottawa, Ottawa, Canada, where he has taught courses in business and management since 2002. He has also enjoyed a rewarding career in the Canadian federal public service spanning over thirty years, and retiring as a member of the executive cadre. And is now a farmer □

Dr. Delcorde completed his undergraduate degree in business administration at the University of Ottawa; a Master of Business Administration from Heriot-Watt University, Edinburgh, Scotland; a Master of Arts in International Business Management from the University of Westminster in London, England; and, a Doctorate in Philosophy from London South Bank University, London, England. He is a member of the Chartered College of Teaching, London, England.

PREFACE

With the growing complexity of decision-making and the interdependence of business, political, and social issues, effective management requires not only an understanding of processes inside a company, but also of how business, government, and civil society interact. Many treatments of this subject are overly generalized, or conversely take a narrowly focused approach. Some authors focus on selected stakeholders, others on particular tracts of interest such as, for example, ethics. Many include a seemingly endless treatment of a barrage of government acts and legislation in their attempt to contextualize "business" in "society." While all of these are meritorious approaches to exploring "business and society" there is a need to present a more fulsome but yet focused view that is more closely representative of the organizations and their interactions occurring in the macro-environment in which future business managers will be required to operate in creating a sustainable competitive advantage for their organizations.

This book is organized on the following logic: that to understand business and society in Canada it is necessary first to partition the Canadian domestic macro- environment into recognizable segments, and then to develop an understanding of what is included in each segment, key issues peculiar to the segment, how each segment influences and is influenced by the other segments, and emerging issues that influence all three segments.

Such an approach more accurately portrays the complexity of the macro-environment. At the same time, it provides the opportunity to control and focus the treatment of this very complex terrain. The ultimate goal is for the future manager to develop an understanding and appreciation of each segment in the Canadian business macro-environment - its unique characteristics, challenges, and interactions – the knowledge of which is essential for success in today's businesses.

As may be appreciated the subject of business, government, and civil society is complex and the landscape is in a condition of perpetual change. The purpose of this book is not to provide a "womb-to-tomb" treatment of every possible detail concerning each of these three segments or every possible iteration of their interactions; rather the intent is to give the business and/or management student a general appreciation of the complexity of this terrain but with sufficient detail to allow for a greater understanding of the segments. Some of the key issues found in each segment, the complexity of inter-segment interactions, and how some key issues transverse all three segments will be discussed. It is hoped that this will provoke a greater appreciation of the complexity of management and inspire business students to become better managers in whatever segment they choose.

No work is the product of one individual. In this I am particularly indebted to the early work on governance in Canada by the late Professor Gilles Paquet and Professor Jeffrey Roy who established and operated the then - Centre on Governance at the University of Ottawa that was the inspiration for this book – in particular the depiction of Canada as the co-evolution of "economy, polity and society" based on the *Boulding Triangle*, introduced by economist Kenneth Boulding in his 1970 publication *A Primer on Social Dynamics* (New York: The Free Press). This book will therefore present the Canadian domestic macro- environment as consisting of three key segments: business, government, and civil society, patterned after the *Boulding Triangle*. In addition to exploring each key segment the book will consider key issues unique to each segment as well as how each segment interacts, influences, and is influenced by the others and how each segment is affected by key cross-segment issues such as the knowledge-based economy, globalization, corporate governance, changes in governance paradigms, and ethics.

I am also grateful for the work of several individuals who reviewed portions of this work and/or provided a practitioner's perspective on the subject matter;

Mr. Jason Flick, CEO of Youi.TV

The Hon. Joe Jordan, P.C., Senior Associate, BlueSky Strategies

Lori MacDonald, Associate Deputy Minister, Immigration, Refugees and Citizenship Canada

Heather Norris, President & CEO of the Ottawa Network for Education

Mr. Paul J. DeVillers, LL.B., P.C. former federal Cabinet Minister

CHAPTER 1

An Introduction to the Canadian Domestic Macro-environment: A Business, Government and Civil Society Perspective

wk1003mike/Shutterstock.com

Business, Government & Civil Society in the News

Civil Society Leaders Applaud Government Commitment to Establish Social Finance Fund (November 22, 2018)[1]

In November 2018, the article entitled "Civil Society Leaders Applaud Government Commitment to Establish Social Finance Fund" addressed the federal govern-

1. "Civil Society Leaders Applaud Government Commitment to Establish Social Finance Fund," McConnel Foundation, Cision, published November 22, 2018, https://www.newswire.ca/news-releases/civil-society-leaders-applaud-government-commitment-to-establish-social-finance-fund-701093632.html, accessed June 18, 2019.

ment's announcement to establish a $755 million *Social Finance Fund* as recommended by the Social Innovation and Social Finance Strategy Co-Creation Steering Group. The Fund is the first of several recommendations that the government has committed to implementing that align the public sector and civil society around inclusive growth.   Charitable organizations such as Imagine Canada, MaRS Discovery District, the McConnell Foundation and the United Way Centraide Canada welcomed the announcement with enthusiasm.

The Social Finance Fund is expected to improve social and environmental outcomes for communities and individuals nationally through:

- New social finance models to accelerate construction of housing units
- Socially-motivated investors to finance Indigenous social entrepreneurs who will in turn address challenges like food insecurity and clean energy generation
- Increased investment by social organizations to create more businesses and social enterprises that will in turn provide jobs and training to persons with disabilities.

The Fund will encourage the formation of networks of relationships to enable people to work together to make their communities more sustainable and inclusive places through social innovation and social finance. Social finance refers to the practice of investing in endeavours expected to have an impact on the social or environmental environment. The article notes that over 3 million Canadian families live in poverty; 570,000 Canadians do not have reliable access to safe drinking water; and total greenhouse gas emissions were only reduced by 2 percent between 2005 and 2015. Addressing these issues is expected to drive economic growth for all Canadians.

The full article can be reviewed at https://www.newswire.ca/news-releases/civil-society-leaders-applaud-government-commitment-to-establish-social-finance-fund-701093632.html.   The full report "Inclusive Innovation" including all twelve recommendations can be viewed at the Government of Canada's webpage.

The introductory news article provides an excellent foundation from which to launch the subject of business, government and civil society, and their interaction. The introductory business student is intuitively focussed on business's role in operating efficiently and effectively, in order to maximize profits. What becomes rapidly apparent is that defining efficiency and effectiveness involves many dimensions, one of which is coming to terms with how business efficiency and effectiveness depends, among other things, on the extent of influence government and civil society can exert, either directly or indirectly on business outcomes.

In reviewing the news article above, consider the following key players and some thought-provoking perspectives:

1. *The Federal Government* – established a $755 million Social Finance Fund. What was the source of the money? In general, tax payers – whether individual or corporate. Were *all* taxpayers consulted on the use of this money? No; not only would this be impractical, it is also not necessary: voters elect a government that is representative and voter support for a government at election time would imply concurrence with the government platform that provides information, inter-alia, on its policy, program and fiscal priorities. Were key constituents consulted? Absolutely. These key constituents would have included representatives of business and civil society. What might motivate a government to invest taxpayers money in such an initiative? Apart from 'vote yield' a government could be motivated to provide a foundation from which to catalyze strategical alliances that would lead to innovation by melding the important knowledge contributions of civil society organizations with business acumen, while simultaneously strengthening civil society and social capital output. Innovation is critical to continued economic prosperity and requires an intellectual contribution from all of society's stakeholders. Readers should note that this brief perspective is simplified for the purpose of introducing the subject matter; there are many more complex dimensions that will be considered later in this book.

2. *Civil Society* (referred to in the news article as the *charitable sector*) – has a number of key roles including, but not limited to advocating for public rights and representing the rights and concerns of smaller and in some cases, disenfranchised stakeholders; making the actions of government and business transparent; and preserving and enhancing social relations with the overall goal of making society a better place, with a higher quality of life for all its members. Over the years, a persistent challenge to civil society organizations is funding. At the same time, civil society collectively represents a wealth of intellectual capital, ideas and capacity that could be harnessed to further government policy. Civil society yields considerable influence over public opinion that in turn can affect the public's perception of the integrity of government and business.

3. *Business* – how does business benefit from the establishment of such a fund? A starting point could be society's expectation of business in general. A strong business segment is profitable, ethical, and socially responsible. To be profitable a business must establish a sustainable competitive advantage that requires continuous innovation, learning and adapting that is only possible through synergistic relationships with other businesses, government, and civil society organizations. Profitability must derive from efficient, effective, and ethical business operations. Both the public and investors expect business to be socially responsible and to be committed to sustainability actions. Working with civil society and becoming involved with the Social Finance Fund could result in new forms of innovation and additional profits, some of which could

CHAPTER 1: An Introduction to the Canadian Domestic Macro-environment: A Business, Government and Civil Society Perspective

3

be reinvested in the fund itself or in spin-offs that benefit both government and civil society that in turn, demonstrates social responsibility.

The observations above represent the tip of the iceberg in a very complex mosaic of actions and reactions on many levels. But one thing should be made very clear: the best possible outcome for all stakeholders depends on an understanding and appreciation of how government, business and civil society work, as well as how they influence each other. Within each segment are different realities: motivations, agenda, timelines, power, influence, and the list goes on. Realizing that any one segment cannot operate in complete isolation of the other two, an understanding of each segment is critical for success.

Introduction

This textbook considers Canadian business in its social context. More than ever before developing a sustainable competitive advantage requires that future managers understand that success depends on strategic partnerships and collaboration as it is not possible to "go it alone". As well, the partnerships required are not limited to partnerships with other businesses, but rather can take the form of partnerships with government as well as with organizations and individuals. To ensure mutually beneficial and strategic partnerships, managers must understand the entire expanse of the Canadian domestic macro- environment.

Over the years several writers have proposed models through which to explain the interactions of the key segments of the macro-environment; however, the majority tends to focus on business and government. While business and government are important segments, in recent times a third segment has arguably achieved equal stature – that segment is "civil society". The concept of "civil society" provokes considerable debate among academics and practitioners alike in terms of what is included in this segment. However, most agree that charities, volunteer groups and other forms of civic engagement are appropriately considered to be eligible for inclusion in this "third" segment.

In recent years business and government are facing increasingly complex issues that can be resolved only with the assistance and important input of a "third party" that is closest to many key stakeholders. What type of complex issues?

Consider just a few:

- Climate change, global warming, greenhouse gas emissions
- Affordable housing
- Disenfranchised stakeholders

- Increased labour costs and increased offshore sourcing
- Governance failures that adversely affect society
- Sustainability
- Society's expectations for ethical business and government, and measurable social responsibility actions
- Intellectual property rights
- Regulation and monitoring of communications – including social media

These issues provoke important questions for which no simple answer exists:

- Who in society has the greatest influence?
- Who has the right to dictate how business should operate?
- What exactly is ethical behavior?
- What exactly is social responsibility? What is the correct amount?
- How do globalization, multiculturalism, and advances in information and communication technologies - including social media - impact business, government, and their relationships

Civil society can provide important insight into these and other complex challenges to enable business and government to make the best decisions, while at the same time forcing transparency of the decisions.

In recent times expectations of business are driven by a more informed, affluent, 'connected' and litigious society. Information and communications technology advances, most recently social media, have placed both business and government under the public microscope and Canadians expect business and government to deal with civil society issues. As well, both business and government frequently need interaction with the third segment to develop closer contact with stakeholders, to broker new forms of collaborative partnerships, and as a means through which to provide alternative service delivery mechanisms.

It is therefore insufficient to view the Canadian domestic macro-environment only through the lens of the interaction between government and business. The third segment, civil society, provides significant contributions and continues to demonstrate the greatest relative increase in its ability to influence the other two segments. Civil society is often viewed as the "neutral broker" between government and business, engendering greater trust from the public. A decision by government or an action by business endorsed by civil society would often be perceived as appropriate.

In order to gain a full and balanced appreciation of the Canadian domestic macro- environment as the total of the activities and efforts of all key representatives, a modification of Kenneth Boulding's triangle can be applied.

CHAPTER 1: An Introduction to the Canadian Domestic Macro-environment: A Business, Government and Civil Society Perspective

5

The Boulding Triangle – An Approach to Representing the Three Segments of the Canadian Domestic Macro-environment

In 1970 Kenneth Boulding proposed the simple concept of a triangle to which a minor modification can be made to depict three segments of a country's domestic macro- environment.[2]

FIGURE 1

Modified Boulding Triangle

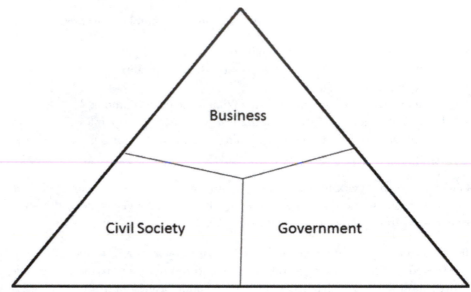

Source: David H.J. Delcorde

This concept portrays three generic ensembles of organizations and institutions, each with its own unique characteristics, membership, challenges, opportunities, and contributions and each holding equal importance to Canada and Canadians. In this regard the contextual description of what is included in each segment is as follows:

> The *business segment* generally includes all forms of "for profit" business ownership in Canada, including corporations, franchises, partnerships, and sole proprietorships.

> The *government segment* generally includes all levels of government in Canada, federal, provincial, and municipal.

2. Kenneth E. Boulding, *A Primer on Social Dynamics* (New York: Basic Books, 1970).

The *civil society segment* generally includes organized and unorganized social networks, non-government organizations (NGOs), volunteer organizations, charities, and philanthropic efforts.

The operation of each segment features different rules, arrangements, or mechanisms of coordination, or *sorting* mechanisms. For the business segment these sorting mechanisms take the form of supply and demand or *quid pro quo exchange*. For the government segment *coercion* and *redistribution* are the prevalent mechanisms, and for civil society these mechanisms include *solidarity, reciprocity, collaboration,* and *trust.*[3] The purest form of a sorting mechanism occurs at the apex of a segment.

It can be seen therefore that the sorting mechanisms in each segment are very different and based on different principles: business where supply and demand forces and price mechanism are the norms; government where coercion and redistribution represent the rules; and civil society where cooperation, reciprocity and solidarity are the integrating principles.[4] This suggests that it is not sufficient to understand the operation of any one segment, and to be able to comprehend fully the domestic macro-environment it is necessary to understand the independent operations of each of the three segments, as well as the interrelationships between each of the three segments, and how they influence each other.

It is important to note that the boundaries between each of the segments are not always well-defined and they are not necessarily rigid as depicted in Figure 1. Rather the boundaries are fluid and continually evolve through interaction and interdependency. In Figure 1 each segment appears to occupy approximately the equivalent amount of space in the macro-environment. This was not always the case. A century ago the government segment was dominated by business and civil society segments in the Canadian domestic macro-environment. From the late 19th century to the 1970s the government segment grew in importance to occupy a much larger area in the triangle. Later movements toward privatization and deregulation resulted in approximate parity now realized between the three segments.[5]

Changes in Canada's Domestic Macro-environment

Changes in Canada's social context have been driven by several developments including, for example, an aging population, diminishing labour pool that consists of multiple generations of workers, continuing advances in the enabling effect of information and communications technologies, multi-culturism and globalization. These developments have affected all three segments in the macro-environment.

3. Gilles Paquet, *States, Communities and Markets: The Distributed Governance Scenario* (Ottawa: University of Ottawa Faculty of Administration, 1997), 5.
4. Paquet, States, Communities and Markets, 5.
5. Gilles Paquet, *Governance through Social Learning* (Ottawa: The University of Ottawa Press, 1999).

CHAPTER 1: An Introduction to the Canadian Domestic Macro-environment: A Business, Government and Civil Society Perspective

7

Canadian business can no longer expect to be bolstered by government support, and must learn to be globally competitive or cease to exist. To be globally competitive requires new governance relationships – partnering and collaborating with suppliers and even working with competitors are examples of this maturing requirement.

The government is under continuous pressure to provide better stewardship of taxpayers' money and to act in the best interests of Canadians. At the same time government activities are under increasing public scrutiny and its international obligations are changing the way in which government has traditionally participated in international initiatives. The Earth Summit (1992), the Kyoto Protocol (2002), the Copenhagen Accord (2009), and the Paris Agreement (2015) provide some tangible examples of these modern pressures in the area of global warming. Additionally, more demands are being made on the services of civil society than ever before, as the issues faced by communities and stakeholders are increasing in complexity. An increasingly diverse population with the associated cross-cultural challenges and an aging population are examples of these demands. The challenges experienced within each segment are significant. These challenges become even more complex when the focus shifts from a single segment to the broader Canadian macro-environment where interactions begin to occur between segments.

In the broader macro-environment, each segment can exert influence on the other two. Business applies pressure to government through lobbying activities in an attempt to influence public policy. Business funds think-tanks and undertakes advocacy advertising in order to exert influence over government. Business is also a significant supporter of civil society, through financial and in-kind contributions, encouraging employees to participate in third-sector activities, and by offering expertise through the transfer of knowledge that would be the inevitable result of business working closely with civil society organizations.

Similarly government has a range of policy instruments available through which to influence business and civil society. Government can regulate, subsidize, tax, loan money and invest in certain activities, procure goods and services, and take ownership of the delivery of products and services to influence business. To influence civil society, government can offer funding for certain activities, modify its tax policy, collaborate to develop alternative service delivery mechanisms, or work to develop national third-sector strategies that would in turn bolster the government's policy direction. (Such as for example, the Social Finance Fund, noted in 'In the News' article at the opening of this chapter).

Civil society can influence business and government in many ways. As the trusted "neutral broker" in dealings between business and government, civil society can influence both segments to move in a specified direction in delivering programs, services, contracts and other matters. Civil society can bring public credibility to the actions of both business and government and, by being closer to stakeholders, serve as an important conduit on public opinion in matters of business activity and public policy.

Stakeholders in the Canadian Domestic Macro-environment

It may appear to be obvious that there are many stakeholders in Canada's domestic macro-environment. Miriam-Webster defines a *stakeholder* as "one that has a stake in an enterprise".[6] Generally, the concept of "stakeholders" is addressed in the context of the activities of a corporation or other business entity, although the concept of a stakeholder goes well beyond the relatively narrow confines of the *corporate stakeholder*. That said the corporate stakeholder concept provides arguably the most intuitive approach to understanding the role of the stakeholder. Corporate stakeholders can be classified in many ways – direct, indirect, primary, and secondary among others – but all stakeholders regardless of classification can to some degree influence or be influenced by the company, business, or corporation. The most common stakeholders from the perspective of the corporate enterprise include but are not limited to shareholders, employees, suppliers, unions, competitors, and government.

Somewhat less intuitive are stakeholders derived from the perspective of government. Every citizen of Canada is a stakeholder to government, and this is further complicated when one expands the stakeholder concept to include not only individuals but also the combinations of individuals into more organized forms – business organizations, including sole proprietorships, partnerships, corporations, cooperatives; civil society groups - large and small, charitable organizations, volunteer organizations, hospitals, universities, and non-government organizations to name a few. All these stakeholders have their own agendas that may or may not align with the policy direction of government and in fact may not be aligned even within the socioeconomic segment of which they are members. Managing stakeholders of the government means attempting to satisfy as many potential voters as possible from an enormous group of individuals - both organized and unorganized, with a wide diversity of interests and uncoordinated agendas, who may come from diverse regions across a significantly large country.

Even less intuitive are stakeholders from the perspective of civil society. While a vitally important segment of the domestic macro-environment, this group is com-

6. "Merriam-Webster, An Encyclopedia Britannica Company," accessed March 15, 2013, http://www.merriam-webster.com/dictionary/stakeholder.

CHAPTER 1: An Introduction to the Canadian Domestic Macro-environment: A Business, Government and Civil Society Perspective

9

paratively the most fragmented and least understood. Yet stakeholders of the civil society segment have enormous power to influence both business and government and, as noted earlier, in recent years have experienced an increasing ability to influence the other two segments. It could be said that as with the government segment, every Canadian citizen is a potential civil society stakeholder since civil society represents the social consciousness of the people.

Stakeholders and Boulding

The treatment of the Canadian domestic macro-environment through a modified Boulding triangle implies the need for a stakeholder approach targeted to each segment. Further, when this perspective is applied to the Canadian society what becomes obvious is a wide diffusion of power among members of a society characterized by diverse ethnic and social groups, which represent the fabric of Canada itself. In other words what emerges is the existence of a *pluralistic society*, a society in which power is distributed, not centralized; a society that consists of a multitude of stakeholders directly or indirectly influencing each other through a range of social relationships. This pluralistic society involves a deepening interdependence of all facets in the wake of increasing interconnectedness, complexity, and uncertainty.

To set the stage for the discussions that follow a brief overview of some key characteristics and data concerning Canada is provided. This overview is useful to provide an appreciation for Canada's geography, population, style of government, and its civil society collectively providing a 40,000-foot view of Canada's domestic macro- environment.

Canada at a Glance

Population

According to Statistics Canada, Canada's population was estimated at 37,412,852 persons in the second quarter of 2019; up 522,683 from the year before, and 2,410,405 from the last printing of this book in 2013. It is interesting to note that Ontario, Quebec, British Columbia and Alberta continue to account for 86 percent of Canada's total population year over year.

Estimates of population, Canada, provinces and territories					
Geography	Q2 2018	Q3 2018	Q4 2018	Q1 2019	Q2 2019
	Persons				
Canada	36,890,169	37,058,856	37,242,571	37,314,442	37,412,852
Newfoundland and Labrador	526,462	525,355	525,073	523,790	522,537
Prince Edward Island	152,009	153,244	154,750	154,748	155,318
Nova Scotia	955,708	959,942	964,693	965,382	966,858
New Brunswick	768,865	770,633	772,238	772,094	773,020
Quebec	8,356,699	8,390,499	8,421,698	8,433,301	8,452,209
Ontario	14,246,035	14,322,757	14,411,424	14,446,515	14,490,207
Manitoba	1,346,851	1,352,154	1,356,836	1,360,396	1,362,789
Saskatchewan	1,158,836	1,162,062	1,165,903	1,168,423	1,169,131
Alberta	4,288,327	4,307,110	4,330,206	4,345,737	4,362,503
British Columbia	4,967,375	4,991,687	5,016,322	5,020,302	5,034,482
Yukon	40,087	40,476	40,333	40,369	40,208
Northwest Territories	45,011	44,541	44,445	44,598	44,420
Nunavut	37,904	38,396	38,650	38,787	39,170

TABLE 1

Estimates of Population[7]

Statistics Canada

Immigration contributed significantly to Canada's population growth in 2016, numbering over 1.2 million persons, and widely dispersed across the globe.

Top 10 countries of birth of recent immigrants, Canada 2016		
	Number	%
Recent immigrants	**1,212,075**	**100.0**
Philippines	188,805	15.6
India	147,190	12.1
China	129,020	10.6
Iran	42,070	3.5
Pakistan	41,480	3.4
United States	33,060	2.7
Syria	29,945	2.5
United Kingdom	24,445	2.0
France	24,155	2.0
South Korea	21,710	1.8
Other countries	530,195	43.7

TABLE 2

Top 10 countries of birth of recent immigrants[8]

Statistics Canada

7. Statistics Canada, Table 17-10-0009-01 Population estimates, quarterly. Doi: https://doi.org/10.25318/1710000901-eng, accessed June 27, 2019.
8. Statistics Canada, Census of Population, 2016, https://www150.statcan.gc.ca/n1/daily-quotidien/171025/t002b-eng.htm, accessed June 27, 2019.

CHAPTER 1: An Introduction to the Canadian Domestic Macro-environment: A Business, Government and Civil Society Perspective

11

TABLE 3

Population
by Broad Age
Groups[9]

Statistics Canada

Population by broad age groups and sex, 2016 counts for both sexes, Canada, provinces and territories, 2016 Census					
Geographic name	Total	Broad age groups			
		0 to 14 years	15 to 64 years	65 years and over	85 years and over
Canada	**35,151,730**	**5,839,570**	**23,376,530**	**5,935,635**	**770,780**
Newfoundland and Labrador	519,715	74,440	344,250	101,025	9,360
Prince Edward Island	142,905	22,685	92,510	27,715	3,080
Nova Scotia	923,600	133,830	605,950	183,820	21,645
New Brunswick	747,100	110,495	487,820	148,785	17,625
Quebec	8,164,360	1,333,255	5,335,910	1,495,190	188,685
Ontario	13,448,495	2,207,975	8,988,870	2,251,655	301,075
Manitoba	1,278,365	243,825	835,580	198,965	29,210
Saskatchewan	1,098,355	215,685	712,240	170,430	26,945
Alberta	4,067,175	779,155	2,787,800	500,220	63,385
British Columbia	4,648,055	691,385	3,107,680	848,990	109,195
Yukon	35,870	6,280	25,335	4,260	300
Northwest Territories	41,785	8,875	29,690	3,220	225
Nunavut	35,940	11,690	22,895	1,365	55

The 2016 census provides some very insightful information about the Canadian population.

FIGURE 2

Canadian popula-
tion by age[10]

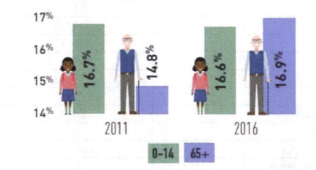

For the first time in census history, the share of seniors aged **65 years and over** exceeds the share of children **under 15 years**...

Our population is aging and yet in Western Canada the number of less than 15 year olds still exceeds the number of person 65 years and over.

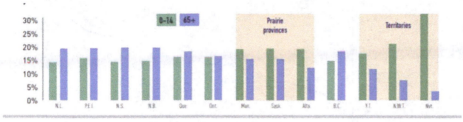

FIGURE 3

Age distribution by province

The number of women far exceeds the number of men particularly among seniors.

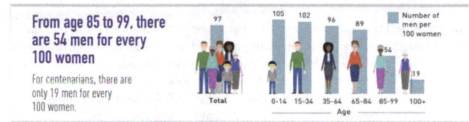

FIGURE 4

Ratio of Men to Women

Labour Force and Education

Canada's unemployment rate in May 2019 was 5.6% as compared to 7% in February 2013, and the lowest since 1976.[11]

Canada		
Indicator	**May 2019**	**Year-over-year change**
Population (15+)	30,623 6 thousands	1.4%
Labour force	20,135 4 thousands	1.9%
Employment	19,002 8 thousands	2.2%
Unemployment	1,132 6 thousands	-2.1%
Unemployment rate	5.6%	-0.3 pts
Participation rate	65.8%	0.4 pts
Employment rate	62.1%	0.5 pts
Syria	29,945	2.5
United Kingdom	24,445	2.0

TABLE 4

Canada Labour Force

11. Statistics Canada, Labour Force Survey, May 2019, https://www150.statcan.gc.ca/n1/daily-quotidi-en/190607/dq190607a-eng.htm?HPA=1&indid=3587-2&indgeo=0, accessed June 27, 2019.

CHAPTER 1: An Introduction to the Canadian Domestic Macro-environment: A Business, Government and Civil Society Perspective

13

FIGURE 5

Employment in
Canada year over
year[12]

Statistics Canada

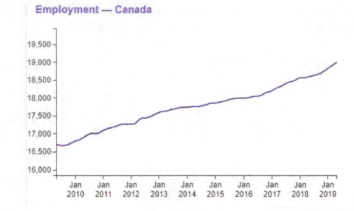

Employment — Canada

In 2012 the Canadian service sector employed (13,635,700) over three and a half times the number of Canadians employed by the goods-producing sector (3,872,000).[13] In May 2019 more people were working health care and social assistance, professional, scientific and technical services; and employment decreases were being experienced in the fields of business, building and other support services, accommodation and food services, and public administration.[14]

Employment by class of worker and industry			
	April 2019 (000s)	**April 2018 to April 2019 change in 000s**	**April 2018 to April 2019 (% change)**
Class of worker			
Employees	16,155.9	402.5	2.6
Public sector employees	3,826.0	47.1	1.2
Private sector employees	12,329.9	355.4	3.0
Self-employed	2,873.2	23.9	0.8
Total employed, all industries	**19,029.1**	**426.4**	**2.3**
Goods-producing sector	3,988.0	54.5	1.4
Agriculture	287.1	5.9	2.1
Natural resources	344.1	6.0	1.8
Utilities	143.5	1.8	1.3
Construction	1,465.1	32.1	2.2

12. Statistics Canada, Labour Market Indicators, May 2019, https://www150.statcan.gc.ca/n1/pub/71-607-x/71-607-x2017001-eng.htm, accessed June 27, 2019.

13. "Employment by industry," Statistics Canada, date modified January 4, 2013, https://www150.statcan.gc.ca/t1/tbl1/en/tv.action?pid=1410002301, accessed June 27, 2019.

14. Statistics Canada, Labour Market Indicators, May 2019, https://www150.statcan.gc.ca/n1/pub/71-607-x/71-607-x2017001-eng.htm, accessed June 27, 2019.

TABLE 5

Employment by
class of worker
and industry

Employment by class of worker and industry			
	April 2019 (000s)	April 2018 to April 2019 change in 000s	April 2018 to April 2019 (% change)
Manufacturing	1,748.2	8.7	0.5
Services-producing sector	15,041.1	371.9	2.5
Wholesale and retail trade	2,861.3	74.6	2.7
Transportation and warehousing	1,032.7	55.9	5.7
Finance, insurance, real estate, rental and leasing	1,196.2	30.1	2.6
Professional, scientific and technical services	1,525.0	62.5	4.3
Business, building and other support services	799.3	32.4	4.2
Educational services	1,348.8	39.4	3.0
Health care and social assistance	2,446.6	50.1	2.1
Information, culture and recreation	776.9	-8.1	-1.0
Accommodation and food services	1,208.2	-33.7	-2.7
Other services (except public administration)	833.5	27.9	3.5
Public administration	1,012.5	40.8	4.2

TABLE 6

Participation Rate
in Education

Participation rate in education, population aged 15 to 29, by age group and type of institution attended (%)						
Age group	Type of institution attended	2013 / 2014	2014 / 2015	2015 / 2016	2016 / 2017	2017 / 2018
15 to 19 years	Total, type of institution attended	83	83	83	85	84
	Elementary/High School	59	58	60	59	59
	College	12	12	12	13	11
	University	12	13	12	13	13
20 to 24 years	Total, type of institution attended	40	41	41	41	42
	Elementary/High School	2	2	2	2	1
	College	13	12	12	12	11
	University	25	27	27	28	29
25 to 29 years	Total, type of institution attended	12	12	12	12	12
	Elementary/High School	1	1	1	0	0
	College	4	4	4	4	4
	University	7	8	8	8	8

While unemployment rates overall have decreased over the past few years, the attendance at Universities or the 20 to 29 years group has increased ever so slightly. Additionally, the number of graduates has generally increased, as seen in the table below.

TABLE 7

Postsecondary graduates[15]

Postsecondary graduates					
	2012	2013	2014	2015	2016
Canada	478,980	499,563	511,281	522,318	532,158
Newfoundland and Labrador	6,480	6,549	6,372	6,393	6,597
Prince Edward Island	2,100	2,199	2,400	2,103	2,148
Nova Scotia	14,805	14,598	15,168	14,904	15,597
New Brunswick	8,460	8,811	8,391	8,295	8,175
Quebec	126,831	136,488	144,345	150,285	153,312
Ontario	193,032	200,607	206,514	209,571	213,873
Manitoba	12,306	12,699	12,780	12,516	12,519
Saskatchewan	10,293	10,332	10,503	10,785	11,100
Alberta	40,737	42,768	41,277	41,634	42,177
British Columbia	63,582	64,242	63,246	65,466	66,294
Territories	348	267	291	366	369

Geography

Geographically Canada is the largest country in the world with an area of 3.85 million square miles, and has an estimated 2 million lakes, occupying approximately 9% of the total land mass.[16] Canada also has the longest coastline of any country in the world with a total length of 243,042 kilometers.[17]

From the above characteristics Canada could be described as a *vast* country with a primarily urban, educated, and aging population concentrated in a small number of key geographic areas and featuring a labour force primarily employed in pursuits not related to the production of goods. As complicated as this initial overview appears, it is incomplete without a consideration of two other important aspects: the country's government and the contributions of its civil society.

15. Statistics Canada, Postsecondary graduates, by institution type, status of student in Canada and sex, Table 37-10-0020-01, https://www150.statcan.gc.ca/t1/tbl1/en/tv.action?pid=3710002001, accessed June 27, 2019.
16. World Atlas, "Canadian Provinces and Territories", https://www.worldatlas.com/articles/canadian-provinces-and-territories-by-land-and-freshwater-area.html, accessed June 27, 2019.
17. Statistics Canada, "International Perspective," https://www150.statcan.gc.ca/n1/pub/11-402-x/2012000/chap/geo/geo01-eng.htm, accessed June 27, 2019.

Style of Government

Canada features a modified Westminster style of government in which legislation can be advanced either federally or provincially. The government's influence on the Canadian socio-economy is significant. In 2009 the federal government generated total revenues of $237.4 billion.[18] Revenues in 2017-2018 were recorded as $313.6 billion with 93% being generated from some form of taxation.[19] The Canadian government spent $164.3 billion on transfer payments to persons, or other levels of government; the remaining balance was applied to direct program costs and public debt charges.[20] Thus the government is a key player in Canada and an understanding of how government works is essential for a manager.

Civil Society

The Canadian civil society exemplified by the volunteer sector and charitable organizations is also a formidable force. For example, in 2010 over 22 million Canadians made a financial donation to a charitable or other non-profit organization with the amount donated totaling $10.6 billion.[21] The majority of these donations were made to religious organizations, health organizations, and social services organizations.[22] Overall Canadians give approximately 1.5% of their income to charity; however donations are on the decline and have dropped by 5% between 2006 and 2015.[23] Socio-economic factors, gender, age, religion, solicitation method and geographical location are important factors in identify donor rates and levels. The civil society segment is an important segment and knowledge of this third segment is equally important for a manager.

The Approach to this Book

Business and society as a subject area is very complex and it would not be possible to provide an in-depth treatment of this subject between the confines of the covers of this book. What this book is intended to do is to present an overview of

18. "Federal general government revenue and expenditures (Revenue)," Statistics Canada, date modified January 6, 2011, http://www.statcan.gc.ca/tables-tableaux/sum- som/l01/ind01/l3_3055_3059-eng.htm?hili_govt02.
19. Finance Canada, "Annual Financial Report of the Government of Canada, Fiscal Year 2017-2018." https://www.fin.gc.ca/afr-rfa/2018/report-rapport-eng.asp, accessed June 27, 2019.
20. Ibid.
21. Martin Turcotte, "Statistics Canada, Charitable giving by Canadians - Component of Statistics Canada Catalogue no. 11-0008-X Canadian Social Trends," accessed April 16, 2012, http://www.statcan.gc.ca/pub/11-008-x/2012001/article/11637-eng.pdf.
22. Turcotte, "Statistics Canada, Charitable giving by Canadians," accessed April 16, 2012.
23. Canada Helps, https://www.canadahelps.org/en/the-giving-report/giving-facts/, accessed June 27, 2019.

CHAPTER 1: An Introduction to the Canadian Domestic Macro-environment: A Business, Government and Civil Society Perspective

17

Canada's domestic macro-environment through an intuitive and logical approach that explores this complex terrain. First we will consider the Canadian domestic macro-environment and some key issues associated with each of the business, government, and civil society segments. A "Practitioner's Perspective" will be provided for each segment. The business segment will feature a perspective from an entrepreneur. The government segment will feature perspectives from a former federal Cabinet Minister and an active federal Deputy Minister. The civil society segment will feature perspectives from a civil society organization.

With this knowledge and understanding, we will then explore the concept of stakeholders and consider how each segment influences each of the other two. Finally, we will consider issues that affect all three segments, including for example the need to collaborate, globalization and multiculturalism, and ethics.

At the end of each chapter, opportunities to reinforce the principles and subject matter will take the form of End of Chapter questions, Application Questions, Research Questions, and a Team Discussion Project.

Of course at the heart of all this is the thesis that whether one is a manager in business, government, or civil society, in order to be an effective manager there is a need to understand each segment of the macro-environment, how it works, and how the contemporary challenges of today's world impact these segments and their relationships with each other. It is, quite simply, not possible to develop a sustainable competitive advantage without this knowledge.

The next chapter will begin the journey through the Canadian domestic macro-environment starting with a description of the business segment and some of the key issues it faces.

Chapter Summary

Canada is large country with many diverse cultures. Canada's domestic macro- environment can be described as consisting of three key segments – business, government, and civil society – each with its own unique characteristics and membership, and holding equal value in terms of importance. Canada's society is pluralistic with no single segment holding exclusive power. As the simultaneous and harmonious interaction of all three segments is necessary, the domestic macro-environment is essentially a set of ongoing relationships between persons and organizations with a deepening interdependence and an increasing interconnectedness. In order to create a sustainable competitive advantage managers require a full understanding of each of the three segments. Given the complexity of society it is simply not possible to 'go it alone'.

End of Chapter Questions

1. Describe Canada's socio-economy in terms of the *Boulding triangle* and explain the *sorting mechanisms* of each segment.

2. Discuss what is meant by *pluralism*. What evidence might exist to support Canadian society as being pluralistic?

3. Describe five key stakeholders for each segment of the Canadian domestic macro-environment and identify their "stake."

Application Questions

1. Returning to the opening news article, discuss how each of the following concepts applies:

    • Pluralism

    • Sorting mechanisms

    • Stakeholders

    • Interconnectedness

    • interdependence

CHAPTER 1: An Introduction to the Canadian Domestic Macro-environment: A Business, Government and Civil Society Perspective

19

Research Questions

1. How does Canada's domestic macro-environment compare to that of the United States of America from the perspective of each macro-environment segment?

2. Review the full report entitled "Inclusive Innovation"; available at www.sisfs. ca, and the Government of Canada website. Outline the major challenges that could be faced by government, civil society, and business.

Team Discussion Project

Bre-X was a Canadian mining company that orchestrated what has been referred to as one of the biggest frauds in capital market history. An interesting presentation of the Bre-X story can be found at: https://www.mining.com/web/bre-x-scandal-a-history-timeline/, and an article from the Globe and Mail can be found at: https://www.theglobeandmail.com/report-on-business/industry-news/the-law-page/the-bre-x-case-finally-closes/article18124172/.

After reviewing this presentation and consulting other on-line resources concerning Bre-X, respond to the following questions:

1. Discuss the roles of Business, Government, and Civil Society applied to this case.

2. Did government discharge its responsibilities?

3. How might have business, government and civil society worked collaboratively to help investors?

4. Today, given the comparatively further developed information and communications technology, in its various formats including social media, would you expect the outcome to be any different?

CHAPTER 2

The Canadian Business Segment

BalkansCat/Shutterstock.com

Canadian Business in the News

Inside Shopify's vision of an e-commerce system to rival Amazon (April 11, 2019)[1]

The article discusses the vision of Shopify to reshape commerce by creating advantage for the "little guys" and change the prevailing ideology that Amazon.com is the alone the future of retail. Harley Finkelstein, the COO of Shopify notes that if we're not careful, and we're not focused, then the future of commerce will be

---

1. Financial Post, "Inside Shopify's vision of an e-commerce system to rival Amazon," published April 11, 2019, https://business.financialpost.com/technology/inside-shopifys-vision-of-an-e-commerce-system-to-rival-amazon, accessed June 21, 2019.

held in the hands of a few monolithic players who will decide when, where and how commerce takes place. And for the future of commerce to not only survive, but to thrive, it needs to be in the hands of the many, not the few."

What is interesting is that while Amazon and Shopify are competitors, they are also partners in that Shopify's e-commerce software is integrated in Amazon's Marketplace to allow merchants to sell their produces on Amazon. Amazon is indeed the largest player in the field with net sales of over US$230 billion in 2018. Shopify is catching up with a platform serving more than 800,000 merchants, who in 2018 collectively sold $41.1-billion worth of products and services.

Shopify executives say the company's whole raison d'être is about empowering entrepreneurs. Shopify's software platform also serves merchant dashboard providing a whole range of functions via an app store where customers can access thousands of third-party developer apps to manage social media advertising, shipping, product reviews and upselling. The company also services that connect merchants with photographers, web designers and marketing professionals.

The full article can be reviewed at https://business.financialpost.com/technology/inside-shopifys-vision-of-an-e-commerce-system-to-rival-amazon.

Introduction

Business drives the economy of a nation. As noted, Canada occupies a land area of over 9 million square kilometers with over 243,000 kilometers of coastline. Its population of over 37 million collectively forms an affluent, technologically adept industrial society with a labour force of almost 19 million and an estimated GDP of approximately $1709 billion US dollars, representing 2.76 percent of the world economy.[2] GDP in Canada averaged 652 USD billion from 1960 to 2018, and was at an all-time high of 1842 USD billion in 2013.[3]

Over 84% of all Canadian dwellings are in one of four provinces including Quebec, Ontario, Albert and British Columbia.[4] Over 67% of Canadians live in one of 33 metropolitan areas with Toronto, Montreal, and Vancouver accounting for

---

2. Trading Economics,"Canada GDP", https://tradingeconomics.com/canada/gdp, accessed July 10, 2019.
3. Ibid.
4. Statisics Canada, "Population and Dwelling Count Highlight Tables, 2016 Census," https://www12.statcan.gc.ca/census-recensement/2016/dp-pd/hlt-fst/pd-pl/Table.cfm?Lang=Eng&T=108&S=50&O=A, accessed July 10, 2019.

approximately one-third of Canada's population.[5] The economic system in Canada is a private enterprise system where firms are rewarded for effectively and efficiently meeting the wants and needs of customers. Characteristic rights of a private enterprise system include: private property, freedom of choice, profit, and competition.

Against this backdrop business is conducted in a well-diversified economy with the goods sector and services sector employing 21 and 79 percent of Canadians respectively.[6] In terms of industry, in 2019 not surprisingly the Service-producing industries contribute the greatest value to Canada's GDP.[7]

The earliest versions of Canadian business pre-date confederation and in the brief 152 years since confederation, Canada and its businesses have transitioned from parochial trade to one of the major international trading economies. The earliest European contact with Canada effectively started "business," beginning with simple trade with the indigenous peoples and progressing to trade in fur and fish. *The Compagnie des Cent- Associés* founded in 1627 and the Hudson's Bay Company established in 1670 were followed by timber companies and wheat traders in the late 1700s through the early 1800s.[8] This initial growth catalyzed the need for banking (the Bank of Montreal in 1817), early manufacturing concerns (Montreal Nail and Spike Works in 1839) and John Molson's in 1810. The early 1900s witnessed the establishment of Westinghouse in response to hydroelectricity and the Crown Corporation Trans-Canada Airlines in 1937.[9] The mid 1900s witnessed the establishment of Canadian conglomerates such as Power Corporation and George Weston and in 1942 the establishment of Bombardier Inc.[10] From the early to mid-nineties to the present day, Canadian business has transitioned from a period of significant government regulation to the prevailing period of government deregulation.

The Current Canadian Business Environment

Today the Canadian business environment can be described as a private market system anchored in the doctrines of capitalism that provide for the private owner-

5. "Population and Dwelling Count Highlight Tables, 2011 Census," Statistics Canada, date modified January 10, 2013, http://www12.statcan.gc.ca/census-recensement/2011/dp-pd/hlt- fst/pd-pl/Highlights-eng.cfm?LANG=Eng.
6. "Employment by industry," Statistics Canada, date modified July 10, 2019, http://www.statcan.gc.ca/tables-tableaux/sum-som/l01/cst01/econ40-eng.htm.
7. Statistics Canada. Table 36-10-0434-02 Gross domestic product (GDP) at basic prices, by industry, monthly, growth rates (x 1,000,000), accessed July 10, 2019.
8. Canada's First Peoples, "The Hudson's Bay Company and the North West Company, The Beginning of Commerce in Canada," http://firstpeoplesofcanada.com/fp_furtrade/fp_furtrade3.html, accessed July 10, 2019.
9. "BMO Financial Group, Celebrating 200 Years," accessed July 10, 2019, https://history.bmo.com/
10 The Canadian Encyclopedia, "Bombardier, Inc." https://www.thecanadianencyclopedia.ca/en/article/bombardier-inc, accessed July 10, 2019.

ship of the factors of production with profits determined through the laws of supply and demand in a generally unrestricted market. Business activities are found across Canada.[11] Atlantic Canada comprising New Brunswick, Newfoundland and Labrador, Nova Scotia and Prince Edward Island, features companies involved in marine-based energy, oceans technology, aquaculture, aerospace and defence and renewable energy. In Central Canada, companies are involved in aerospace, manufacturing, financial services, multi-media and artificial intelligence. Western Canada is the home to Canada's digital technology and protein superclusters, with companies involved in clean technology and agricultural technology. Northern Canada is home to companies involved in oil and gas, mining and exploration, and mineral and resource development, as well as film, video, and digital media.[12]

Given the range of economic activity in Canada it is not surprising that many companies are active in many sectors. The following industrial sectors are key areas for Canada: Aerospace, Agri-food, Biopharmaceuticals, Digital media, Machinery and equipment, Mining, Renewable energy, and Software.[13]

Aerospace

This important industrial sector involves over 700 companies and 85,000 persons, generating $29 billion in revenues (2017).[14]

AgriFood

This industrial sector is the largest Canadian manufacturing sector employing 2.3 million persons and contributing in excess of $110 billion to the Canadian economy.[15]

Biopharmaceuticals

The world's ten largest pharmaceutical companies have a presence in Canada, and the biopharmaceutical industry generates in the order of $20 billion in production revenues, of which approximately half is exported.[16]

---

11. Invest in Canada, https://www.investcanada.ca/, accessed July 10, 2019.
12. Invest in Canada, "Discover What Canada's Provinces, Territories and Cities have to Offer," https://www.investcanada.ca/locations, accessed July 10, 2019.
13. Invest in Canada, "Explore Canada's Key Industries and the Companies Already Thriving Here," https://www.investcanada.ca/industries, accessed July 10, 2019.
14. Invest in Canada, "Aerospace," https://www.investcanada.ca/industries/aerospace, accessed July 10, 2019.
15. Invest in Canada, "Agri-Food," https://www.investcanada.ca/industries/agri-food, accessed July 10, 2019.
16. Invest in Canada,"Biopharmaceuticals," https://www.investcanada.ca/industries/biopharmaceuticals, accessed July 10, 2019.

Digital Media

Canada is a world leader in the development of video games, animation and visual effects. This sector employs 120,000 persons and generates revenues of $22 billion.[17]

Machinery and Equipment

This sector features over 10,000 establishments, employing 160,000 persons and generating revenues of over $42 billion in 2015.[18]

Mining

Canada's mining operations occur in gold, copper, potash, iron ore, and coal, employing over 370,000 persons and contributing over $60 billion to Canada's Gross Domestic Product.[19]

Renewable Energies

Canada boasts the world's fifth largest capacity for renewable energy, and is the sixth largest consumer of electricity in the world. This sector features the presence of a number of the largest wind energy companies.[20]

Software

Several global companies are operating and conducting R&D in this important sector in Canada, including IBM, Microsoft, Samsung and Adobe.[21]

Business in Canada: Importance of Small Business

Given the degree of sophistication required of businesses in Canada's key industrial sectors, it might be tempting to assume that the majority of Canadian businesses are large. In fact, quite the opposite is true – of the 1.2 million employer business establishments in Canada in 2017, 97.9 percent were small business (1-99 employees), 1.9 percent were medium-sized businesses (100-499 employees), and

---

17. Invest in Canada, "Digital Media," https://www.investcanada.ca/industries/digital-media, accessed July 10, 2019.
18. Invest in Canada, "Machinery and Equipment," https://www.investcanada.ca/industries/machinery-and-equipment, accessed July 10, 2019.
19. Invest in Canada, "Mining," https://www.investcanada.ca/industries/mining, accessed July 10, 2019.
20. Invest in Canada, "Renewable Energies," https://www.investcanada.ca/industries/renewable-energy, accessed July 10, 2019.
21. Invest in Canada, "Software," https://www.investcanada.ca/industries/software, accessed July 10, 2019.

only 0.2 percent were large business (greater than 500 employees). Approximately eight million Canadians or almost 70% of the total private sector labour force are employed in small businesses.[22]

Seventy-eight percent of Canadians employed in small businesses are in the services sector.[23]

Canada's Workforce

Key Challenges for Business

As the world evolves, so must business. Building a sustainable competitive advantage is key to business success and while Michael Porter's five forces models still very relevant, businesses face challenges that are not always directly related to competitors.[24]

An Aging Population and the Labour Pool

For the first time ever, in 2016 seniors outnumbered children in Canada's population. According to Statistics Canada, by 2031 nearly 25 percent of Canadians will be over aged 65 years.[25] The aging population is attributed to the aging of the massive number of persons born between 1946 and 1964 (the baby boomers), longer life expectancies and lower fertility rates. Older Canadians are continuing to work longer. Consider some observations made by Statistics Canada:

- In 2016, individuals aged 55 and over accounted for 36% of the working-age population;

- From 1996 to 2016, the labour force participation rate of individuals aged 55 and over increased from 24% to 38%, reaching a record high in 2016.[26]

Today's labour pool is a mixture of baby boomers, Generation X (1965-1981), and Generation Y (1982-2005); each generation with different views of "work", lifestyles, and backgrounds. Although many baby boomers are retiring, a signif-

22. Industry Canada, "Key Small Business Statistics – January 2019," https://www.ic.gc.ca/eic/site/061.nsf/eng/h_03090.html#toc-02, accessed June 27, 2019.
23. Industry Canada, "Key Small Business Statistics – January 2019", https://www.ic.gc.ca/eic/site/061.nsf/eng/h_03090.html#toc-02 accessed June 27, 2019.
24. Business Fundas, "Michael Porter's 5 forces model," http://www.business-fundas.com/2011/michael-porters-5-forces-model/, accessed June 27, 2019.
25. MacLean's, "Aging," https://www.macleans.ca/tag/aging/, accessed June 27, 2019.
26. Statistics Canada, " The impact of aging on labour market participation rates," https://www150.statcan.gc.ca/n1/pub/75-006-x/2017001/article/14826-eng.htm, accessed June 27, 2019.

icant number continue to work beyond retirement age for a variety of reasons, among these to preserve health benefits that exist under employer benefit plans, to maintain a salary to deal with increasing and unexpected costs of supporting adult children and, in some cases, aging parents, or to build private pension plans necessary to maintain a current standard of living. As well it is not unusual to find already retired persons re-entering the workforce.

A November, 2017 report by Statistics Canada highlighted that almost 20 percent of Canadians aged 65 years and older reported working at some point during 2015, and almost 6 percent of seniors worked fulltime/full year. [27] This same report indicated that immigrants accounted for almost twenty-five percent of Canada's 2016 labour force, and that youth between the ages of 15 and 24 were less likely to work in 2016. The report also noted that fewer men and women aged 25 to 54 were working full time in 2015, signaling a shift toward part-time and part-year work.

Today's manager will therefore need to be able to manage older workers, younger workers, and virtually everything in between, and this will require an understanding of the expectations, work ethic and motivators that are attributable to each generation. For example, the older worker might be a career company employee who defines himself or herself to a large extent by the job he or she is doing; the younger worker by comparison may be motivated by pay raises and be much more ready to change companies frequently. For the older worker the job is perceived as a career for which loyalty is owed to the company in exchange for a reliable position; in some cases, the job *defines* the person – the person is who they are because of their title or position; for the younger worker the job is perceived as a stop-over enroute to the utopian job of choice. Obviously managing each of these workers will require different skills and one managerial style will not work effectively for everyone.

Increasingly Diverse Workforce, Flexibility and Mobility

In 2016, immigrants accounted for nearly twenty-five percent of Canada's labour force.[28] Historically Canada is a country of immigrants; however, as the source of immigration changes, greater challenges are developing in terms of cultural differences. Language is one obvious challenge but multiculturalism in the workplace requires considerable cultural sensitivity in areas such as verbal and non-verbal communication, superior- subordinate relations, individualism vs. collectivism, the perception of time and deadlines, work-life balance, and gender differences.

27. Statistics Canada, " Labour in Canada: Key results from 2016 Census," https://www150.statcan.gc.ca/n1/en/daily-quotidien/171129/dq171129b-eng.pdf?st=2a7qT3ET, accessed June 27, 2019.
28. Statistics Canada, " Labour in Canada: Key results from 2016 Census," https://www150.statcan.gc.ca/n1/en/daily-quotidien/171129/dq171129b-eng.pdf?st=2a7qT3ET, accessed June 27, 2019.

More discussion on these important aspects of multiculturalism will follow in a later chapter.

The Changing Nature of Work

Notwithstanding the continuing outsourcing of manufacturing jobs, the third highest share of employment occurred in the manufacturing sector in 2016, although compared to 2006 the manufacturing sector employed 20 percent fewer persons.[29] The 50-year trend of strongest employment growth in service-producing industries continued in 2016 with the health care and social assistance industry representing the main employer, followed by retail trade; combining to represent over 23 percent of all workers.[30]

Innovation through Collaboration

Businesses must create a sustainable competitive advantage at a time when competition is fierce and can come from anywhere. In addition innovation by itself is not enough – innovation must be commercialized in order to provide society with the perceived benefits of the product or service offering and to generate revenues. To innovate, commercialize, and provide competitive products and services requires specialization and, in today's complex business world, most businesses do not have the resources to have in-house specialization in every area necessary. In response businesses are increasingly making use of collaboration with strategic partners that could include support business, competitors, and supply chain members. In order to ensure the ongoing generation of innovative ideas many businesses use a variety of team structures to encourage full knowledge contributions from all key stakeholders.

Business Ownership

Building on the forgoing overview of the Canadian business landscape, it is useful to consider the forms of business ownership in Canada. Given the importance of small business to Canada, a special consideration of the Canadian *entrepreneur* is warranted. Regardless of what legal form of business ownership prevails, the starting point is an idea – this falls in the realm of the entrepreneur.

Entrepreneurship and Entrepreneurs

Entrepreneurs have been defined in several ways: *people who risk their time, money, and other resources to start and manage a business*[31]; *people who accept the opportunities and risks in-*

---

29. Ibid, p.11, accessed June 27, 2019
30. Ibid.
31. Kelly, Marce, McGowen, Jim, MacKenzie, H.F., and Snow, Kim:BUSN, Second Canadian Edition. Nelson Education Limited, Toronto, ON: p.75

volved in creating and operating businesses.[32] Entrepreneurs are therefore, self-confident risk-takers with the capacity to convert an idea into a tangible product or service that people want and will pay for. These ideas may fall anywhere on the spectrum between 'new to the world' products or services, and new applications for existing products or services. In other words, entrepreneurship involves innovation and/or improvement – key components of the backbone of the Canadian business segment.

Being an entrepreneur is not easy. Start Up Canada, in its 2018 Entrepreneur Census Summary, provides a number of important observations from the 780 respondents to the census, representing entrepreneurs from 10 provinces and 2 territories:

- The 780 respondents collectively contributed in excess of 3,000 jobs to the economy in 2018;

- The main challenges faced by entrepreneurs are funding, sales, and cash flow;

- The respondents perceive that there are limited funding options in Canada and that investors and lenders in Canada are too conservative.[33]

Forms of Business Ownership

There are essentially four main types of business ownership in Canada: *sole proprietorships, partnerships, corporations,* and *co-operatives.* Another type of specialized form of business ownership is the *franchise*, usually found in the corporate form but with some unique operating characteristics. A brief review of these business structures is important as their different characteristics have an impact not only on how they operate but also on how they interact with each other as well as with the other segments of the Canadian domestic macroeconomic environment.

The Sole Proprietorship

The simplest form of business ownership is the sole proprietorship – a form of business owned and operated by one person such that "the sole proprietor's status as an individual is not legally separate from his or her status as a business owner".[34] The sole proprietorship falls under the jurisdiction of provincial and municipal governments and is available to anyone legally able to enter into a binding contract. If operating under a person's legal name, there is no need to file a name declaration. This form of business ownership offers several advantages and disadvantages, some of which are provided below.

---

32. Ebert, Griffin, Starke, Dracopoulos: Business Essentials Eighth Canadian Edition, Pearson Canada Inc. Don Mills, ON, p.5
33. https://www.startupcan.ca/our-work/census/ accessed June 27, 2019
34. Boone, Kurtz, Khan and Canzer: Contemporary Business, Second Canadian Edition, John Wiley and Sons Canada, Ltd. Toronto, ON. P. 138

Advantages	Disadvantages
Simple and inexpensive	Unlimited liability – to satisfy business liabilities creditors can turn to the proprietor's personal assets as well as any business assets
Minimal investment required	The proprietor is usually the sole manager which could limit the available management talent
Control of the business rests completely with the proprietor	Sole proprietorships are perceived as being of higher risk than other forms of business ownership and it is comparatively more difficult to obtain financing from lending institutions
All income generated by the proprietor belongs to the proprietor – no need to share	Staffing can be difficult since the proprietorship usually cannot afford to remunerate employees at the level and with the benefits that larger businesses can offer thus limiting the talent pool
No separate "business tax" as the profits become part of the proprietor's individual tax return	Enormous time commitment – while the proprietor, as the sole operator, may hire people and empower them with decision-making authority, s/he cannot delegate accountability for those decisions made and remains liable for any outcome or result
Easy to terminate	The sole proprietorship dies if the owner dies; however the "business" is an "asset" in itself and can be inherited or sold by a beneficiary if so legally designated by the proprietor
Freedom from government regulation	

The Partnership

The second form of business ownership is the partnership. In a partnership, two or more people share ownership of a single business. As with the sole proprietorship the law does not distinguish between the business and its owners; however, provincial laws require that a partnership must legally register its name and give information about the partners (except in Newfoundland and Labrador where only incorporated businesses are required to register with the Provincial Registry of Companies and Deeds).[35]

According to The Balance Small Business, a good partnership agreement must provide answers to 10 key questions:

1. What Is the Financial Contribution of Each Partner?

2. What Is the Division of Work Between the Partners?

3. What Constitutes Income in the Partnership?

---

35. "Newfoundland and Labrador, Registry of Companies," date modified January 10, 2013, http://www.servicenl.gov.nl.ca/registries/companies/corp_about.html, accessed July 10, 2019.

4. What Property Is Included in the Partnership and How Is It Defined?

5. How Will/Can Partnership Property Be Used by Individual Partners?

6. How Will Bank Accounts Be Set up and How Will Accounting and Tax Matters Be Handled?

7. How Will Disputes Related to the Partnership Be Resolved?

8. What Happens If One Partner Dies or Becomes Disabled or Incapacitated?

9. What Happens If One Partner Wants to Leave the Partnership?

10. How Will the Sale of the Business Be Handled?[36]

Common law provinces in Canada recognize two types of partnership – the *general partnership* and the *limited partnership*. In a general partnership all partners manage the business and are jointly responsible for partnership liabilities. General partners are also personally liable for the consequences of the actions of the other partners – they are said to be *jointly* and *severally* liable. In a limited partnership some members are general partners (at least one) who control and manage the business while other partners are "limited" - typically to the extent of their investment in the partnership. Limited partners take no part in control or management. In Canada a Limited Liability Partnership (LLP) is often used by groups of professionals such as public accountants, lawyers, and physicians. LLPs are governed by provincial legislation.

Within the limited partnership structure there are several types of partners. *Silent partners* are known to the public, but have no active role in the management of the business itself. *Secret partners* are unknown to the public, but do take an active role in the management of the enterprise. *Nominal partners* lend their name for public relations purposes to the enterprise, but are actually not involved in the operations. *Dormant partners* are neither known to the public, nor active in the management of the business.

---

36. The balance small business, "10 Questions Partnership Agreements Need to Answer," https://www.thebalancesmb.com/questions-for-partnership-agreements-2948119, accessed June 28, 2019

Advantages	Disadvantages
While more involved than a sole proprietorship to establish, simpler than a corporation	As a general partner, unlimited liability and jointly and severally liable
Different partners offer different specialties that combine to enrich the managerial expertise	When a partner dies or withdraws, the partnership dies; however if there are more than two partners a "Partnership Agreement" would in all likelihood address and spell out the rights and obligations of the surviving partner
A partnership offers the benefit of raising private funds brought in by each partner, more funds than would be available to a sole proprietorship	Authority typically must be shared between partners
The potential to become a partner in the organization can serve as an enticement to high-calibre talent	Inter-partner conflict resolution can be difficult to resolve
Limited regulation	The ability to raise capital is restricted to the partners – an improvement over the sole proprietorship but highly restricted compared to the corporation
Flexibility	Profits must be shared
No special "business" taxes – the profits become part of each partner's personal income in accordance with the partnership agreement	

The Corporation

A corporation is a business that is recognized as legally distinct from its owners with most of the rights of an individual person under the law. A corporation can enter into agreements, be taxed, sue, and be sued. Normally, if there is more than one shareholder a "Shareholders' Agreement" would set out what would happen in the event of death of a shareholders, for a breakdown in communications between shareholders, etc. Examples of a situation where there would be only a single shareholder include "private" corporations such as a medical or legal practice. The owners of a corporation are called *shareholders* and ownership of a corporation is in the form of shares or stock. Shareholders elect a board of directors to oversee the governance of the corporation and to hire and supervise a management team. In Canada a corporation can be incorporated under provincial laws or under federal laws. Federally incorporated businesses may function anywhere in Canada and are not restricted by jurisdiction. In other words a provincial government cannot prevent a federally incorporated company from exercising those powers conferred on it by federal authority, including conducting business in that province. However, there are additional registration requirements that must be complied with in each province.

A corporation is identified by the terms "Limited," "Ltd.," "Incorporated," "Inc.," "Corporation," or "Corp." appearing after its name. Corporations can be private or public. A *private corporation* can be formed by one or more persons, but cannot sell shares or securities to the general public. Generally, the number of shareholders is limited to fewer than 50, and the right to transfer shares is restricted.

A *public corporation* is one that sells ownership shares to the public through a public stock exchange such as the Toronto Stock Exchange (TSX). Generally, a public corporation is subject to stricter regulations for filing financial reports, must follow specified audit procedures, and must file a prospectus if shares are being sold to the investing public.

A corporation's board of directors is responsible for corporate governance – elected by the shareholders they are accountable for how the organization steers itself. They do not, however, generally manage the day-to-day operations of the corporation: this is the responsibility of senior management whom the board hires for this purpose. However in smaller corporations (i.e. private corporations such as a medical practice) directors may indeed be shareholders, and be directly involved in the day-to-day operations. Further discussion of the responsibilities of a corporation's board of directors will follow in subsequent sections.

As with the forms of business ownership discussed earlier, there are several advantages and disadvantages of the corporate form.

Advantages	Disadvantages
Perhaps the greatest advantage from an owner's perspective (in this case, a shareholder) is that liability is limited to the amount of his/her investment.	Taxation - the corporation as a separate legal entity pays taxes on its earnings **and** the shareholder (owner) pays taxes personally on any dividends received from the corporation. This is referred to by some writers as "double taxation."
Creditors of the corporation may not turn to a shareholder's personal assets to settle a claim. No shareholder is personally liable for the debts, obligations, or acts of the corporation Continuity – if a shareholder dies, the corporation continues and the shares owned by the shareholder can be willed or sold.	Compared to the sole proprietorship and the partnership, a corporation is more closely "regulated" by government in terms of filing requirements and other legal requirements. The private corporation faces fewer government-imposed requirements.
Greater access to capital – in simple terms the corporation can raise funds by selling more shares. This may result in the dilution of interest of current shareholders.	Compared to a sole proprietorship and a partnership, setting up a corporation is more complex and, as a result, more costly.
Greater resources can provide for retaining higher-calibre managers and employees, including specialists that can greatly increase the management calibre of the organization.	To meet the reporting requirements of shareholders, stock exchanges, and government, corporations must maintain extensive records and in proper form.

Cooperatives

A co-operative is a legally incorporated corporation that is owned by an association of persons seeking to satisfy common needs such as access to products or services, sale of their products or services, or employment. There are several types of cooperatives including financial (e.g. credit services), Retail (e.g., food, hardware), Service (e.g., daycare, funeral), Producer (e.g., farm supply, fisheries), Worker (e.g., construction, forestry), and Multi-stakeholder (different categories of members such as employees, clients, and other interested individuals and organizations e.g., homecare services).[37]

In Canada, a co-operative must incorporate under a specific co-operative Act at the provincial, territorial or federal level.[38]

The Cooperative is an important form of business ownership in Canada, with over 9,000 cooperatives, credit unions and mutuals, employing over 150,000 persons.

The co-op sector has deep roots in Canada. In the late 19th century, farmers in Quebec, Ontario and Atlantic Canada developed co-operative creameries and cheese factories to meet the needs of the growing dairy industry. Alphonse Desjardins founded Canada's first caisse populaire in Lévis, Quebec in 1900. And in the first decade of the 20th century, farmers in western Canada organized co- operatives in an effort to market their products.

As with other forms of business ownership, co-operatives have advantages and disadvantages.

Advantages	Disadvantages
Cooperatives are owned and controlled by members	Potential conflict between members
Members' liability is limited to the ownership share	Compared to a sole proprietorship or partnership, more extensive record keeping
Any profits are distributed to members only	Being managed by members could result in a longer decision-making process than found in a sole proprietorship or partnership

37. Industry Canada, "Various kinds of co-operatives," https://www.ic.gc.ca/eic/site/106.nsf/eng/00046.html, accessed June 28, 2019.
38. Industry Canada, " Hos is a co-operative different from other business forms?" https://www.ic.gc.ca/eic/site/106.nsf/eng/h_00073.html#how, accessed June 28,2019

Franchises – A Specialized Form of Business Ownership

A franchise can be defined as a business established or operated under an authorization to sell or distribute a company's goods or services in a particular area. The ten largest franchises in Canada in 2017, as reported by Franchise Direct, are:

1. Tim Hortons – 3,665 units in Canada
2. Subway – 3,200 units in Canada
3. McDonald's Restaurants of Canada – over 1,400 units in Canada
4. JAN-PRO Canada – 1,281 units in Canada
5. A&W Food Services of Canada – 879 units in Canada
6. RE/MAX Canada – 785 units in Canada
7. Pizza Pizza – 752 units in Canada
8. KFC Canada – 650 units in Canada
9. Dairy Queen Canada – 638 units in Canada
10. Country Style – 500 units in Canada[39]

Franchises make up an important and significant part of the Canadian macro-economic environment. According to Franchise101 Inc.:

- Canada has the 2nd largest franchise industry in the world, led only by the U.S.A.
- There are between 1,200 and 1,300 franchise companies operating approximately 76,000 franchised outlets in Canada.
- Approximately $1 of every $5 is spent on goods or services at franchise.
- The franchise business in Canada represents over $100 billion in sales annually and continues to grow.
- Franchising employs over 1.5 million people in Canada
- Of all the franchises opened in Canada within the last 5 years, 86% are under the same ownership and 97% are still in business.
- In the restaurant sector, 35% of all sales are from franchise operations.
- In the retail sector, 45% of all sales are from franchise operations. Franchising is active in over 30 businesses, retail and service sectors.[40]

---

39. Franchise Direct, " The 10 Largest Franchises in Canada," https://www.franchisedirect.ca/blog/the10largestfranchisesincanada/?gclid=EAIaIQobChMIgqrdkYaN4wIVC8DICh0IVQC_EAAYASAAE-gKjh_D_BwE , accessed June 28, 2019
40. Franchice101, "Canadian Franchise Statistics", http://www.franchise101.net/canadian-franchise-statistics Accessed June 28, accessed June 28, 2019.

Advantages	Disadvantages
A proven operating methodology with a widely recognized product, service, or name	Establishing a franchise can require significant investment
Extensive franchisee training and support	The same common training and support can also greatly restrict freedom in operations – to depart from the standard way of doing business may not be possible, even if it seems like a good idea
Supplies are sourced from an established supply chain with reliable suppliers who meet quality requirements	Reporting requirements to the franchisor can be extensive

The dominant form of business ownership in Canada is the corporation, and while this may seem somewhat incongruent with earlier claims of small business being the most frequently encountered business size in Canada, it should be noted that a private corporation can consist of one or two shareholders who are also employees of the corporation. Business size therefore is not a reliable indicator of form of business ownership!

Key Issues for the Business Segment: Governance and Social Responsibility

While small business provides considerable employment, services, and product the form of business that garners the greatest interest from stakeholder groups is the corporation. While not all corporations are giant multinationals, corporations are typically viewed as having the greatest resource base and therefore the greatest ability to wield influence on other segments of the macro-environment. To provide some context in this regard consider which company could cause more environmental harm: a multinational tire manufacturer or a local garage? Who could cause the greatest grief to investors – a poorly managed large publicly traded corporation or a partnership? As such there is keen interest in how corporations are governed and how their actions (or inaction) affect the broader society. This forms the basis for the exploration of two key issues in the Canadian business segment – governance and social responsibility.

These issues combine to reflect both the slippery terrain upon which corporations operate and the complexity of the Canadian business segment. Note that the business segment is also affected in significant ways by other key issues – the need to collaborate with other businesses and other segments of the Canadian domestic macro-environment, globalization and multiculturalism, and ethics provide some examples. However, as these issues touch all segments, later chapters will consider these issues in greater detail in the context of how each segment is affected.

The Governance of Business Organizations

What exactly is governance?

According to the Institute on Governance:

"The need for governance exists anytime a group of people come together to accomplish an end. Though the governance literature proposes several definitions, most rest on three dimensions: authority, decision-making and accountability. At the Institute, our working definition of governance reflects these dimensions:

Governance determines who has power, who makes decisions, how other players make their voice heard and how account is rendered.

Governance is how society or groups within it, organize to make decisions."[41]

As such, matters of governance are not restricted to business organizations but are germane to all segments of both the domestic and global macro- environment.

The Philanthropic Foundations of Canada defines governance in the strictest sense as the "framework of rules, relationships, systems and processes within and by which authority is exercised and controlled."[42] From these definitions it should be obvious that there are several definitions and perspectives on a rather complicated subject, and it would be unlikely that one single acceptable definition of governance could be advanced. The common theme that emerges is that essentially governance is concerned with how an organization steers itself.

Corporate Governance

The most common treatment of governance occurs in the context of *corporate governance*. According to the Organization for Economic Cooperation and Development (OCED), corporate governance "helps to build an environment of trust, transparency and accountability necessary for fostering long-term investment, financial stability and business integrity, thereby supporting stronger growth and more inclusive societies".[43] More recent descriptions of corporate governance move beyond members of the board of directors, shareholders and managers. Zabinhollah Rezaee portrays corporate governance as defining "a set of contracts and relationships between the company, its directors, its officers, and its stakehold-

---

41. Institute on Governance, https://iog.ca/what-is-governance/, accessed July 10, 2019.
42. Hillary Pearson, PFC and Peter Broader, *The Muttart Foundation, Good Governance: A Guide for Canadian Foundations* (Philanthropic Foundations Canada: Canada, June 2011), 2.
43. OECD, "Corporate Governance", http://www.oecd.org/corporate/, accessed July 10. 2019.

ers"[44] describing effective corporate governance: "ensures corporate accountability, enhances the reliability and quality of public financial information, enhances the integrity and efficiency of the capital market, and, thus, improves investor confidence."[45] One of the simplest descriptions of governance is "how an organization steers itself". As mentioned above, from this some key themes emerge when discussing governance: stakeholders, values, rules, processes, impact, accountability, and responsibility. With the collapse of giant corporations such as Enron and WorldCom, the 2010 BP oil spill, as well as the increasingly public challenges faced by comparatively smaller corporations such as, for example, Hollinger International, the governance of corporations is increasingly subjected to public scrutiny. Against this backdrop three key stakeholders are involved in corporate governance: shareholders, directors, and officers.

Shareholders

Shareholders are the de-facto owners of a corporation and as such hold a significant stake in corporate governance. Shareholders primarily are interested in receiving a return on their investment in the corporation. All corporations are required to have at least one class of shares, usually referred to as *common shares*, which represent the residual ownership of the corporation. Common shares have three basic rights including but not limited to: the right to attend a shareholders' meeting and vote; the right to share in residual assets of the corporation, if any, at dissolution; and the right to receive any declared dividend. In addition to common shares, corporations may issue preference shares or special or hybrid shares.

Regardless of the type of share, various rights or conditions may attach to any class of share including dividend, convertibility, participating, and redemption, retraction, voting rights and restrictions, and sharing in distributable assets.[46]

More recently investors are becoming more "governance concerned". Some investors prefer to invest in corporations that are socially responsible with a track record of ethical operations, concern for sustainability, and a positive media presence. There are a number of reasons for this, including for example, a genuine concern for mankind, upholding a position of profitability but only if profit is generated in a manner consistent with their own beliefs and practices, and also to protect their investment – unethical corporations with poor governance structures and practices can face significant financial penalties that ultimately are felt by investors in a diminishing investment value.

---

44. Zabihollah Rezaee, Corporate Governance and Ethics: John Wiley and Sons, 2009 MA, USA, p.17
45. ibid
46. Irv Ash and Ani Abdalyan, *Corporate Law Study Guide*, 2nd Canadian Edition (Chartered Secretaries: Canada, 2006).

Boards of Directors

The steering of a corporation has long been the purview of the *board of directors* or those individuals elected by the shareholders to represent shareholder interests in the governing of the corporation. It is the board of directors who are responsible for hiring the senior management team who are, in turn, responsible for managing the day-to-day operations of the corporation. Corporate directors have many roles and responsibilities that are not related to the day-to-day management of the operations of the corporation, and include those associated with: management of control systems, required disclosure, financial reporting, accountability to shareholders, respect of shareholder rights, recognition, and management of risk and performance.

The CCH Canadian Corporate Secretaries Guide (paragraph 7005 – 7095) highlights two important and overarching duties imposed on directors at common law: *fiduciary duty* and *duty of care*. Fiduciary duty is the duty to act honestly and in good faith with a view to the best interests of the corporation, to exercise powers properly for the purpose for which they were conferred, to avoid conflict of interest and to prevent improper payments; whereas the duty of care is the duty to act prudently and on a reasonably informed basis.[47] It is interesting to note that, while directors are obliged to act "in the best interest of the corporation," such acts may not be in the best interest of the shareholder!

It is noteworthy that directors are exposed to substantial liabilities – to the corporation or the state for any *breaches of duty* – and can also be held personally liable for obligations arising from improper financial dealings. Examples of such liabilities include but are not limited to the improperly authorized payment of dividends, improper redemption of shares, inappropriate paying commissions for the purchase of shares, and employee wages and benefits, and taxes. It is not surprising that there is a prevailing shortage of individuals willing to serve as directors on corporate boards!

The CCH Canadian Corporate Secretaries Guide (paragraph 7225 – 7239) provides that the board of directors may delegate many of its powers to committees of directors who are members of the board of directors possessing the necessary skill, experience, and independence to discharge the responsibilities of the committee. Common committees include the audit committee and the nominating committee.

Officers

Directors may delegate their duties to officers of the corporation who are the senior employees overseeing the day-to-day operations of the corporation. When

---

47. Ash, *Corporate Law Study Guide*.

this occurs, the officers become subject to many of the same duties and liabilities imposed on directors. The board of directors will typically hire the President and/ or the Chief Operating Officer who then hires members of the senior management team. These senior employees are included as key players in the corporate governance structure because they can influence the direction of the corporation through the conduct of their responsibilities.

Examples of Corporate Governance Failures

Norbourg was a Montreal, Quebec-based trust fund company whose founder and Chief Executive Officer, Vincent Lacroix, was found guilty of diverting investors' funds for personal interests. Triggered by a discovery made by the Autorité des marchés financiers (Quebec's top financial regulator) and confirmed by Ernst & Young, $130 million of investors' money was unaccounted for. It was reported that several false reports were filed with securities regulators to conceal operating deficits and the manipulation of mutual fund values. Nearly 9,200 investors in Quebec lost millions of dollars in what is considered to be one of the largest Canadian financial scandals in history and the largest in Quebec. The Globe and Mail reported in September 2011 that two more former Norbourg execs were sentenced to eight years each in the fraud case. Previously, on October 9, 2009, Mr. Lacroix was sentenced to 13 years in jail after pleading guilty to about 200 fraud charges. To date the Lacroix sentence is thought to be one of the most severe Canadian penalties handed out in the area of white-collar crime.[48]

WorldCom originated as Long Distance Discount Service Inc (LDDS), beginning in Clinton, Mississippi in 1983 and growing primarily through acquisitions during the 1990s. The merger of WorldCom and MCI Communications in late 1997 represented the largest merger in US history. In the late 1990s the telecommunications sector entered a downturn. In an attempt to offset declining share values, fraudulent accounting masked financial reality – costs that were customarily expensed were improperly capitalized and revenues were reported that were not actually revenues. In 2002 WorldCom filed for bankruptcy protection – the largest such filing in US history. Approximately 20,000 people were out of work, and shareholders lost approximately $180 billion. Bernard Ebbers, former WorldCom boss, was found guilty of fraud and conspiracy in March 2005 following revelations of an $11 billion accounting fraud. Ebbers was one of five executives charged.[49]

Enron began as the Northern Natural Gas Company in 1931 in Omaha, Nebraska, and evolved into seven different business units. It traded in more than 30 differ-

---

48. CBC News, "Ex-Norbourg CEO gets sentence reduced," https://www.cbc.ca/news/canada/montreal/ex-norbourg-ceo-gets-sentence-reduced-1.778451, accessed July 10, 2019.
49. "WorldCom's ex-boss gets 25 years," *BBC News*, http://news.bbc.co.uk/1/hi/business/4680221.stm, accessed April 12, 2013.

ent products – from products traded on EnronOnline (such as plastics, power, and steel) to shipping/freight, computer chips, and water and wastewater. Its holdings were vast – 38 electric power plants worldwide, 11 pipelines, three electric utilities/distributors, six natural gas related businesses, and three pulp and paper companies, as well as other major assets. In the midst of a scandal that alleged irregular accounting procedures bordering on fraud through which many of its debts and the losses it suffered were not reported on its financial statements, its once blue-chip stock dropped from over US$90.00 per share to just pennies. Enron filed for bankruptcy in December, 2001 after admitting to accounting errors, and inflating income by $586 million. Auditors Arthur Andersen were included in the official investigation after admitting to destroying Enron files.[50]

Principles of Good Governance - Learning from Fiascos

On the surface Enron and WorldCom (and others, such as Tyco International and Peregrine Systems) reflect governance failures anchored in the mismanagement of funds an important area that is the responsibility of the board of directors but also the shared responsibility of company officers. Additionally those failures included dissemination of misinformation, failure to manage risk, making of improper payments, conflicts of interest, and the failure to be accountable to shareholders and other stakeholders.

One of the characteristics of the corporate form of business ownership that has contributed to governance challenges is the separation of *ownership* from *control*. It was emphasized above that shareholders are the de-facto owners of the corporation and the votes attached to the common shares permit shareholders to exercise control over the corporation. However, in large public corporations such as WorldCom and Enron share ownership may become so dispersed that no one shareholder or group of shareholders actually has voting control of the corporation, and the only viable control available to shareholders is in the election of the board of directors who are expected to watch over management, protecting the shareholders' interests. Combine the dispersion of share ownership with large and decentralized boards who meet only a few times per year, what results is that the actual authority, power, and control of the corporation rests with *managers* of the corporation – the very group the board of directors must direct – who may pursue corporate goals that are more reflective of *self-interest* than the best interests of the shareholders. While this should in no way represent an excuse for poor governance or blatant fraudulent activities, it may help contextualize the complexity of corporate governance.

---

50. "Behind the Enron Scandal," *Time*, accessed April 12, 2013, http://www.time.com/time/specials/packages/article/0,28804,2021097_2023262,00.html

In the wake of these and other governance scandals considerable focus has been given to improving governance. For example, the *Sarbanes-Oxley Act of 2002 (SOX)*, also known the *Company Accounting Reform and Investor Protection Act of 2002*, is a United States federal law intended to increase public confidence in accounting and reporting practices, and establish new or enhanced standards for all US public company boards, management, and public accounting firms. In 2015 the *Organization for Economic Cooperation and Development* (OECD) updated its *Principles of Corporate Governance*. These principles address important areas such as:

- Ensuring the basis for an effective corporate governance framework
- The rights and equitable treatment of shareholders and key ownership functions
- Institutional investors, stock markets and other intermediaries
- The role of stakeholders in corporate governance
- Disclosure and transparency
- The responsibilities of the board.[51]

In March 2013, the Australian Stock Exchange published a document entitled *Principles of Good Corporate Governance and Best Practice Recommendations* which includes a discussion of ten basic principles as follows[52]:

1. Lay solid foundations for management and oversight
2. Structure a board of directors that adds value
3. Promote ethical and responsible decision-making
4. Safeguard integrity in financial reporting
5. Timely and balanced disclosure
6. Respect the rights of shareholders
7. Recognize and manage risk
8. Encourage enhanced performance
9. Remunerate fairly and responsibly
10. Recognize the legitimate interest of stakeholders

In 2016, Business Roundtable posted the following guiding principles of corporate governance arising from Harvard Law School's Forum on Corporate Governance and Financial Regulation:

---

51. OESC (2015), G20/OECD Principles of Corporate Governance, OESC Publishing, Paris, https://www.oecd.org/daf/ca/Corporate-Governance-Principles-ENG.pdf
52. ASX Corporate Governance Council, "Principles of Good Corporate Governance and Best Practice Recommendations," https://www.asx.com.au/documents/asx-compliance/principles-and-recommendations-march-2003.pdf, accessed July 10, 2019.

Guiding Principles of Corporate Governance[53]

Business Roundtable supports the following core guiding principles:

1. The board approves the corporate strategy, appoints the CEO and senior management, and sets the "tone" for ethical conduct.
2. Management develops and implements corporate strategy and operates the company's business.
3. Management produces financial statements and makes timely disclosures to investors.
4. The audit committee manages the relationship with the external auditor, oversees the company's annual financial audit and internal financial controls, and oversees the company's risk management program.
5. The corporate governance committee strives to build an engaged and diverse board whose composition is appropriate in light of the company's needs and strategy, and actively conducts succession planning for the board.
6. The compensation committee develops an executive compensation philosophy, adopts and oversees the implementation of compensation policies.
7. The board and management should engage with long-term shareholders on issues and concerns that are of widespread interest to them and that affect the company's long-term value creation.
8. In making decisions, the board may consider the interests of all of the company's constituencies, including stakeholders such as employees, customers, suppliers and the community in which the company does business.

In Canada, following the Norbourg scandal of 2005 that involved diverting money from a trust fund, the Canadian Foundation for Advancement of Investor Rights (FAIR) is lobbying for the creation of an industry-wide, inclusive investor's indemnity fund, arguing that the current system for compensating victims of investment fraud in Canada is underfunded, confusing, and inadequate. On October 20, 2009, the Minister of Justice and Attorney General of Canada announced new legislation to crack down on white- collar crime that, among other things, introduces mandatory jail sentences for those who commit fraud over $1 million. Much of the emphasis on more effective governance is intended to protect stakeholders.

---

53. Harvard Law School Forum on Corporate Governance and Financial Regulation, "Princples of Corporate Governnace", https://corpgov.law.harvard.edu/2016/09/08/principles-of-corporate-governance/ accessed July 2nd, 2019.

As demonstrated in the Enron, WorldCom, and other governance scandals, more than shareholders were adversely affected, and many parties, including employees, suppliers, pensioners (through pension funds), communities, government, and civil society at large, are both directly and indirectly affected.

Corporate Social Responsibility

Businesses' concern for stakeholders is anchored in the doctrines of businesses' social responsibility, typically described as *corporate social responsibility*. But can a corporation actually have social responsibilities? Can a corporation be morally responsible for its actions? As previous noted the key features of a corporation are:

1. it is an artificial person under the law,
2. it is owned by shareholders but exists independently of its owners, and
3. it has a board of directors and managers who have fiduciary responsibilities to protect the investment of its shareholders.[54]

Given these parameters to what degree can a corporation act in its own self-interest? Andrew Crane and Dirk Matten claim that corporations do have some level of moral responsibility. The argument proposed is as follows: 1) corporations have an organized framework of decision-making that transcends an individual's framework of responsibility, and 2) corporations manifest a set of beliefs and values – an organizational culture that among other things prescribes what is right or wrong. Therefore, the level of a corporation's moral responsibility is more than the responsibility of the individuals who constitute the corporation.[55]

Corporate Social Responsibility Defined

Corporate social responsibility can be framed in many ways. Some definitions are instructive:

> *The social responsibility of business encompasses the economic, legal, ethical and discretionary expectations that society has of organizations at a given point in time.*[56]

> *Corporate social responsibility is about businesses and other organizations going beyond the legal obligations to manage the impact they have on the environment and society.*[57]

---

54. Andrew Crane and Dirk Matten, *Business Ethics*, Third Edition (Oxford University Press, 2010).
55. Crane and Matten, *Business Ethics*.
56. Archie B Carroll, "A Three-Dimensional Conceptual Model of Corporate Performance", *Academy of Management Review*, Vol. 4, No.4 (1979): 500.
57. Ruth Lea, "Corporate Social Responsibility: IoD Member Opinion Survey," *The Institute of Directors, UK* (November 2002): 10.

Generally, corporate social responsibility is understood to be the way firms integrate social, environmental and economic concerns into their values, culture, decision making, strategy and operations in a transparent and accountable manner and thereby establish better practices within the firm, create wealth and improve society.[58]

... the degree of moral obligation that may be ascribed to corporations beyond simple obedience to the laws of state...[59]

... the capacity of a corporation to respond to social pressures.[60]

Pros and Cons

Common to these definitions is a message that businesses have a responsibility beyond profit maximization. There are many arguments for and against corporate social responsibility.

Pros	Cons
• Business must satisfy society's needs business exists to provide society with the goods and services society demands to increase quality of life • Corporate social responsibility is a good investment, minimizes public criticism and dissuades government involvement • Business and society have a symbiotic relationship: one cannot exist without the other • Corporate social responsibility is profitable in the longer term • In recent times investors prefer investing in a socially responsible company for reasons ranging from belief in socially responsible business activities to minimizing risk of loss from unscrupulous activities • Business opportunities can occur as a result of considering social problems that a company might be able to resolve – the classic example is decreasing pollution spawning recycling industries that evolve requiring R&D investments and increasingly leading-edge technology applications • A company seen as visibly taking a proactive role to be socially responsible will be perceived positively by the public, enhancing its public image and building a goodwill bank of "credits" from which to draw on in the event something negative concerning the company surfaces • Business has problem-solving skills that can be brought to bear to assist in solving social problems	• The efficiency and effectiveness of business is maximized when profits are maximized – maximizing profits means more taxes paid to government which is there for the purpose of solving social problems • Accountability of business is clear: to its owners. In the case of a corporation, the business is accountable to shareholders, no other stakeholders • Social policy is the domain of government, not business • Business lacks training in social issues • Requiring business to resolve social issues would ultimately detract from its original purpose, cause it to become inefficient, and ultimately compromise the ability of government to resolve social issues: business would have too much power • Social responsibility is not free and it is not cheap – someone must pay for it. As costs increase in order that businesses undertake social responsibility activities either the price goes up (consumers pay) or profits go down (investors pay – and many will sell their shares and reinvest in a company offering better returns on investment) • There is no uniformly agreed-upon approach to socially responsible action – it varies by company, by culture, by country, by industry, and by government – so how will business know for certain it is doing the right thing and by whose standards will its actions be measured? • Business cannot be held accountable unlike social institutions – a corporation cannot be "voted out" like a government

58. "Corporate Social Responsibility: An Implementation Guide for Canadian Business," Industry Canada, date modified December 1, 2012, www.strategis.ic.gc.ca/csr.
59. M. Kilcullen and J. Kooistra, "At least do no harm: Sources and the changing role of business ethics and corporate social responsibility", *Reference Service Review* (1999): 158-179.
60. Andrew Crane and Dirk Matten, *Business Ethics*, 3rd edition (United Kingdom: Oxford University Press, 2010).

While there is general agreement that business should operate in a socially responsible manner, there is much debate over the *degree* of social responsibility that is appropriate. Geoffrey Lantos identifies three levels of corporate social responsibility: *ethical, altruistic,* and *strategic.*[61] First, at the ethical level of corporate social responsibility the mantra is "avoid harm to society." This recognizes that profit should not be maximized without regard to the means used. Secondly, the altruistic level of corporate social responsibility suggests that companies should give back to society regardless of whether a firm will recognize any gain from doing so. Finally, the strategic level of corporate social responsibility is an approach that invests in socially responsible activities or ventures that are good for both the company and society.

Elizabeth Redman advances three models of corporate social responsibility –

1. the *Traditional Conflict* model,
2. the *Corporate Social Responsibility Brings in the Cash* model, and
3. the *Multiple Firm Goals, All Created Equal* model.[62]

The traditional conflict model proposes that "private expenditures on environmental or social objectives represent dollars stolen from either employees or stockholders" and is consistent with the views of Milton Friedman. Companies following the second model choose to be socially responsible for profit-oriented reasons – attracting new customers, enhancing networks, fostering innovation, and anticipating future legislation.[63] Companies following the third model identify social and environmental responsibilities as being as important as profits and which should be pursued with the same enthusiasm.

In a study of longer-term global trends in corporate social responsibility for VanCity Credit Union, Strandberg Consulting gathered the views of 47 "corporate social responsibility leaders" from the United Kingdom, Canada, the United States, the Netherlands, Hong Kong, Belgium, Switzerland, Australia, and Italy. The result was a defined range of corporate social responsibility representing a view of future corporate social responsibility (CSR) behaviours:

*   *CSR Lite* represents companies with a marginal commitment to corporate social responsibility, concerned with responsiveness to complaints;
*   *CSR Compliant* expects companies will be compliant with prevailing corporate social responsibility standards but no more;

---

61. G. Lantos, "The Boundaries of Strategic Corporate Social Responsibility", *Journal of Consumer Marketing*, Vol. 18, No. 7 (2001): 595-649.
62. Elizabeth Redman, "Three Models of Corporate Social Responsibility: Implications for Public Policy", *The Roosevelt Review* (2005): 95-108.
63. Redman, "Three Models of Corporate Social Responsibility: Implications for Public Policy", 96.

- *CSR Strategic* predicts companies will develop business strategies within certain aspects of corporate social responsibility that can offer a competitive advantage;
- *CSR Integrated* expects companies will fully integrate corporate social responsibility throughout their business, but will not be driven by a view to develop a strategic advantage but by a genuine concern for social responsibilities; and
- *Deep CSR* describes examples of companies who will adopt business models whose goal is to improve social conditions.[64]

There is increasing evidence that corporate social responsibility is becoming recognized as an essential phrase in the corporate lexicon. For example, Toyota invested in hybrid cars as a way to show responsibility for the environment; PepsiCo acquired Tropicana and Quaker Oats to position itself as a more health-oriented company; McDonalds actively pursues the development and offering of healthier menus for its customers. All these companies demonstrate, through their actions, a concern for society and their commitment to social responsibility. However, despite society's growing interest and concern with how companies operate, some philosophical questions remain:

- Given the costs of being socially responsible are companies truly concerned with the welfare of society, or is this a tactical attempt to create the perception of social responsibility in order to remain competitive?
- Is the motivation toward being socially responsible actually anchored in discovering new market opportunities?
- Are the costs of being socially responsible *truly* borne by shareholders who are willing to take less of a return on their investment – does the market actually reward socially responsible companies?
- How much social responsibility is the right amount, and according to which, or whose, standards?

Corporate Social Responsibility Theory

Another view of corporate social responsibility is proposed by Klonoski, where he considers three theories: the *amoral view*, the *personal view*, and the *social view*.[65] The amoral view, or traditional view, states that an activity such as profit maximization lacks a moral quality. In other words, it is neither moral nor immoral. The corporation is a profit-making entity legitimized by the prevailing laws of society and therefore it is not about being socially responsible or not.

---

64. Coro Stranberg, "The Future of Corporate Social Responsibility", *Report for VanCity Credit Union* (2002), accessed April 15, 2013, http://www.corostrandberg.com/pdfs/Future_of_CSR.pdf

65. Richard J. Klonoski, "Foundational Considerations in the Corporate Social Responsibility Debate," *Business Horizons* (1991, July/August): 16, accessed April 15, 2013, http://web.ebscohost.com/ehost/pdfviewer/pdfviewer?sid=fb8da8d3-b686-42ea-a35e-6eb23449e3b3%40sessionmgr110&vid=2&hid=118.

The personal view proposes that corporations are like people and can therefore be held accountable for their actions. Corporations are either *moral persons* or *moral agents*. If they are moral *persons*, a corporation can be blamed in the same way a natural person can be blamed. If the corporation is a moral *agent*, then it is exempt from moral punishments.

The social view holds that corporations are social institutions with social responsibilities. The corporation is a social institution because it provides goods and services demanded by society and because society, through its prevailing laws, implicitly sanctions the corporation to operate in that form.

A further view of corporate social responsibility was proposed by Archie Carroll. According to Carroll a corporation must be economically, legally, ethically and philanthropically responsible to demonstrate corporate social responsibility.[66]

FIGURE 6

Pyramid of Corporate Social Responsibility

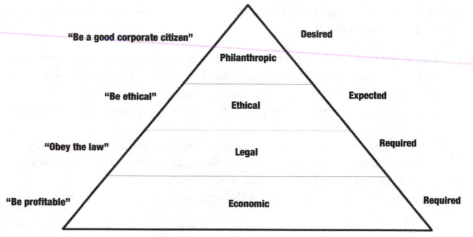

In other words, Carroll's view of corporate social responsibility requires that in order to be socially responsible, corporations should strive to be profitable, not break any laws, proactively embrace the emerging values and norms that society expects, and participate in activities or programs to promote human welfare.

66. Archie B. Carroll, "The Pyramid of Corporate Social Responsibility: Toward the Moral Management of Organizational Stakeholders," *Business Horizons* (July-August, 1991), accessed April 15, 2013, http://cobacourses.creighton.edu/businesscommunity/new773/pyramid_of_corporate_social_resp.htm

Contemporary Social Responsibility Concepts

In addition to the concept of corporate social responsibility, Robert W. Sexty brings together a number of related contemporary concepts: *corporate sustainability*, *reputational management*, *social impact management*, and *triple bottom line*.[67] Each of these concepts will be considered below.

Corporate Sustainability

Corporate sustainability occurs when social, environmental, and economic activities are considered in the context of their impact on stakeholders. Marrewijk proposes five levels of corporate sustainability:

1. *Compliance-driven* occurs where a corporation meets the requirements of the law, and supports charity to the minimal level viewed acceptable by society.
2. *Profit-driven* occurs where a corporation invests in social, ethical, and environmental areas only to the extent that such investment improves the corporation's bottom line.
3. *Caring* occurs where initiatives exceed minimum legal requirements and transcend concern for profit with a view to taking a balanced approach to economic, social, and environmental concerns.
4. *Synergistic* occurs when well-balanced and realistic solutions are derived that generate economic, social, and environmental value that results in gains for all stakeholders.
5. *Holistic* reflects fully integrated corporate sustainability into every corporate activity.[68]

These five levels of corporate sustainability, when considered from the perspective of a publicly traded company with shareholders demanding a competitive rate of return on investment, raise some interesting questions: [69]

---

67. Robert Sexty, *Canadian Business and Society: Ethics & Responsibilities,* 2nd edition (Canada: McGraw-Hill, 2011), 151.
68. Marcel van Marrewijk, "Concepts and Definitions of CSR and CorporateSustainability:Between Agency and Communion," *Journal of Business Ethics,* 44, No.2 (2003):102-103.
69. Marcel van Marrewijk, "Concepts and Definitions of CSR and CorporateSustainability:Between Agency and Communion," *Journal of Business Ethics,* 44, No.2 (2003):102-103.

Level of Corporate Sustainability	Interpretation	Rationale	Questions
Compliance-driven	Minimalist	Meeting the minimum legal requirements meets the expectations of society as laws reflect the prevailing sentiments of society	Is merely meeting the legal minimum sufficient for corporate sustainability?
Profit-driven	Tactical	Investments in social, ethical, and environmental areas mean that fewer resources are available to meet economic responsibilities. While these areas re not mutually exclusive there needs to be a positive impact on the bottom line to appease shareholders.	To what extent should return on investment be compromised in order to meet social, ethical, and environmental concerns?
Caring	Accommodating	Balancing social, environmental, and economic concerns suggests that each is of equal importance.	Does the market agree that each of these components is of equal importance and are firms who take a balanced approach aptly rewarded?
Synergistic	Collaborative	Collaboration implies a win-win situation for stakeholders in all areas – this requires each to have equal voice, power, and influence.	Are solutions to diverse problems that yield gains for social, environmental, and economic concerns truly feasible?
Holistic	Visionary	Full integration is an honourable but utopian goal, similar to a company vision statement: a picture of where the organization hopes to go, but can only arrive there in the longer term and under ideal conditions – in this case that economic, social and environmental stakeholders will see the value of and agree to each taking less in order to make greater progress for all.	Is this realistic?

Reputational Management

In its simplest form the management of a company's reputation involves any focused effort to improve the company name in the eyes of its key stakeholders. This could involve both proactive and reactive approaches. A company that is perceived to be socially responsible can enhance its reputation and bolster its ability to weather the storm when issues occur that detracts from its positive reputation.

Social Impact Management

Social impact management is defined by the Aspen Institute as "the field of inquiry at the intersection of business needs and wider social concerns that reflects and respects the complex interdependency of the two."[70] From a corporate social responsibility perspective this view emphasizes that society and business cannot exist without each other and that both must recognize that while business influences society, society also influences business, and both must work together to maximize the returns for each.

Triple Bottom Line

The phrase "the triple bottom line" was first put forth by John Elkington, founder of British Consultancy SustainAbility.[71] This approach to corporate social responsibility advocates that performance should be evaluated not only by a corporation's *economic* success, but also by the value it creates (or destroys) *environmentally* and *ethically*. The goal of the triple bottom line is corporate sustainability. The view is that a company only acknowledges the full cost of its operations when it takes into account each element of its triple bottom line.[72] Despite the intuitive appeal of this approach, some argue that the markets are not sufficiently mature to assess and reward companies for the "value created or destroyed" in these areas, in that reward is still anchored in profitability. Norman and MacDonald argue that this approach is not adding value to corporate social responsibility discussions, and can actually assist corporations in avoiding ethical and environmental responsibilities.[73]

Community Investment

Community investment is becoming increasingly important to companies as these organizations see the enormous value of working with community stakeholders. Community investment definitions abound, but generally are concerned with strategic philanthropic efforts in communities affected by the operations of the organizations. One definition of community investment is a company's long-term strategic involvement in community partnerships to address social issues chosen by the company to protect corporate interests and enhance reputation. Such a definition presents, perhaps somewhat clinically, the notion that community investment accrues benefits to

---

70. Robert Sexty, *Canadian Business and Society: Ethics & Responsibilities*, 2nd edition (Canada: McGraw-Hill, 2011), 153.
71. "Triple Bottom Line – It Consists of three Ps: profit, people and planet," *The Economist* (November 2009), accessed April 22, 2013. http://www.economist.com/node/14301663.
72. J. Elkington, "Cannibals with Forks: the Triple Bottom Line of 21st Century Business," Oxford: Capstone Publishing Ltd. (1997), accessed May 15, 2013.
73. Wayne Norman and Chris MacDonald, "Getting to the Bottom Line of 'Triple Bottom Line,'"*Business Ethics Quarterly*, 14, Issue 2 (2004): 243-262.

both the company and the community. Other definitions, such as that proposed by the International Centre for Corporate Social Responsibility, Nottingham University Business School for CAF (Charities Aid Foundation), presents [corporate] community investment a "...business' involvement in social initiatives to meet the needs of the communities in which they operate... [and proposes that corporate community investment] is more than making financial contributions to charities. It is also about companies giving local people or charitable organisations access to:

- equipment or infrastructure (e.g. computers, meeting space)
- human resources (e.g. time, skills, knowledge)
- business capacity (e.g. marketing and customer reach)"[74]

The emerging themes from these and other definitions can be generalized as follows:

- community investment involves giving back to the community,
- community investment involves more than donating money and other philanthropic activities, and
- community investment is widely regarded as a sound investment that produces measurable returns for the organization.

The Conference Board of Canada in its April 2013 *Canadian Corporate Community Investment Benchmarking Report* cited the four most common types of community investments as being:

1. contributing money to community organizations;
2. providing contributions through sponsorships or marketing activities;
3. providing in-kind resources, services and goods; and
4. supporting employee volunteering programs.[75]

In its December 2017 report, Corporate Community Investment in Canada, The Conference Board of Canada indicated the top 4 reasons organizations engage in community investment were as follows:

1. To create trust and a positive reputation
2. To enhance brand awareness and media attention
3. To help with employee retention and motivation
4. To nurture strategic relationships.[76]

---

74. "An evaluation of Corporate Community Investment in the UK. Current developments, future challenges," International Centre for Corporate Social Responsibility, Nottingham University Business School for Charities Aid Foundation (December 2006), accessed June 13, 2013, http://www.cafonline.org/pdf/CCI%20research%20report.pdf.
75. "Canadian Corporate Community Investment Benchmarking Report," Conference Board of Canada (April 2013), https://www.conferenceboard.ca/e-library/abstract.aspx?did=5389 accessed July 2, 2019.
76. "Canadian Corporate Community Investment Benchmarking Report," Conference Board of Canada (April 2013), https://www.conferenceboard.ca/e-library/abstract.aspx?did=5389, p.39, accessed July 2, 2019

In addition to the reasons for business involvement in the community cited by the conference board, there are a number of other drivers of community investment. First, many communities are expecting companies that operate in their communities to take an active role in solving social challenges. Second, company-community interaction and community issues are increasing in complexity; some examples include age demographics and resulting community needs and cross cultural trends. Companies often need to draw from a global pool of human resources in order to fill vacancies and this requires facilitating the entry of persons from different cultural backgrounds into the community in which the company is located. Despite the often quoted mass retirement expected of the baby boomers, many have decided not to retire for a variety of reasons and the workforce can frequently be comprised of multiple generations with varying expectations from the company and the community. Third, communities themselves are becoming more sophisticated in many respects including their ability to provide important contributions to companies, as well as to professionally articulate community expectations of companies, and to bring parochial, national and international focus to community issues involving companies through continued advancement in information communication technologies.

Some examples of Canadian companies active in community investment activities include Alectra Utilities who, through its alectraCARES Community Support Program, offers funding to a limited number of charities and non-profit organizations that foster healthy, diverse and sustainable communities within the Alectra service territory[77]. Price Waterhouse Coopers' (PWC) Young People Project helps address the issue of youth unemployment.[78] Alterna Savings distributes 1 percent of pre-tax profits to worthy organizations.[79]

The Natural Environment and Business

In any discussion of corporate social responsibility, the natural environment must be considered. To what extent do consumers understand the full economic footprint left in the production of every good they consume? If the product is made in another country and the environmental impact is felt in that country, does this mean there is no environmental impact?

---

77. Alectra. https://alectracares.smapply.io/, accessed July 2, 2019
78. PwC Corporate Responsibility Highlights 2019, https://www.pwc.com/ca/en/corporate-responsibility/publications/P501338-CR-FY18-Highlights-EN.pdf#page=6, accessed July 2, 2019
79. Alterna Savings, "Helping our Communities", https://www.alterna.ca/AboutUs/Community/CommunityInvestments/HelpingOurCommunities/ accessed July 2, 2019

In his book, *The Future*, former US Vice-President Al Gore positions environmental deterioration as no longer a theoretical concern and points to declining Arctic sea ice, melting glaciers, extreme temperature movements and vacillations in precipitation as proof.[80] According to Kathleen Rogers, president of the Washington, DC-based Earth Day Network, a melting polar cap has far-reaching repercussions that affect weather, air quality, fish, and animals, and also dumps toxic methane into the atmosphere.[81] In January 2013, when the second term of the Kyoto Protocol, a movement to reduce world carbon output believed to be contributing to global warming, came into effect – some notable countries dropped out, including Canada, Japan, Russia, New Zealand, the United States and China, the latter two positioned as the world's two largest emitters. Consider China: just how polluted is it? *Maclean's* provides this perspective:

> *"At 8 p.m. on January 12, 2013, an air-quality-monitoring device in Beijing registered 886 micrograms of small airborne particles per cubic metre, which translates into an air quality index (AQI) of 755. The Environmental Protection Agency in the United States advises people to stay indoors when the index goes beyond 300."*[82]

Environmental issues present serious risks to business. In Ecuador, for example, an environmental lawsuit launched twenty years ago against Texaco Petroleum (acquired by Chevron in 2001) by Ecuadorean locals culminated in a 2012 US$19 billion judgement against Chevron. Chevron appealed the verdict handed down in a Lago Agrio courtroom and, while the situation is complicated, it emphatically demonstrates, among other things, the reality of environmental risk that rests with corporations.[83]

A key debate has always been productivity versus pollution. Pollution is the inevitable result of increases in productivity. Consumers buy the products, but are they aware of the environmental costs associated with the production of those desired items that feed our western lifestyle? How much of a premium are consumers willing to pay for a clean environment? How should environmental protection and environmental responsibility be financed? This latter question leads to two schools of thought 1) government intervention is required to ensure company compliance (standard environmentalism), and 2) the opposing school of thought: market forces will result in companies choosing to protect the environment without government intervention (market environmentalism). These two approaches can be explained as follows:[84]

---

80. "Environmentally Yours," *MacLeans*, April 29, 2013, 34.
81. "Environmentally Yours," *MacLeans*, April 29, 2013, 35.
82. "Environmentally Yours," *MacLeans*, April 29, 2013, 35.
83. Tim Shufelt. "A Dirty Fight," *Canadian Business*, October 29, 2012, 61-63.
84. Robert W. Sexty, *Canadian Business and Society – Ethics and Responsibilities*, First Edition (Canada: McGraw Hill Ryerson, 2008), 295.

Standard Environmentalism

Standard environmentalism occurs when government regulation or intervention is required to remedy the market's failure to provide sufficient environmental protection. This implies that government intervention or regulation is needed to protect the environment.

Market Environmentalism

Market environmentalism occurs when economic incentives created by the market are more effective at protecting the environment than government intervention. In contrast with standard environmentalism, market environmentalism implies that there is sufficient profit incentive, or cost incentives, to protect the environment without government intervention.

Challenges of Corporate Social Responsibility

Notwithstanding the considerable progress that has been made in recent years, the social responsibility of business remains a contentious area. Apart from whether social responsibility adds value to a company, at the core of the debate is also whether business is genuinely interested in social responsibility or whether the entire effort is about creating the perception of social responsibility under the guise of "public relations." The entire macro-environment has a ways to go. Consider the following questions for contemplation:

1. Has governance fully embraced social responsibility or does it continue to reflect the interests of shareholders as the most important stakeholder?
2. Do markets truly reward socially responsible companies and, in order to reinforce the importance of social responsibility, should the market not recognize more than the financial bottom line – to include, for example, social responsibility, and environmental responsibility as having equal importance in determining the value of a company?
3. Is there any consensus regarding the meaning of corporate social responsibility?

Toward a Model of Social Responsibility

Given the challenges associated with social responsibility, how might a company develop a social responsibility program? While any such program will differ between companies and between industries, Pava and Krausz propose four characteristics of the ideal social responsibility program that could apply to any program:[85]

1. The program is informed by a significant degree of local knowledge
2. It is designed to deal with problems for which the company is directly responsible
3. All stakeholders are informed, involved, and agree about means and ends
4. The program will have a positive effect on the company's financial bottom line

This complex managerial terrain is not a simple one to navigate. The issue is not whether a company should be socially responsible – a company must be socially responsible. The challenges are more in the area of what constitutes socially responsible actions in the view of key stakeholders, and what is the correct amount of "social responsibility"?

---

85. Moses L Pava, and Joshua Krausz, "Criteria for Evaluating the Legitimacy of Corporate Social Responsibility", (*Journal of Business Ethics*, 16, 1997): 346.

Chapter Summary

Canada's business environment can be described as a generally unrestricted private market system anchored in the doctrines of capitalism that provides for the private ownership of the factors of production with profits determined through the laws of supply and demand. The Canadian government has identified nine key industrial sectors: aerospace, agri-food, biopharmaceuticals, digital media, machinery and equipment, mining, renewable energies, and software. While the Canadian business segment is dominated by small businesses, the private corporation is the preferred form of business ownership.

There are four common forms of business ownership in Canada: sole proprietorships, partnerships, corporations and cooperatives – each with their own set of advantages and disadvantages. Governance and social responsibility are two of the more significant issues facing Canadian corporations. The way a corporation is "steered" by its board of directors reflects its approach to governance. The key players in corporate governance include shareholders, the board of directors, and officers. The board of directors is elected by the shareholders to protect shareholder interests and act in the best interests of the corporation. Members of the board of directors have two important overarching duties: a fiduciary duty and a duty of care. The increasing number of corporate failures has increased the scrutiny the public is placing on governance and has provoked legislation, particularly in the United States, to tighten governance in publicly traded companies and to anchor responsibility to the boards of directors.

Corporate social responsibility has been defined in many ways, but germane to the idea of corporate social responsibility is the need for corporations to do more than maximize profits. In essence corporate social responsibility calls for profit maximization, but not "at any social cost" and the recognition that the corporation has many more stakeholders than just shareholders.

A Practitioners' Perspective: An Interview with Jason Flick, Co-founder and CEO of Youi.TV

Jason Flick is Co-founder and CEO of Youi.TV and a successful serial entrepreneur. Jason brings 25 years of technical and business leadership to the role. Youi. TV has continued to double in size each year and now calls the biggest media and technology companies in the world as their customers. Jason also sits on a number of both non-profit entrepreneur focused entities and private sector company boards. He also founded Flick Software in 2002 which continues as a leader in mobile development services today. Prior to this he was co-founder and CTO at N-able Technologies which exited to solarwinds.

Canadian Business & Society: *What motivates you to do what you do?*

Jason Flick: Making a difference, for the better, at scale through my businesses.

Canadian Business & Society: *As an entrepreneur, what form of business ownership do you use?*

Jason Flick: Federal incorporation.

Canadian Business & Society: *In your view, what is your most significant challenge?*

Jason Flick: Organization design. Getting the right people in the right roles, empowered and motived to succeed with each other.

Canadian Business & Society: *Do you believe it is important to understand how government and civil society organizations work to help you meet your business goals?*

Jason Flick: Very much so. Specially in Canada where capital, execs, key partners and other things that say Silicon Valley have so easy access too.

Canadian Business & Society: *From your perspective as an entrepreneur, if there was one message you would like to give to introductory business students, what would it be?*

Jason Flick: Everything is a mixture of Art and Science a.k.a. gut and data. The "soft" things matter as much as the "hard".

End of Chapter Questions

1. Discuss the importance of small business to the Canadian economy.

2. Describe each form of business ownership in Canada, provide examples of advantages and disadvantages for each form, and discuss the circumstances under which each form of business ownership might be preferred.

3. Define governance and identify the key players in corporate governance.

4. Define corporate social responsibility and compare and contrast the shareholder view with the stakeholder view.

Contributed by Jason Flick. © Kendall Hunt Publishing Company

5. Compare and contrast Lantos' levels of corporate social responsibility with Strandberg's continuum.

6. What are key challenges associated with business social responsibility?

Application Questions

Returning to the opening news article, discuss how each of the following "concepts" apply:

a. The effect of information and communication technologies on small businesses

b. The changing nature of work and what this means to managers

c. Shopify and social responsibility

d. Shopify and community investment

Research Questions

1. Pick a Canadian franchise of your choice and prepare a detailed report. From your report findings discuss the greatest element of risk that you would perceive to exist in purchasing such a franchise.

2. Analyze any family-owned business of your choice. In your analysis describe the form of business ownership, the governance structure, and the advantages and disadvantages of this being a family-owned business.

3. Using on-line resources, analyze information on Shopify to determine:

   • 5 key Shopify stakeholders and their stakes

   • 2 Shopify stakeholder that, in your view, are at the greatest risk from a corporate governance perspective.

Team Discussion Project

Nortel Networks was founded in 1895 as the Northern Electric and Manufacturing Company. In 2008 police laid fraud-related charges against a number of Nortel executives relating to an accounting scandal that occurred in 2004. Nortel filed for bankruptcy protection in 2009, and in January 2014 three top executives were acquitted of the charges.

Required:

1. Using reliable on-line resources, discuss whether, in your view, the death of Nortel Networks was due to a governance failure.

2. Had social media been developed then, to the level it has now, do you feel the outcome for Nortel would have been different?

CHAPTER 3

The Government Segment

Wangkun Jia/Shutterstock.com

Canadian & Provincial Government in the News

Trans Mountain Expansion will fund Canada's future clean economy[1]

A news release from the Prime Minister's office announced that Government of Canada has approved the Trans Mountain Expansion (TMX) and that every dollar the federal government earns from this project will be invested in Canada's clean energy transition.

---

1. Justin Trudeau, Prime Minister of Canada, "New Release", https://pm.gc.ca/eng/news/2019/06/18/trans-mountain-expansion-will-fund-canadas-future-clean-economy, accessed July 3 2019.

The Government of Canada believes that the environment and the economy must be managed together and that investing in clean jobs, technologies, and infrastructure of the future will benefit Canadians. Supporting the discovery of new energy markets will diversify the energy sector, where 99 per cent of Canadian resources are currently sold to one market. Opening the sector up new international markets will support workers and their families, and foster competitiveness.

Every dollar the federal government earns from this project will be invested in Canada's clean energy transition. It is estimated that the project could generate as much as $500 million per year once completed.

Moving forward with the TMX, will create jobs, diversify markets, accelerate the clean energy transition, and open up new avenues for economic prosperity.

The full article can be reviewed at https://pm.gc.ca/eng/news/2019/06/18/trans-mountain-expansion-will-fund-canadas-future-clean-economy.

Introduction

The previous chapter considered the Canadian business segment as well as two of the more important issues faced by this segment – governance and social responsibility. In this chapter the Canadian government segment will be explored as well as a number of key issues faced by the government segment in Canada.

The *Concise Oxford English Dictionary* defines government as "the system by which a state or community is governed."[2] From the perspective of business and civil society it is very difficult to find a subject or area that is not touched in some way by government, yet for many business students their intuitive understanding of what government is, how it works, and its importance is often lacking and more often incorrect.

Many students of business perceive the government as an entity bent on interfering with the marketplace; a barrier-creating, rules-laden, inefficient regulating bureaucratic labyrinth that offers little support for business. The periodically sensationalized and publicly displayed bungling of both politicians and bureaucrats alike are often cited by business students in responding to the "innocent" suggestion that they might consider spending some time working for government during the course of their careers – responses that range anywhere from a polite smile to a loud and occasionally impolite oration of why he or she would never consider

---

2. *Concise Oxford University English Dictionary*, (Oxford University Press, 2002), 614.

working for such an organization. This only anchors the view that, despite their claims to the contrary, many business students as well as many business managers do not truly understand the government: what it is, why it is the way it is, and why it is essential for business managers to understand the government in order to manage their organizations effectively.

Government is a complicated business. This chapter is not intended to provide students with an in-depth understanding of everything to do with government. Entire courses and, indeed, entire programs address government in all its intricate details. This chapter is intended to provide students with a brief overview of the Canadian government segment with its main focus on the Canadian federal government, to provide answers to the questions that frequently remain unanswered: what it is, why it is the way it is, what some of the issues are, and why knowledge of this segment is important. To set the context a consideration of the differences between government and business will be developed.

This will be followed by an examination of the different levels of government in Canada with the federal government given a more in-depth treatment. Next, some key challenges for the federal government will be explored. The chapter will conclude with a rationale on why an understanding of the government is critical for business success.

Government versus Business

Areas of Common Ground

To say that government is different from business is a significant understatement and yet both segments share some important commonalities. First, both the government and the business segment strive to maximize the wealth of their stakeholders. Socially responsible and ethical businesses seek a shareholder-stakeholder balance that maximizes the wealth of their shareholder owners as well as their key stakeholders that include inter- alia, employees, suppliers, and the community. Government seeks to maximize the wealth of its constituents ensuring, among other things, safety and security, social equality, economic prosperity, and a decent quality of life.

Both business and government strive to implement best practices in what they do. For business to remain viable and to develop a sustainable competitive advantage prudent and responsible approaches to governance demand increasing efficiency and effectiveness measures. Government must also operate with due regard to the most appropriate use of tax-payer money and strive to support and invest in those things deemed to be in the best interest of the greatest number of constituents.

Business and government seek the best and the brightest to populate their ranks and frequently compete with each other for highly trained professionals and new graduates, as both segments recognize that their success is rooted in their people, and must come to terms with the new employer-employee paradigm: one in which younger workers are highly mobile, more risk-tolerant, indifferent toward job security, and less likely than previous generations to remain with an organization, either public or private or both, to forge a long-term career. Forty years ago firms such as Bell Canada and IBM were well-known for offering life-long careers and secure employment; the government segment was also well-known for offering life-long careers with opportunities for advancement, as well as job security, early retirement, and rich benefits. It was not unusual for employees to spend thirty years in these organizations – today this is no longer the case. Unlike their predecessors, younger workers today neither expect job security nor offer their services with a view toward making a long-term commitment, regardless of whether they are working in the business segment or the government segment.

Another area of commonality concerns transparency. Both business and government are operating in an increasingly transparent environment, facilitated in no small part by continuing developments in information and communications enabling technologies, a most recent example being Social Media, where the actions of government and business leaders are instantly exposed to public scrutiny and can be beamed around the world instantaneously. Stakeholders in both segments are easily connected to business and government leaders and expect timely responses to their queries. It is easier for the public to get information on issues, more difficult for business and government to bury unpopular outcomes, and the consequences of perceived indiscretions are serious, more immediate, and inescapable. One only needs to consider a few highly publicized scandals in both segments for context: the Gomery Commission, Enron, and WorldCom.

The ever-increasing complexity of the issues that each segment must deal with is common to both business and government. For example, business has long been criticized for not doing enough in the area of social responsibility – but what is the right amount and in what form? Similarly government has been criticized for implementing policies that meet the requirements of some stakeholders and not others. Both segments must deal with phenomena such as climate change, global warming, energy issues, and globalization and multiculturalism that can further complicate already complicated issues.

Differentiating Business and Government

Despite the common ground shared by business and government there are several important differences. The reality of stakeholder management in government is that actions to meet the needs and expectations of the greatest number of stakeholders will come at the expense of other stakeholders who arguably would have the same access to elected officials, the Internet, social media and the mainstream media, and who could, bolstered by media attention and in a very short span of time, bring public attention to the actions or decisions of government decision makers causing them to publicly defend their policies in front of all constituents. From the government's perspective every eligible voter is an involuntary shareholder – in excess of 37 million for the federal government and involuntary in the sense that not paying taxes is not an option – whereas from the perspective of a company, shareholders typically voluntarily invest in a company in anticipation of a return on their investment and for the most part can pull their investment at any time if expectations are not met. Catering to the expectations of the largest shareholders and other key stakeholders, arguably those with the greatest interest and power to influence company outcomes, while complicated, is at least possible.

How often have the words "…let the government fix it" been heard? Society generally expects business to fix social problems it has caused, but this same society expects the government to fix problems it has not directly caused and these are frequently problems for which there is no obvious, immediate, or simple solution, such as for example, unemployment, the shortage of physicians and other skilled workers, the price of fuel, global warming, climate change, arctic sovereignty, an aging population and associated demands on services, and any corporate financial meltdowns to name a few.

Another difference concerns the sheer size of government – according to Statistics Canada the federal general government employed approximately 380,700 individuals in 2006, down slightly from nearly 382,000 in March 1995; and this does not include employees of provincial and municipal governments across Canada.[3] In 2018 the Canadian federal service, excluding the RCMP and members of the Canadian Forces, numbered 273,571; down from 274,370 in 2009.[4] In contrast, Canada's largest private sector employer is the Royal Bank of Canada, also Canada's largest bank, employing almost 84,000 full-time and part-time individuals in 2019; up from 75,000 in 2013.[5] While the functions of management between

3. Statistics Canada, "Federal general government", https://www150.statcan.gc.ca/n1/pub/11-621-m/11-621-m2008066-eng.htm, accessed July 11, 2019.
4. Treasury Board of Canada, "Populationof the federal public service", https://www.canada.ca/en/treasury-board-secretariat/services/innovation/human-resources-statistics/population-federal-public-service.html, accessed July 11, 2019.
5. "The World's Biggest Public Companies," Forbes.com Global 2000, https://www.forbes.com/companies/rbc/?list=global2000#6b3c989b556a, accessed July 11, 2019.

public and private sector organizations are generally similar, the actual managing of an organizational structure of 380,000 is more complicated.

A discussion of the size of the bureaucracy leads naturally to a discussion of the difference in timelines between business and government as the next difference between the segments. Business, regardless of size, must necessarily be nimble in order to react to the realities of the marketplace. This requires the capacity to make swift non- programmed decisions that in turn requires considerable delegation of authority, responsibility, and accountability. To business, "fast" means acting quickly; a definition used by government usually only in situations of emergency or dealing with emerging political crises. "Fast," "quickly," "as soon as possible" are expressions with different meanings in the government segment, which is generally attributed to the number of rules and operating procedures necessary to ensure and demonstrate that politicians and public servants are discharging their "fiduciary" duties of efficiency, economy, effectiveness, and stewardship over taxpayers' assets, and also necessary to effectively manage very complex issues in large and complicated organizations.

The sources and uses of money also differentiate business from government. Investors have a choice in determining which company to invest in; taxpayers do not – as indicated earlier not paying taxes is *not* an option. Further, companies are accountable to shareholders for the expenditure of company money sourced from the capital investments of its shareholders, investment activities as well as revenue from sales; all private activities in the marketplace. Arguably most shareholders would be indifferent to the type of expenditure, provided the return on their investment was at least at the level of the competition. The government, on the other hand, spends *public* money and therefore is accountable to every taxpayer.

Generally businesses operate in their area of specialty – an area typically well understood and reasonably predictable with common activities such as marketing, sales, and financing undertaken to maximize the wealth of shareholders. In contrast, the government's business is public policy – the term in itself rather vague and intangible to the business segment, but refers to the development of programs, regulations, and other approaches to deal with complex public issues for the benefit of all Canadians, either directly or indirectly, with far-reaching and longer-term consequences. Despite the best analyses, the "ripple" effects of public policy may not be apparent for years – consider, for example, the relatively recent global financial meltdown that arguably occurred as a consequence of inexpensive and easy credit policies (among other things).

Finally, elections can result in whole-scale changes to program priorities that require a bureaucratic change in direction in a very short timeframe as when for example a different political party assumes power. As well, whether a government achieves majority or minority status in the House of Commons will also affect program direction and program priority, the latter situation typically resulting in a more short-term focus. Regardless of which political party is in power, public servants are non-partisan and work to deliver programs for Canadians that are consistent with the political direction provided. While overnight the governing party can change, the government programs in place must continue to run.

The differences between government and business can be summarized as follows:

Business	Government
Discernible key stakeholders	Every voter is a stakeholder
Problems usually within business's purview to fix	Problems for which no obvious solution exists
Comparatively smaller organizations	Comparatively larger organizations
Timelines: fast means "quick"	Timelines: fast does not necessarily mean "quick"
Private money from voluntary investors	Public money from involuntary taxpayers
Output is products and services, and methodologies are well understood and predictable; impact on key stakeholders is known	Output is public policy dealing with very complex issues that affect every Canadian; longer-term effects are not always correctly predicted
Boards of directors are elected by shareholders but the change in directors rarely causes a complete change of corporate direction, and minor changes are phased in over reasonable time periods	Elections can result in new governments with majority or minority status that can result in major changes to program direction in a very short period of time

From Whence We Came

Canada is a comparatively young country that began as a collection of British North American colonies with equal powers and differing interests. Prior to confederation in 1867, despite the differences between the colonies, all were concerned with the threat of expansion from the United States and the lack of interest Britain had in the affairs of the colonies. These two factors catalyzed the movement to join together as a country.

In 1867 the *British North America Act*[6] created the Dominion of Canada in the British Commonwealth through which three provinces joined the confederation: the Province of Canada (later becoming Ontario and Quebec), Nova Scotia, and New Brunswick. A number of important elements were contained in the Act, most noteworthy the division of powers between the federal parliament and the provinces

---

6. "British North American Act, 1867," Department of Justice, https://www.justice.gc.ca/eng/rp-pr/csj-sjc/constitution/lawreg-loireg/p1t11.html, accessed July 11, 2019.

and the recognition that the federal parliament could assume any powers not already specifically allocated and had the power to act for "peace, order and good government".[7] The last province to be established was Newfoundland in 1949 and the most recent territory established was Nunavut in 1999. There are currently 10 provinces and three territories in Canada.

As indicated previously the *British North America Act* prescribed the division of powers between the federal parliament and the provinces:

Federal Responsibilities	Provincial Responsibilities
Central bank and monetary policy	Health
Defence	Education
Foreign relations	Property and civil rights
Trade	Administration of justice
Criminal law	Social security
	Municipal institutions

Over the years a number of areas have emerged where federal and provincial responsibilities overlap, and these usually involved national issues that cross provincial boundaries, including aviation, marine transport, rail, highways, vehicle registration, and driver licensing. Over time, the courts have interpreted federal residuary power to include the incorporation of businesses with federal objectives, as well as aeronautics, radio, television, nuclear energy, responsibility for the national capital, offshore mineral rights, official languages within the federal sphere, citizenship, foreign affairs and the control of drugs, and emergency powers in peace and war.[8]

The *Constitution Act of 1982* had the effect of Britain surrendering the power to make laws affecting Canada, including the Constitution.[9] The *Act* did not give Canada a new constitution, but provided some important amendments to the old constitution, including the *Charter of Rights and Freedoms* that guarantees, among other things, the fundamental freedoms of conscience, religion, thought, expression, assembly, and association, as well as democratic rights including the right to vote and mobility rights for Canadian citizens.[10]

---

7. Ibid.
8. The Canadian Encyclopedia, "Distribution of Powers", last edited October 23, 2015, https://www.thecanadianencyclopedia.ca/en/article/distribution-of-powers, accessed July 11, 2019.
9. "Constitution Act, 1867," Justice Laws Website, date modified: 2013-04-18, https://laws-lois.justice.gc.ca/eng/const/fulltext.html, accessed July 11, 2019.
10. Forsey, How Canadians Govern Themselves, 9.

Canadian Government

There are generally three levels of government in Canada: *municipal, provincial,* and *federal,* each having its own area of exclusive power.[11] Municipal governments are without constitutional standing and are generally responsible for fire protection, garbage collection, local roads, local land use, local recreation, and other activities that affect parochial regions.

Provincial government powers and duties, internal organization and structure of municipalities, as in Ontario for example, are governed by the *Ontario Municipal Act* which took effect on 1 January 2003, or some other similar legislation. The head of a local municipal council is either called the mayor or the reeve (or the warden in the case of a country council and a regional chair in the case of a regional council) with members of council being called councillors or aldermen.[12]

Provincial governments have exclusive power in the following areas:

*   Direct taxation in the province for provincial purposes
*   Natural resources
*   Prisons, excluding federal penitentiaries
*   Hospitals, excluding marine hospitals
*   Health care, excluding Aboriginal peoples, the Canadian Forces, and veterans for whom the federal government has responsibility
*   Incorporation of provincial companies
*   Creation of courts and the administration of justice
*   Education

The federal government, in addition to its general power, has been given explicit exclusive national power, compliments of the Fathers of Confederation, in a number of key areas, some of which are:

*   Taxation
*   Regulation of trade and commerce
*   Public debt and property
*   The post office
*   National defence
*   Patents, copyrights
*   Money and banking
*   Incorporation of Canadian corporations

11. Forsey, How Canadians Govern Themselves, 9.
12. "Municipal Act," Ontario, Ministry of Municipal Affairs and Housing, date modified: January 25, 2013, http://www.mah.gov.on.ca/Page184.aspx, accessed July 11, 2019.

While all three levels of government provide important services to Canadians, the treatment of the government segment in the discussion that follows will focus on Canada's federal government.

FIGURE 7

The Canadian
Political Landscape

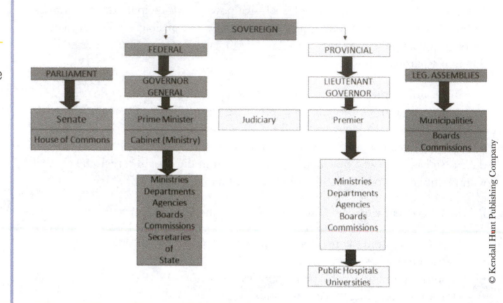

The Westminster Model

The Westminster model derives from the seat of British Parliament in Westminster in London, England, and prescribes a representative and responsible government of which members are elected by citizens and responsible to Parliament for their actions. This model of government has been adapted in Canada to recognize two sources of law: *federal parliament* and *provincial legislatures* both of which operate through the *Westminster model*.[13]

Canada is described as a *constitutional monarchy*, a *federation*, and a *democracy*. Queen Elizabeth II is Canada's Head of State represented federally by the Governor General and provincially by Lieutenant Governors to whom her powers have been delegated.

There are three branches of the federal government: the *legislative branch* consisting of the Queen, the House of Commons and the Senate; the *executive branch* consisting of the Prime Minister, Cabinet and the Public Service; and the *judicial branch* consisting of the court system.[14]

---

13. The Government of Canada, "The Crown in Canada", https://www.canada.ca/en/canadian-heritage/services/crown-canada.html, accessed July 11, 2019.
14. Parliament of Canada, "Our Country, Our Parliament", https://lop.parl.ca/about/parliament/education/ourcountryourparliament/html_booklet/canada-s-system-government-e.html, accessed July 11, 2019.

The Legislative Branch

House of Commons

The *House of Commons* is a component of the legislative branch of government and has 338 seats held by members elected by their constituents. The Constitution requires that a general election be held at least every five years at the call of the Prime Minister.[15] In May 2007, Parliament passed a law requiring the establishment of fixed dates for federal general elections. Under this law a general election must be held on the third Monday in October in the fourth calendar year following the previous general election. The number of seats is generally based on population (but can be affected by redistricting) and is informed based on census information.[16] The breakdown of the 338 seats is currently as follows:

Area	Seats
Alberta	34
British Columbia	42
Manitoba	14
New Brunswick	10
Newfoundland and Labrador	7
Northwest Territories	1
Nova Scotia	11
Nunavut	1
Ontario	121
Prince Edward Island	4
Quebec	78
Saskatchewan	14
Yukon Territory	1
Total	338

---

15. Parliament of Canada, "Party Standings in the House of Commons", https://www.ourcommons.ca/Parliamentarians/en/partystandings, accessed July 11, 2019.
16. Forsey, How Canadians Govern Themselves, 36.

The occupants of these seats, Members of Parliament, have enormous responsibilities. In addition to sitting in the House of Commons, participating in debates, and bringing forth the concerns of their constituents in matters of public policy, Members of Parliament must also undertake committee work, participate in caucus meetings, and maintain both a parliamentary and a constituency office. Members of Parliament also participate in activities occurring in their constituencies and regularly meet with their constituents on a range of matters.

After a general election the political party with the most seats forms the government. A *majority government* occurs when a political party holds more than half of the available seats in the House of Commons (i.e. 170 seats). In majority government situations, the vast majority of legislation tabled by the governing party will be passed in the House of Commons since the House *approves* legislation on the basis of majority vote, not consensus. Since confederation, Canadians have elected 32 majority governments. In instances where a party receives less than 170 seats, but more than any other party and can demonstrate to the Governor General that it has the confidence of the House of Commons, this party leads the government. Such situations are more likely to be shorter term and more conciliatory since a minority government can be defeated on a confidence motion if the other parties agree to combine their votes and the aggregate number of votes exceeds the votes of the minority government.

If a minority government falls on a *vote of confidence* – a vote on a piece of legislation before the House of Commons which, if not passed by a majority of Members, means the Prime Minister has effectively lost the confidence of the House of Commons, which is essential to remain in power, then the Prime Minister typically asks the Governor General for an election or pirogues Parliament. The Governor General can either grant an election, or turn to the leader of the official opposition to form a government if that leader can demonstrate he or she has the confidence of the House of Commons.

The Senate

A place of "sober second thought," the Senate is a revising and investigatory body for legislation and other matters of public policy. Bills or legislation tabled in the House of Commons pass through the Senate and Senate Committees for discussion, amendment and recommendation before receiving Royal Assent in the House of Commons.

Senators are not elected but rather appointed by the Governor General on the recommendation of the Prime Minister.[17] Key criteria for one to become a sen-

---

17. Forsey, How Canadians Govern Themselves, 33.

ator state that, "senators must be at least 30 years old, and must have real estate worth $4,000 net, and total net assets of a least $4,000. They must reside in the province or territory for which they are appointed; in Quebec, they must reside, or have their property qualification, in the particular one of Quebec's 24 senatorial districts for which they are appointed. Till 1965, they held office for life; now they hold office until age 75 unless they miss two consecutive sessions of Parliament."[18]

Historically, there was a level of allegiance between an appointed Senator and the Prime Minister, and the party that appointed them. Prime Minister Trudeau began the process of appointing Senators through an independent panel and removed existing "Liberal" Senators from the Government Caucus. It remains to be seen what the legislative impacts of this chamber of independent Parliamentarians will be going forward.

The breakdown of the 105 seats in the Senate is as follows:[19]

Area	Seats
Alberta	6
British Columbia	6
Manitoba	6
New Brunswick	10
Newfoundland and Labrador	6
Northwest Territories	1
Nova Scotia	10
Nunavut	1
Ontario	24
Prince Edward Island	4
Quebec	24
Saskatchewan	6
Yukon Territory	1
Total	105

According to Canada Guide.com, "*in 2014 Prime Minister Justin Trudeau expelled all Liberal senators from the Liberal Senate caucus, with most identifying as "independents". In 2016 several of the formerly Liberal independent senators created the* **Independent Senate Group** (**ISG**), *which is now recognized by the Senate rules as something with basically*

---

18. Forsey, How Canadians Govern Themselves, 33.
19. Government of Canada, "About the Senate", https://www.canada.ca/en/campaign/independent-advisory-board-for-senate-appointments/about-the-senate.html, accessed July 3, 2019.

the same rights as a political party."[20] As of May, 2019, the distribution of senators by political affiliation is as follows: [21]

Affiliation	Number of Senators
Independent (ISG)	59
Conservatives	30
Liberal	9
Non-affiliated	6
Vacancies	1

The Executive Branch

The Prime Minister

The Prime Minister has the strongest policy voice in Canada and immense responsibility and power. Among the Prime Minister's responsibilities is the appointment of Senators, Cabinet members, Parliamentary secretaries, judges, the Governor General, Lieutenant Governors, Deputy Ministers, ambassadors, and heads of government agencies and Crown corporations.

The Prime Minister is supported by two key offices. The *Prime Minister's Office* or the PMO is the political office that provides political advice. The *Privy Council Office* or the PCO is responsible for providing the Prime Minister with advice concerning the coordination of government policy.

The Prime Minister's Deputy Minister (who is NOT the Deputy Prime Minister) is the Clerk of the Privy Council and is Canada's top bureaucrat.

Cabinet

Cabinet Ministers are selected by the Prime Minister on the basis of experience as well as the need to form a Cabinet representative of Canada's geographic and ethnic diversity.

Cabinet Ministers are given responsibility for a department and they are accountable to the people of Canada through the House of Commons for all the actions of the department. There are currently 35 Ministers, including the Prime Minister.[22]

20. Canada Guide, "The Senate of Canada", http://www.thecanadaguide.com/government/the-senate/, accessed July 3 2019.
21. Canada Guide, "The Senate of Canada", http://www.thecanadaguide.com/government/the-senate/ , accessed July 3 2019.
22. Parliament of Canada, "The Ministry (Cabinet)", https://www.ourcommons.ca/Parliamentarians/en/ministries?page=2, accessed July 3, 2019.

The Federal Public Service

The largest component of the Executive Branch is the public service broadly consisting of approximately 259 organizations including departments, agencies, Crown corporations, and other organizations for which departments and agencies are responsible.[23] Public servants work in all these organizations providing service to the public in many different important areas. Public servants bring tangibility to public policy outcomes by designing and managing programs to serve the public and to meet public needs.

Running a country means that certain public goods and services must be provided to all Canadians at the same price and with the same vigour regardless of where Canadians live. Certain public goods and services are obvious such as, for example, national defence where the government must provide defence to every part of Canada and all Canadians. The private sector would likely be unable to do this. There are other areas where the private sector would be unwilling or unable to provide services thought to be in the public interest and for which the government establishes *Crown corporations* – corporations established and run by the government that have no competitors and receive government funding or that operate competitively and receive no government funding.

Some examples of Crown corporations include the Bank of Canada, the Canadian Broadcasting Corporation, the Canadian Deposit Insurance Corporation, Atomic Energy of Canada Ltd., Canada Post, and the Royal Canadian Mint.

The federal bureaucracy is a complicated landscape. Many writers are fond of criticizing any bureaucratic structure citing inefficiencies, duplication, ineffectiveness, waste, and any number of other observations that support the contention that this style of organization is simply bad. Yet there are important applications of the bureaucratic organizational design, most notably in highly decentralized and complicated organizations. The largest private sector organizations are organized bureaucratically, and of course, the government is thought to exemplify bureaucracy, albeit not always in the most positive way.

Generally a typical federal government department would likely be organized more or less as follows.

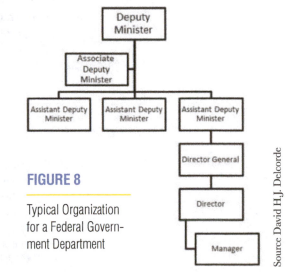

FIGURE 8

Typical Organization for a Federal Government Department

Source David H.J. Delcorde

23. Government of Canada, "The Government at a Glance", https://www.tbs-sct.gc.ca/ems-sgd/edb-bdd/index-eng.html#partition/org_info_by_ministry/org_info, accessed July 11, 2019.

It should be noted that Deputy Ministers are appointed by the Governor General on the recommendation of the Prime Minister in the same way that Cabinet Ministers are appointed.

Some Key Central Federal Government Offices

While every federal government department has its own specific operational mandate such as, for example, Transport, Fisheries and Oceans, Public Safety, there are some important departments whose mandates concern the oversight and operation of the government itself. Some of these offices include the Privy Council Office, Treasury Board of Canada Secretariat, Finance Canada, and the Office of the Auditor General.

The Privy Council Office effectively supports the development of the government's policy agenda and the effective operation of Cabinet. It is headed by the *Clerk of the Privy Council*, who is also the head of the public service, Deputy Minister to the Prime Minister, and Secretary to the Cabinet.

The *Treasury Board of Canada Secretariat* is a government department that supports the *Treasury Board* (which is a Cabinet committee) by providing support to Ministers in their role of ensuring prudent financial management and value-for-money. The deputy minister of the Treasury Board Secretariat is the Secretary who reports to the President of the Treasury Board who in turn is a Cabinet Minister.

The *Department of Finance* is responsible for providing advice and analysis to the government on the economic, fiscal, and tax implications of its policies. Its ten program activities include tax policy, economic and fiscal policy, financial sector policy, economic development and corporate finance, federal-provincial relations and social policy, international trade and finance, public debt, domestic coinage, transfer payments to provinces and territories, and international financial organizations.

The *Office of the Auditor General of Canada* is an independent office responsible for holding the federal government accountable for its stewardship of public funds.[24] The Auditor General reports directly to Parliament.

The Judiciary

The *Constitution Act* of 1867 divides the authority for the Canadian judicial system between the federal government and the provinces. The federal government has the responsibility to appoint, remunerate, and remove judges in all superior courts as well as the authority to establish a General Court of Appeal and additional

---

24. Office of the Auditor General of Canada, " What We Do", http://www.oag-bvg.gc.ca/internet/English/au_fs_e_371.html, accessed July 11, 2019.

courts such as the *Supreme Court of Canada*, the *Federal Court of Appeal*, and the *Tax Court of Canada*.[25]

TABLE 8

The Canadian
Judicial System

Organization of Courts in Canada	
Supreme Court of Canada	• Serves as the "General Court of Appeal for Canada" and hears appeals for all other Canadian courts of law • Has jurisdiction over constitutional, administrative, criminal and private law • Sits only in Ottawa • Comprises a Chief Justice and eight puisne (means "ranked after") judges appointed by the Governor-in-Council • At least three judges must come from Quebec • All judges must live within forty kilometers of the National Capital Region
Federal Courts	• Federal Court of Appeal and Federal Court succeeded the appeal and trial division of the Federal Court of Canada (established 1971), which had succeeded the Exchequer Court of Canada (established 1875) • Federal Court has jurisdiction over revenue, the Crown in Right of Canada as litigant, industrial and intellectual property and other areas regulated by federal legislation, and holds power of judicial review over decisions of federal tribunals and other matters including, for example, provincial transportation and aeronautics.
The Tax Court of Canada	• (established 1983) is responsible for hearing appeals regarding income tax concerns
Provincial and Territorial Superior Courts	• Courts of general trial jurisdiction and provincial courts of appeal • Jurisdiction over disputes arising in areas where the federal government has legislative jurisdiction such as, for example, criminal law and banking
Provincial and Territorial Courts	• The "lowest" level of court in Canada • Deal with the vast majority of court cases in Canada including criminal matters, family law and civil litigation
Administrative Tribunals	• Not formally part of the Canadian judicial system, but are an integral component of the system created to resolve disputes • Limited in supervisory jurisdiction

Public Policy and the Legislative Process

Public policy has been defined by Thomas Dye as "whatever governments choose to do or not do."[26] When an issue brought forward is thought to affect a significant number of Canadians, or be of significance to the public interest, government moves toward developing a policy to deal with the issue. More practically *public policy* is the government's response to an existing or emerging social problem that directly or indirectly affects a significant number of Canadians. It might include such issues as taxation, regulation, and redistribution and may involve the devel-

25. Supreme Court of Canada, "Role fo the Court", https://www.scc-csc.ca/court-cour/role-eng.aspx, accessed July 11, 2019.
26. T.R. Dye, *Understanding Public Policy* (Englewood Cliffs, NJ: Prentice-Hall, 1972).

opment of legislation. Governments become aware of issues in a number of ways, however, there are five key sources that can often prompt the making of policy:

1. The public at large or public interest groups;
2. The government, in the form of the government caucus, research bodies, Royal Commissions;
3. The public service through the evolution of existing programs;
4. Parliament via committee reports or private member's bills; or,
5. The judiciary as a consequence of judicial decisions. [27]

Public policy itself can take many forms, and can be categorized in four ways:

1. *Distributive* – whereby benefits are solicited by and awarded to specific groups but the costs are borne equally by the general population (tariffs and subsidies);
2. *Regulatory* – in which behaviour is modified through government sanction (environmental controls);
3. *Redistributive* – whereby wealth is transferred from one segment of the population to another (income taxation); and,
4. *Constituent* – whereby benefits and costs are widely dispersed (monetary and fiscal policy).[28]

The *legislative process* describes the steps through which proposed legislation must pass before becoming law. This process is complicated and time-consuming.

Pieces of legislation are referred to as *government bills*, which are drafted by the Department of Justice with input from the responsible federal department, the Federal Cabinet and tabled in the House of Commons by a Cabinet Minister. Bills may also take the form of *private members' bills*, which are public bills and are concerned with matters of public policy and introduced by Members of Parliament who are not Cabinet Ministers. Private senators' bills can be introduced in the Senate. There are also *private bills* that specifically benefit an individual or company, and which do not concern public policy. This type of bill is usually introduced in the Senate.

All bills usually go through the following process in both the House of Commons and the Senate. The legislative process and, more specifically, the steps that occur inside Cabinet before a piece of legislation is introduced to the House of Commons (or the Senate, except for legislation involving the spending of public monies) and the steps that occur inside the House of Commons (and the Senate) are presented below.

27. Gilles Paquet and Jeffrey Roy, Government in Canada – Competition, Cooperation, and Co- evolution in Business-Government –Society Relations (Ottawa: University of Ottawa, 1998).
28. D. Wayne Taylor, Allan A. Warrack and Mark C. Baetz, *Business and Government in Canada – Partners for the Future* (Canada: Prentice Hall, 1999).

The Cabinet Stage

The introduction of a bill.

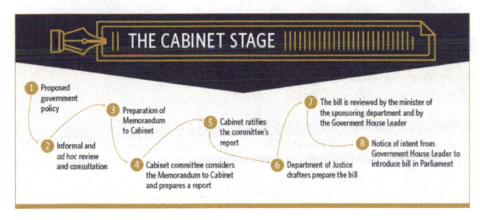

The primary purpose of the Cabinet stage is to review and decide which measures the government wants to implement through legislation. Government policy – often announced in the Throne Speech, the budget, international or federal/provincial agreements, ministerial proposals and other sources – is the point of origin for most federal government legislation.[29]

The Parliamentary Stage

The bill must pass through both houses of Parliament, going through 'readings', debates, and committee reviews.[30]

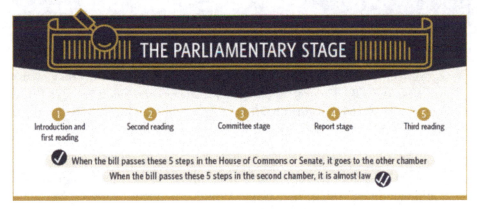

29. Parliament of Canada,"The Legislative Process: From Government Policy to Proclamation", https://lop.parl.ca/sites/PublicWebsite/default/en_CA/ResearchPublications/201552E, accessed July 11, 2019.
30. Parliament of Canada,"The Legislative Process: From Government Policy to Proclamation", https://lop.parl.ca/sites/PublicWebsite/default/en_CA/ResearchPublications/201552E, accessed July 11, 2019.

First Reading	The bill is read but no debate ensues
Second Reading	The bill is debated, members vote and the bill is then typically sent to a House of Commons or Senate committee
Committee Stage	Analysis that examines the bill clause by clause, consults with interested stakeholder experts and witnesses, and produces a report that either recommends approval as submitted, amendments, or that it not proceed further
Report Stage	Debate on further amendments
Third Reading	Final debate and vote

If passed, the bill is sent to the other House – bills that are introduced in the House of Commons are sent to the Senate, and bills that are introduced in the Senate are sent to the House of Commons.

Royal Asset and Coming into Force Stages

When both the House of Commons and the Senate have passed a bill in the same form, the bill awaits Royal Assent. Royal Assent is the point at which a bill becomes an Act.[31]

© Library of Parliament

Occurs when the House of Commons and the Senate have passed the bill in the same form and the Governor General, or one of her Deputies on behalf of the Crown, signs the bill. The legislation becomes law either when it receives Royal Assent, on a day specified in the bill, or on a day set by the Governor General (on Cabinet advice).

It is interesting to note that the reference to the reading of a bill evolves from our history books. Early in Canada's history many Members of Parliament were illiterate and one role of the Speaker of the House was to read aloud the bill being presented for consideration.

---

31. Parliament of Canada,"The Legislative Process: From Government Policy to Proclamation", https://lop.parl.ca/sites/PublicWebsite/default/en_CA/ResearchPublications/201552E, accessed July 11, 2019

Any bill that calls for the expenditure of public monies must be tabled only by a Cabinet Minister and only in the House of Commons. Any bill following a legislative process that is interrupted by the termination of a session of Parliament is said to *die on the order paper*. Continuing with the bill at the stage it was at before the Parliamentary session ended is not an option and such bills must be reintroduced in the next session of Parliament, starting at the beginning of the legislative process once again.

Parliamentary Committees

The usual outcome at the second reading of a bill is referral to a government committee. This is an important stage as committees allow for a detailed and considered review of the bill involving input from specialists, experts and interested Canadians and provide an opportunity to validate the principle of the bill. Types of committees are as follows:

Committee	Description
Standing Committees	Permanent committees established by standing orders of the House of Commons, focused on an area of government policy, and reporting to the House of Commons (for example, the Public Accounts Committee)
Subcommittees	Report to the main committee but not to the House of Commons
Legislative Committees	Established as necessary to examine specific government bills after they have passed second reading
Special Committees	Temporary committees focused on specific issues
Joint Committees	Composed of Members from both the House of Commons and the Senate
Committees of the Whole	Composed of all members of the House of Commons or the Senate

Other Commonwealth Governments

Bridgman and Davis provide a fulsome model in the context of the Australian policy experience that suggests eight steps occurring in a cycle. This approach is more explicit and includes specific stages of policy instruments, consultation and coordination, and proposes that issues can be elevated to the policy agenda if they have widespread public attention, a shared belief by the public that action is necessary, and that the matter requires government intervention for resolution. The second stage of this model calls for policy analysis that explores alternative courses of action and the pros and cons associated with each alternative. Policy instruments include laws, regulations, programs and other approaches the government has available to deal with the issue. Consultation with stakeholders ensures a balanced view of both the problem and the emerging alternative solutions, and coordination ensures consistency with the government's overall direction.

FIGURE 9

Bridgman and
Davis' Australian
Policy Cycle
Model

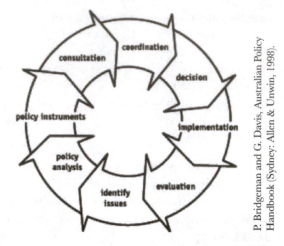

P. Bridgeman and G. Davis, Australian Policy Handbook (Sydney: Allen & Unwin, 1998).

Provincial Government

Provincial governments are responsible for matters such as education, health care and the police. The Ontario government looks after a number of important areas, such as:

- Business and vehicle registration
- Courts
- Health records and organ donation registration
- Property and land registration
- Education and training
- Employment standards, including workplace safety and insurance
- Retail sales tax
- Identification and certification records
- Outdoor services, including provincial parks.[32]

Headed by a premier provincial governments operate very similarly to the federal government, following the Westminster model.

The Constitution Act of 1867 created a Canadian Federation consisting of four provinces – Ontario, Quebec, Nova Scotia and New Brunswick. Ontario has a 'unicameral' or 'one chamber' parliament, which is based on a British model dating back to 1215.[33] In Ontario the Executive Council, also called the Cabinet, consists

---

32. Province of Ontario, "ServiceOntario," https://www.ontario.ca/page/services, accessed July 11, 2019.
33. Ontario, "History of government", https://www.ontario.ca/page/history-government, accessed July 11, 2019.

of the Premier and Cabinet Ministers, develops policies, sets priorities and introduces legislation for the consideration of the Members of Provincial Parliament (MPPs). The 124 Ontario MPPs sit in the Legislative Assembly where, similar to the House of Commons, legislation is debated and laws are made. Provincial elections, as with federal elections, must be held at least every five years and the political party that wins the majority of seats in the legislature forms the government. The provincial judiciary consists of the courts, the judges, and the chief justices and has responsibility for interpreting and enforcing laws and protecting citizens' rights.[34]

The legislative process in the Legislative Assembly is similar to that practiced in the House of Commons. At the first reading the proposed law is introduced and if it merits further discussion it is scheduled for a second reading at which it is debated and either sent for a third reading or referred to a committee. If the bill is referred to a committee, each section of the bill is discussed and voted on by committee members after which the committee reports to the legislature. At this point the bill can either go on to a committee consisting of the entire legislature or into a final debate. After the third reading, the Speaker of the Legislative Assembly calls for a final vote. Once passed, the bill goes to the Lieutenant Governor for Royal Assent on behalf of the Queen – there is no provincial Senate through which the bill must pass before receiving Royal Assent. After a bill receives Royal Assent the bill becomes law and a date is selected for its coming into effect.

Municipal Governments

Municipal governments have no constitutional standing but have played an important role in education, land development, local business regulation, and civic and cultural activities. This level of government in increasingly important to citizens, firms, and organizations because municipal government encourages policy innovation, matches policies with citizen preferences, and works closely with citizens' groups.[35]

In Ontario, the extent of powers and duties, internal organization, and structure of municipalities is governed by the *Ontario Municipal Act of 2001*.[36] Municipal councils govern municipalities and councillors make decisions regarding services

---

34. Ontario, "History of government", https://www.ontario.ca/page/history-government, accessed July 11, 2019.
35. Gilles Paquet and Jeffry Roy, Governance in Canada – Competition, Cooperation, and Co- evolution in Business-Government-Society Relations (Ottawa, Canada: Prime, 1997), 108-109.
36. Ontario, "Municipal Act, 2001, S.O. 2001, C.25", https://www.ontario.ca/laws/statute/01m25, accessed July 11, 2019.

and finances, for such areas as libraries, streets, garbage collection, land use regulations and building codes. The head of a local municipal council is either called the *mayor* or the *reeve* (or the *warden* in the case of a rural council and a *regional chair* in the case of a regional council) with members of council being called *councillors* or *aldermen*. Municipal councillors can be elected *at-large* or by *ward*. If elected at-large, councillors represent the entire municipality in which candidates with the largest number of votes in a municipal election are elected to the council. If the municipality is divided into wards, each ward may have more than one representative on council and voters in each ward can choose only among the candidates running for election in that ward.

The Government versus Business Paradigm

To set the context for a consideration of the challenges that follow it is important to further develop the *government* concept in terms of how it differs from the more intuitive business paradigm. An understanding of the difference is germane to an appreciation of government's complexity and might help explain the frustration experienced by business in its dealings with government.

At the outset it is somewhat of an understatement to say that government differs significantly from business. Whereas business is motivated by profit at the level of each individual firm, the government is motivated by providing the most for the greatest number. Whereas business seeks economic efficiency, the government seeks political efficiency. Occasionally these goals are congruent; most often they are not. At the federal level of government, Timothy Plumptre, in identifying impediments to management in the government, provides useful insight into the differences between government and business.[37] From Plumptre's presentation it is possible to differentiate government from business along three key lines: the *political process*, the *nature of government activity*, and the *institutional context of government*.

The political process

Several characteristics of the political process differentiate government from business, the first of which is elections – which can occur in a predictable fashion every four or five years or in a very unpredictable fashion in the case of a minority government. In situations where governments change, the priorities of the governing party may also change to align with the election platform and the party's key goals and priorities. This has an affect on program delivery which must adjust quickly.

---

37. Timothy Plumptre, *Beyond the Bottom Line: Management in Government* (Nova Scotia, Canada: Institute for Research in Public Policy, 1988).

Business is typically not subject to such extensive wholesale administrative changes in the constrained time period resulting from a change in government.

Related to elections is the difference in timelines perceived by politicians and the civil servants who work to deliver the programs. The number one priority for most politicians is to be successfully re-elected, and this typically involves a focus on the short-term, whereas public servants are typically focussed on the longer term having no vested interest in elections, in view of their neutrality in political matters. Business can exercise short-term and long-term interests anchored in the anticipated return on the bottom line.

In addition to elections and timelines, the government must treat members of the public consistently in its delivery of government programs. The same service level and rigour must be available for all Canadians regardless of where they live. Business has no such obligation except to target markets necessary to sustain a competitive advantage and such target markets generally demonstrate a characteristic cohesiveness.

The nature of government activity

For business its goals are typically well-defined and its activities are clearly congruent with its objectives. The measurement of its performance is clear and feedback measured by capital markets is often instantaneous. Government, by comparison, faces what Plumptre refers to as a "multiplicity of goals and the lack of any clear distinction between means and ends."[38] In recent months the federal government has enacted legislation to enhance accountability and responsibility but it is still frequently difficult to measure performance. Many of the qualitative goals of senior government managers do not lend themselves to the application of precisely measurable performance standards – this is not a criticism but more a statement of reality tied to the "nature of the beast." Related to this is the difficulty in ascertaining the true value-added of many government activities.

Whereas business can relate its activities to a return on the bottom line, the government is not able to do so and, even if it were, there would undoubtedly be situations where certain activities that are of questionable economic efficiency must continue because they are politically efficient.

Business typically partakes in areas it knows well and where a sustainable competitive advantage can be developed. A business operating in any of Canada's key sectors enjoys an advantage not available to the government – operational problems that arise are typically manageable within an understood domain and solutions will be applied to a relatively simple problem. Yet Canadians expect the government

38. Plumptre, Beyond the Bottom Line: Management in Government, 169.

to solve problems for which there are no obvious solutions that would satisfy the unending interests of an unending list of stakeholders – pollution, unemployment, international trade, corporate social responsibility, and solutions for the economic impact of changing population demographics, to provide but a few examples.

The Institutional Context of Government

In this area three key characteristics differentiate the government from business. First, the activities of government are increasingly transparent and its activities are subject to public review by an enormous range of stakeholders. Second, every voter is a stakeholder and in politics every vote matters so it is extremely challenging for the government to dialogue with every stakeholder and take their interests into account. Whereas in business key stakeholders can be determined, for government the number of key stakeholders in any issue of policy is daunting and the management of stakeholders an extremely arduous task.

Finally, government as an institution is far more complex than even the largest business enterprise. Larson and Zussman state that "the policy and management challenges facing the federal government are much more complex than those facing any other organization in the country."[39] And because there is "no other organization in Canada that comes close to the federal government's more than 200,000 employees, or its geographic distribution of those employees, they also suggest that, in addition to the three impediments put forth by Plumptre, a fourth barrier that differentiates the government from business is its size and geographic distribution.[40] The demands of stakeholders, the broad effect of policy decisions, and the time necessary to implement legislation all combine to produce a system that necessarily operates by design more deliberately than business.

Key Challenges for the Federal Government

From the discussion on the differences between government and business it should be obvious that any democratic government will face a daunting number of challenges. At the federal level there are, however, a number of challenges that represent priorities for the Government of Canada. Some of these items can be characterized as general issues concerning the administration of government; others are more specific.

---

39. Peter Larson and David Zussman, "Canadian Federal Public Service: The View From Recent Executive Recruits", *Optimum Online*, Vol.36, Issue 4, (2006).
40. Larson and Zussman, "Canadian Federal Public Service: The View From Recent Executive Recruits".

Decline in Voter Participation

In Canada's 41st General Election held on May 2, 2011 approximately 61 percent of registered electors elected the government. This means that around 40 percent of eligible voters for one reason or another did not exercise their democratic right to vote. In 1958, voter turnout was almost 79.4% and it has steadily declined since; reaching a low point of just 58.8% in October 2008. This is a disturbing trend that shows a general freefall in voter participation over the past 20 years. Over the past two elections voter turnout has rebounded almost ten percent, however, voter participation remains lower now than in 1867.[41]

Voter Turnout at Federal Elections and Referendums

Date of election/ referendum	Population	Number of Electors on lists	Total ballots cast	Voter turnout (%)
7 August - 20 September 1867	3,230,000	361,028	268,387	73.1
20 July - 12 October 1872	3,689,000	426,974	318,329	70.3
22 January 1874	3,689,000	432,410	324,006	69.6
17 September 1878	3,689,000	715,279	534,029	69.1
20 June 1882	4,325,000	663,873	508,496	70.3
22 February 1887	4,325,000	948,222	724,517	70.1
5 March 1891	4,833,000	1,113,140	778,495	64.4
23 June 1896	4,833,000	1,358,328	912,992	62.9
29 September 1898	4,833,000	1,236,419	551,405	44.6
7 November 1900	4,833,000	1,167,402	958,497	77.4
3 November 1904	5,371,000	1,385,440	1,036,878	71.6
26 October 1908	5,371,000	1,463,591	1,180,820	70.3
21 September 1911	7,204,527	1,820,742	1,314,953	70.2
17 December 1917	7,591,971	2,093,799	1,892,741	75.0
6 December 1921	8,760,211	4,435,310	3,139,306	67.7
29 October 1925	8,776,352	4,608,636	3,168,412	66.4
14 September 1926	8,887,952	4,665,381	3,273,062	67.7
28 July 1930	8,887,952	5,153,971	3,922,481	73.5
14 October 1935	10,367,063	5,918,207	4,452,675	74.2
26 March 1940	10,429,169	6,588,888	4,672,531	69.9
27 April 1942	11,494,627	6,502,234	4,638,847	71.3
11 June 1945	11,494,627	6,952,445	5,305,193	75.3
27 June 1949	11,823,649	7,893,629	5,903,572	73.8
10 August 1953	14,003,704	8,401,691	5,701,963	67.5
10 June 1957	16,073,970	8,902,125	6,680,690	74.1

41. Elections Canada, "Voter Turnout at Federal Elections and Referendums", https://www.elections.ca/content.aspx?section=ele&dir=turn&document=index&lang=e, accessed July 11, 2019.

Date of election/ referendum	Population	Number of Electors on lists	Total ballots cast	Voter turnout (%)
31 March 1958	16,073,970	9,131,200	7,357,139	79.4
18 June 1962	18,238,247	9,700,325	7,772,656	79.0
8 April 1963	18,238,247	9,910,757	7,958,636	79.2
8 November 1965	18,238,247	10,274,904	7,796,728	74.8
25 June 1968	20,014,880	10,860,888	8,217,916	75.7
30 October 1972	21,568,311	13,000,778	9,974,661	76.7
8 July 1974	21,568,311	13,620,353	9,671,002	71.0
22 May 1979	22,992,604	15,233,653	11,541,000	75.7
18 February 1980	22,992,604	15,890,416	11,015,514	69.3
4 September 1984	24,343,181	16,774,941	12,638,424	75.3
21 November 1988	25,309,331	17,639,001	13,281,191	75.3
26 October 1992	20,400,896	13,725,966	9,855,978	71.8
25 October 1993	27,296,859	19,906,796	13,863,135	69.6
2 June 1997	27,296,859	19,663,478	13,174,698	67.0
27 November 2000	28,846,761	21,243,473	12,997,185	61.2
28 June 2004	30,007,094	22,466,621	13,683,570	60.9
23 January 2006	30,007,094	23,054,615	14,908,703	64.7
14 October 2008	31,612,897	23,677,639	13,929,093	58.8
2 May 2011	33,476,688	24,257,592	14,823,408	61.1
19 October 2015	33,476,688	25,939,742	17,711,983	68.3

Elections Canada. Reproduced with the permission of Elections Canada.

The percentage of voter turnout might be a deciding factor in who gets elected, particularly in very close races, and would make a difference in the composition of the House of Commons and possibly whether a majority or minority government would result. Any elected government in Canada wants to be certain it is representative of all the people and that its policies are a reflection of the interests of all Canadians.

Indifference on the part of voters compromises this goal. As well, a voter who does not vote because of indifference is not in a particularly credible position to criticize the actions of the elected government.

Implications for Business

For business, the implication of low voter turnout may not be obvious however the following points will demonstrate why this matters to business:

- *People* vote and elect politicians, not *businesses*, therefore it is in business' best interests to ensure as many voters vote as possible, in particular like-minded key stakeholders such as, for example, employees and key suppliers.
- A low number of voters may not truly represent the true sentiments of a community or business environment.

Expectations for greater efficiency, cost-effectiveness, and accountability

Over the years the federal government has been criticized for improper spending of resources. In the aftermath of the widely publicized "sponsorship scandal" around a fund that had been set up in the wake of the 1995 referendum on Quebec sovereignty to assist in promoting federalism and the ensuing report of the Gomery Commission, the federal government introduced new legislation. The *Federal Accountability Act* that became law on December 12, 2006 represents an attempt to dispel the perception of the growing mistrust that exists between the public and the government by instituting as law a number of reforms including the financing of political parties, toughening the *Lobbyists Registration Act*, cleaning up the procurement of government contracts, providing protection for whistleblowers, and strengthening the power of the Auditor General and auditing and accountability within departments. While no one would dispute that making government officials more accountable and responsible to taxpayers is a good thing, some question the effectiveness of the Act's complex paradigm that is "management" in government. Some writers suggest that the Act's approach to solving mistrust is to put in place more mechanisms of oversight in an already over-burdened oversight system and would call into question the motives and behaviours of all public office holders. Others suggest that control is not a substitute for good governance. These insights offer important perspectives on the management of accountability in government. On the one hand there is a need to be fiscally responsible stewards of the public purse and appear to the voting public as a responsible government dedicated to increasing responsibility and accountability on the use of taxpayers' dollars. On the other hand increasing responsibility and accountability will necessarily result in making an already rules-laden and reporting-fatigued bureaucracy more bureaucratic and discourage innovation and creativity that both demand assuming risk.

Implications for Business

Greater accountability will mean the more effective use of corporate tax dollars and this could, arguably result in tax reduction. However greater accountability in a bureaucracy comes with tangible and intangible costs:

- Increasing accountability will result in additional systems of check and balance and there will be a cost to implementation
- As more systems and more rules emerge bureaucrats will spend more time 'feeding the beast' and this will slow the business of government

It is important, however, to balance the control and accountability against the parameters of the scandal. Justice Gomery's report highlighted, among other findings, clear evidence of political involvement in the administration of the Sponsorship Program, inflated commissions amid a complex web of financial transactions involving kickbacks, and insufficient oversight at very senior levels of the public service.[42] Perhaps the sponsorship scandal would qualify as one of CBC News' top ten scandals in Canadian political history, some of which are given below.[43]

Scandal	Descriptions
The Pacific Scandal (1873)	Perhaps, Canada's first political scandal. Sir John A. Macdonald and the Conservatives accused of accepting $350,000 in donations from Sir Hugh Allan during the 1873 election in return for giving Allan's consortium the contract to build the Canadian Pacific Railway.
The King-Byng Affair (1925)	The Minister of Customs and Excise, responsible for ensuring contraband did not cross the Canada-US border during prohibition accused of promoting a bootlegger to a top customs enforcement position.
The Gerda Munsinger Scandal (1966)	Accusations of some Progressive Conservative Cabinet Ministers consorting with an East German playgirl who may have been a spy for the KGB.
The Hospital Document Scandal (1978)	Liberal Solicitor General accused of assisting a woman in procuring an abortion after signing the woman's husband's name on a hospital document.
Tunagate (1985)	Conservative Fisheries Minister accused of overturning an order from his own inspectors and ordering a million cans of StarKist tuna, deemed by his inspectors to be badly spoiled, released for sale to the public.
All the other Mulroney ministers (1984-1993)	The Conservative government lost an average of one Cabinet Minister per year to allegations of wrongdoing.

42. Government of Canada, " Restoring accountability – recommendations / John Gomery, Commissioner", http://publications.gc.ca/site/eng/287355/publication.html, accessed July 11, 2019.
43. CBC News, "Up the skirt or in the till: Top ten scandals in Canadian political history", published February 10, 2005, https://www.cbc.ca/news2/background/cdngovernment/scandals.html, accessed July 11, 2019.

Scandal	Descriptions
Shawinigate (1993)	Questions regarding the Liberal Prime Minister's involvement in the sale of two properties in his riding.
Airbus (1995)	An investigation related to the purchasing of airplanes and helicopters tangled up with allegations of kick-backs and secret commissions.
The APEC Inquiry (1997)	The RCMP pepper sprayed protesters lining the planned route of world leaders attending the APEC Conference in Vancouver. Later the RCMP would be found to have acted inappropriately.
The billion-dollar boondoggle (2000)	Liberal government accused of failing to track employment program grants worth $1 billion to ensure the funds were used as intended.

And later governments appear to continue the trend.[44]

Scandal	Descriptions
Grant Bristow (1994)	The co-founder of one of Canada's most influential white supremacist organizations was revealed to in fact be a spy for CSIS.
The Maxime Bernier Scandal (2008)	MP Maxime Bernier was forced to resigned his post as Minister of Foreign Affairs when it was discovered that he had misplaced a file of secret documents in his girlfriend's home.
F-35 Scandal (2010)	An Auditor General Report revealed that officials had intentionally withheld information including the true cost of the proposed contract.
Elbowgate (2016)	The House of Commons was left in an uproar when Prime Minister Justin Trudeau was accused of 'manhandling' an opposition MP and elbowing another during an important vote.
SNC Lavalin (2019)	SNC-Lavalin faces charges of fraud and corruption in connection with payments made to the Libyan government totaling approximately $48 million. The company had hoped that the charges could be resolved with a Deferred Prosecution Agreement, which would spare the company a trial and possible criminal conviction. SNC-Lavalin employs nearly 9,000 Canadians with the concentration of jobs being in Quebec. The controversy began with the accusation that the Prime Minister's office had "attempted to press" the Justice Minister to intervene in the prosecution of the company.

The horizontal management of issues that cross departmental borders

Many issues in government such as climate change, competitiveness, biotechnology, and border security involve more than one department and could benefit from coordinated and collaborative efforts across departments. Bakvis and Juillet exam-

44. MSN, "The biggest political scandals in Canadian history", https://www.msn.com/en-ca/news/canada/the-biggest-political-scandals-in-canadian-history/ss-BBOwrCs?fullscreen=true#image=3, accessed July 11, 2019.

ined six areas of horizontal management using four case studies as a focus.[45] Among these six areas were the nature of policy domains and management philosophies, catalysts and champions, costs and benefits as factors in the uptake of horizontal management, and accountability. Their conclusions highlight an increasing willingness of public servants to work across departmental boundaries on major policy issues that require such a horizontal approach. At the same time their findings also suggest a number of important challenges. First, while horizontal management is intended to generate better outcomes and cost savings, the research found that the costs of working horizontally are often underestimated.

Second, adding to an already complex management environment, working horizontally requires the management of more complicated performance indicators, reporting relationships, and accountabilities.

The reality is that several evolving complex issues can only be resolved using a horizontal approach to their management that reflects a full knowledge contribution from the key players in the issue regardless of departmental boundaries. This approach would arguably lead to a better informed policy decisions, but would not necessarily generate cost-savings in the management approach.

Effective stewardship of the public purse

There is a need to manage multiple accountabilities and to demonstrate the achievement of performance objectives to Canadians in areas where the very nature of programs complicates the measurement of performance. Given that the source of government funding is effectively individual and company taxpayers, it is critical to reassure Canadians that bureaucrats and politicians are acting as appropriate stewards of the public purse, and can demonstrate this in a coherent and transparent manner. As such federal departments are required to engage in a number of requirements designed to ensure that they are achieving results for Canadians.

In order to ensure accountability from a program perspective, each federal department is required to manage program results, and report those results to the public accordingly.[46]

The new *Policy on Results* was put into effect in 2016 to replace the previous Management, Resources and Results Structure (MRRS) a structured program management framework intended to provide the federal government and the individual

45. Herman Bakvis and Luc Juillet, *The Horizontal Challenge: Line Departments, Central Agencies and Leadership*, (Ottawa, Canada: Canada School of Public Service, 2004), 8.
46. Government of Canada, "Policy on Results", https://www.tbs-sct.gc.ca/pol/doc-eng.aspx?id=31300, accessed July 15, 2019.

departments a means to manage the financial and non-financial information related to programs and corporate services. The new policy also replaced policies on reporting and evaluation.

The government's Policy on Results in intended to "improve the achievement of results across government, and enhance the understanding of the results government seeks to achieve, does achieve, and the resources used to achieve them".[47] In order to accomplish this, departments are required to develop a "Departmental Results Framework", which describes the department's "core responsibilities" and must be approved by the Treasury Board of Canada.[48]

A Performance Measurement and Evaluation Committee oversees the departmental performance against the approved framework. To ensure that performance measurement is robust, the function requires a senior official to oversee the development and maintenance of Program Inventories, and Performance Information Profiles, which includes appropriate data collection for evaluation.

The Head of Evaluation is a neutral function, reporting directly to the Deputy Head. A five year rolling Evaluation Plan is updated and presented annually to ensure that programs and the performance of these programs is appropriately monitored and reported.[49]

Planning and reporting

Planning and reporting in any major government department is challenging and complicated, and involves the integration of many components, including, for example:

- An environmental scan – what is happening in the macro-environment that could impact on a government department's ability to achieve its strategic outcomes
- Senior management strategic and program priorities
- Risk profile – an enterprise risk profile that articulates areas of key risk, and mitigation measures
- Internal audits and program evaluations; external audits conducted by the Office of the Auditor General
- Human resources planning
- Business planning
- Information management and information technology planning
- Capital planning

47. Government of Canada, "Policy on Results", https://www.tbs-sct.gc.ca/pol/doc-eng.aspx?id=31300, accessed July 15, 2019.
48. Government of Canada, "Policy on Results", https://www.tbs-sct.gc.ca/pol/doc-eng.aspx?id=31300, accessed July 15, 2019.
49. Government of Canada, "Policy on Results", https://www.tbs-sct.gc.ca/pol/doc-eng.aspx?id=31300, accessed July 15, 2019.

- Regional planning
- Resource allocation

Departmental Plans are part of the Estimates documents which support the appropriation of funds to be spent by the government. The Estimates document has three parts:

1. Part I provides and overview of federal spending,
2. Part II lists the financial resources required by individual departments, agencies and Crown corporations for the coming fiscal year,
3. Part III consists of the *Departmental Plan* and the *Departmental Results Report*.[50]

The Departmental Plan describes the strategic outcomes, programs, expected results and resource requirements for a three period. The Departmental Results Report are the accounts of actual performance for the most recently completed fiscal year against the plans, priorities and expected results set out in the Departmental Plan. The financial information in the Departmental Plan is drawn from the *Main Estimates* which represent the approved budgetary expenditures for the upcoming fiscal year. The *Main Estimates* comprise the documents used by the government to estimate what it will cost to run the government for the fiscal year, and through which it obtains authority from Parliament to spend public monies. The *Policy on Results* aligns the performance information in the Departmental Plan, with the Estimates documents and the Public Accounts of Canada.[51]

Performance measurement

Both public and private sector organizations strive to measure performance to assess progress in the achievement of goals and objectives. They must be able to demonstrate effectiveness and efficiency in the use of the resources available to them. For businesses, regardless of the nature of the goods or services they provide, performance is relatively easy to measure and report to key stakeholders. This is because the primary performance indicators for businesses are financial ones such as profit and rate of return on investment. Achieving them of course is another matter.

Performance measurement in the public sector, on the other hand, is more difficult to track because performance measures for government organizations tend to be non- financial (e.g., sustainable fisheries, safe food supply, and reliable roadways). Efficiency and staying within budget are important of course for meeting stewardship obligations, but the goals and objectives of government, as written into

50. Government of Canada, "Departmental Plans", https://www.canada.ca/en/treasury-board-secretariat/services/planned-government-spending/reports-plans-priorities.html, accessed July 15, 2019.
51. Government of Canada, "Departmental Plans", https://www.canada.ca/en/treasury-board-secretariat/services/planned-government-spending/reports-plans-priorities.html, accessed July 15, 2019.

legislation, arc much more diverse and the definition of success is more complex. Considerable effort must go into identifying desired results and outcomes, that is, the consequences or impact of a program. There can be short, medium, and long-term outcomes.

Also, the kinds of stakeholders interested in seeing performance results are broader for government as compared to business and more numerous. Whereas shareholders, unions, creditors, some non-government organizations, and regulatory bodies wish to be informed on performance and related issues for businesses, the number of affected and interested parties seeking performance information from government can include others as well such as parliamentarians, voters, taxpayers, and special interest groups.

Risk management

Risk management, the on-going process of seeking to be prepared for serious eventualities that can affect the achievement of goals and objectives, is relatively more difficult for government as compared to business as well. This is because of the difficulties that can be encountered in government into developing useful performance indicators to track progress against objectives. Clarity about objectives and outcomes is essential before organizations can assess the likelihood and impact of risks to the achievement of goals and objectives and then formulate mitigation strategies to respond to the risks.

Becoming more citizen-centric, engaged, and accessible to the public

Earlier discussions regarding the complexity of government, the number of stakeholders, and the difficulty in narrowing down key stakeholders serve to complicate efforts to become more citizen-centric and engaged with the voting public. Clearly significant consultation and public engagement will result in greater perceptions of legitimacy, credibility, and transparency, and, arguably, more effective public policy and better policy outcomes. However, being citizen-centric must be framed in the "bounded reality" in which public sector managers and politicians work – that regardless of the level of consultation undertaken there may not be consensus or full agreement and that both those who agree and those who disagree are all potential voters.

Similar to stakeholder dialogue the logic of this approach is quite sound, and Canadians would undoubtedly appreciate the effort to be consulted. As with stakeholder analysis in general, and stakeholder identification more specifically, the challenges of which public stakeholders to consult remains, and is made even more complex by the very nature of government as entrusted to act in the best interests of society. Moreover very few members of the public fully appreciate the complexity of government both as an institution and as regards the policy issues that must be dealt with. To further complicate the matter, often the stakeholders themselves do not fully understand their stakes nor the reality of government's need to strike a balance between the diverse interests of innumerable stakeholders and the requirement to do what satisfies the greatest number of constituents.

In the era of ongoing development in information and communications technologies the concept of *e-government* has become popular – essentially using the electronic communication tools available to engage citizens, business, and civil society stakeholders. There is considerable merit to this approach; however, a consideration of the way things worked before the information and telecommunications revolution is useful to provide context.

Prior to the advent of e-mail, when a constituent sent an actual letter by post to his/her Member of Parliament or a Cabinet Minister it was generally accepted that a certain inevitable delay would occur as the constituent's letter travelled the perilous route through the bureaucratic chain of command – from the Minister's office's correspondence unit through Deputy Minister's office to the appropriate Assistant Deputy Minister whose staff would forward it to the appropriate Director General whose office, in turn, would send it on to one of his/her Directors who would find some division chief who would in turn find some officer to draft a response. The draft response would then be *typed* by support staff and sent back to the minister through the same chain of command, with every level in the chain of command value-added revisions to the draft such that the final response to the writer signed by the minister likely bore no resemblance whatsoever to the original draft prepared by the civil servant who likely had responsibility for the project that was the subject of the incoming letter in the first place.

As inefficient and humorous as the process from the old days may appear, there were, of course, some merits to the scenario above, not the least of which was that government had time to carefully consider the incoming letter and to develop a considered and fulsome response on likely a very complex policy issue, informed by the various levels of expertise on the subject of the incoming letter. But of course all this was before the internet and e-mail – today any constituent can pull out his or her laptop or cell phone and fire off an e-mail or text message to his/her minister of choice instantaneously, copying everyone imaginable including the press, and of course expect an instantaneous response other than "Your message has been received." While technology has served as the great enabler for communications, in reality the only difference between today and the old days is that the e-mail message (a.k.a. the letter) runs down the chain of command faster. The response still requires all the same value-added input and considered analysis by all the same parties, except the edits can be made without having to retype the entire draft.

Failure to exercise due diligence and attention to detail in responses to the public would be a disservice on the part of public servants to Canadians.

When expectations are managed, technology does offer considerable capacity for greater citizen engagement, although not without certain challenges. Professor Jeffrey Roy suggests there are four challenges associated with effective e-government: service, security, transparency, and trust.[52] Service challenges include the ability to act effectively and reliably with Canadians. Security concerns may compromise a philosophy of efficient customer service. While information and communications technologies certainly enable greater consultation and stakeholder engagement, and can enable increased citizen-centricity, much work remains to be done in this area.

Implications for Business

Greater citizen engagement by government has a number of implications for business:

- Access to politicians and government decision-makers is no longer the cloistered domain of business
- Given that any citizen or civil society stakeholder group has immediate access to politicians and bureaucrats, there is a greater need on the part of business for increased transparency and stakeholder engagement since business stakeholders can more easily *whistle-blow* on the alleged wrongdoings or misdoings of business
- As politicians and bureaucrats must respond to queries of all constituents there is less time for face-to-face exchanges with business
- The work that remains to be done in facilitating greater citizen engagement can present opportunities for business to work with government to innovate solutions to the communications challenges associated with a more citizen-centric government

---

Issues Facing Government

A decade ago the main issues facing government were the economy, infrastructure, national security, and free trade between the provinces. Our world since then has become so much more complicated.

---

52. Jeffrey Roy, *E-Government in Canada – Transformation for the Digital Age* (Ottawa, Canada: University of Ottawa Press, 2006).

The Economy

In 2008 we experienced a global meltdown of the financial markets that resulted in unprecedented actions of national governments to stem the wave of uncertainty and risk in some cases by nationalizing banks and in other cases providing unprecedented injections of taxpayers' money as guarantees against shaky bank debt instruments. This has resulted in bankruptcies of otherwise stable financial institutions and the evaporation of retirement funds for countless Canadians as well as a meltdown in the automotive and manufacturing sectors.

Infrastructure

Increasing population and continued economic growth were combining to tax Canada's infrastructure. Statistics Canada reported that "by 2003, the roads and highways network already had over 50 percent of its useful life behind it."[53] *The Building Canada* plan was to provide $33 billion over seven years, investing in infrastructure to build a stronger economy, cleaner environment, and better communities.

National Security

The world changed on September 11, 2001 and Canada was not immune to the fallout of the actions of terrorists on the World Trade Center. More than a decade later the consequences of that day were still being felt. In April 2004 Canada's *National Security Policy* was released.[54]

Free Trade between Canada's Provinces

Recognizing that internal trade barriers were detrimental to development, in 1994 the Prime Minister as well as the first minister of all provinces and territories signed the Agreement on Internal Trade (AIT) which had, as its goal, the elimination of barriers to trade, investment and mobility in Canada. More specifically the goal of the AIT is to reduce and eliminate, to the extent possible, barriers to the free movement of persons, goods, services, and investments within Canada and to establish an open, efficient and stable domestic market.[55] A decade later, the perception was that barriers still existed and required the attention of government to ensure that internal trade was not overshadowed by international trade.

---

53. "The Daily, Study: The age of Canada's public infrastructure," Statistics Canada, date modified: 2006-01-30, https://www150.statcan.gc.ca/n1/daily-quotidien/060130/dq060130b-eng.htm.
54. Government of Canada, *Securing an Open Society: Canada's National Security Policy, (2004)*, accessed May 10, 2013, http://publications.gc.ca/collections/Collection/CP22-77-2004E.pdf.
55. "Top 10 Barriers to Competitiveness," The Canadian Chamber of Commerce, 16.

Issues Facing Government in 2019

Today the issues are more numerous and more complex.

Social issues including abortion, gay marriage, LGBT adoption rights, gender workplace diversity, women in combat, euthanasia, the death penalty, and the wearing of the Niqàb are all centre-stage, crossing socio-economic and demographic lines.

Environmental issues including renewable energy, pipelines, fracking, plastic product bans, GMOs, animal testing, and environmental regulation are key issues for the voting population, and have and will continue to be heavily debated for many years to come.

Domestic policies relating to gun control, funding of native projects, social media regulation, the Senate and funding of the CBC continue to take up much of the soundbites in chambers. All of these issues have the potential to affect our day to day lives as citizens, but also impact the business and the civil sectors.

Immigration is a hot topic. Deportation of criminal immigrants, immigration bans, immigrant assimilation, skilled immigrants, citizenship testing, dual citizenship and the use of temporary foreign workers are discussions that have all hit the news in recent years.

Healthcare. We live in a world populated by multiple generations – more now than ever before. The health of our citizens is critical to our survival as a nation, and is deeply personal as well. Who funds what, privatization, marijuana, prescription drugs, dental and vision coverage are all topics we can relate to as individuals. The top of mental health and the complexity of this issue alone is so very critical to our overall well-being.

Foreign policy issues are highlighted every day in the news. Military spending, mandatory military service, and foreign aid funding, Canada's relations with the United Nations, Syria, North Korea, Iraq, Israel, and the political climate of the United States – all impact us as Canadians.

The economy will always occupy the minds of our citizens. Government must continually be aware of concerns in regards taxes, wages, free trade, government spending, tariffs, pensions, and jobs.

Electoral issues regarding reform, voters' rights, financing of campaigns, candidate transparency and limitations to terms served are somewhat new in the news.

Crime is always in the news as well. Politicians today are concerned with prison overcrowding, parole hearings, private prisons, and drug trafficking penalties.

Education is always a hot topic as well. Debates around university tuition, should education be a provincial or federal responsibility, etc. are becoming more and more volatile.

Finally transportation issues relating to public transportation systems, including light rail, and the use of drones for commercial purposes all have implications for the way in which government and business influence each other.

Chapter Summary

Created in 1867 through the *British North American Act*, Canada is a comparatively young country that began as a collection of British North American colonies with equal powers and differing interests. Canada is governed through the Westminster model derived from the seat of British Parliament in Westminster in London, adapted to reflect Canada's two sources of law: federal parliament and provincial legislatures. The three branches of the federal government include the legislative branch, the executive branch, and the judiciary. Provincial governments in Canada follow the Westminster model. Local or municipal governments have no constitutional standing.

The Canadian government differs greatly from Canadian business and this difference is what makes the government sector complex and fraught with issues that not only affect every Canadian macro-economic segment, but also affect each segment in profound ways for which no solution that would appease every segment is possible. Canadian business and civil society are continuously pressing for increased efficiency and accountability but achieving these goals is much more difficult in the government segment than in other segments. The recent interest and efforts toward the horizontal management of issues that cross departmental borders, while theoretically sound, are no guarantee of cost savings due to the complexity of the policy issues, the nature of government activity, and the institutional context of government. While the movement toward greater public involvement is important, organizing public participation presents challenges as regards key stakeholder identification, and e-government has created expectations of instantaneous communications with policy decision makers who will provide instant answers to complex questions.

While the issues facing government were of paramount concern a decade ago, the complexity and breadth of issues facing politicians and the bureaucrats serving them are even more numerous representing challenges across the social and economic spectrum. Such is a sampling of the depth, breadth, and complexity of the issues the government segment must deal with in a manner that appeases all segments of the Canadian macro-economic environment.

A Practitioners' Perspective: An Interview with Paul J. DeVillers, LL.B., P.C.

Mr. DeVillers studied at the University of Ottawa and obtained his LL. B. in 1970. While at U of O he played varsity hockey and was Captain of the Gee-Gees in 1966-67 and 1967-68.

Mr. DeVillers practiced law from 1972 to 1993 in Ottawa, Penetanguishene and Midland. In 1993 he was elected Member of Parliament for the riding of Simcoe

North and was re-elected three times in 1997, 2000, and 2004. He was elected Chair of the Liberal National Caucus in 1998 where he served until being appointed by PM Jean Chretien as Secretary of State for Amateur Sport and Deputy Leader of the Government in the House in 2002. In 2003 he was appointed Secretary of State for Physical Activity and Sport as well as Deputy Leader of the Government in the House. In 2003 he was appointed Parliamentary Secretary to PM Paul Martin to complete a report on the creation of a full Ministry of Physical Activity and Sport. This report was presented to the Government in July 2003 and was ignored with Mr. DeVillers resigning in protest.

After retiring from politics Mr. DeVillers spent from 2006 to 2019 as a Lawyer Member of the Ontario Consent and Capacity Board being named a Vice Chair of the Board in 2016.

Canadian Business & Society: *From your perspective, how important is political instincts in decision-making?*

Paul DeVillers: It essential to consider the distinction between "political instinct and political strategy". Instinct is the natural reaction to a political situation without having the luxury of the time to consult or plan. Strategy is the result consulting others and developing a plan when time permits. It is also necessary to consider that both political activities and business involve marketing. In politics it is the marketing of ideas and candidates and in business it marketing goods and services. In my view the person who can make sound decisions instinctively should fare better in both political activity and business.

Canadian Business & Society: *Today it is often said that business, government, and civil society must work together synergistically to create sustainable value for Canadians. How do you go about 'dividing the pie' between business, government, and civil society stakeholders?*

Paul DeVillers: In my view the role of business is to make profits for the proprietors and in the case of corporations for the shareholder. The role of government is to redistribute the wealth in a fair and equitable fashion while providing peace and order. The role of civil society is to ensure that business and government are performing their roles while respecting the rights of the individual. The question implies that business, government and civil society serve different masters who require a piece of the "pie" which in my view is not the case. The sustainable value to Canadians should be the compliance with the Charter of Rights and Freedoms to the benefit of all.

Canadian Business & Society: *How important to business success is an understanding of how government works?*

Contributed by Paul J. Devillers. © Kendall Hunt Publishing Company

Paul DeVillers: As stated previously my view of the role of government is to re-distribute the wealth fairly and to provide peace and order. Government is provided powers to regulate and to tax to accomplish this role. In addition providing peace, order and good government sets the stable conditions for business to complete its role of making profits. To me it therefore follows that business is served well when it understands and works cooperatively with government. Thus it is in my view important to the success of business to understand the role of government and how it works.

Canadian Business & Society: *From your perspective as a former Cabinet Minister, if there was one message you would like to give to introductory business students, what would it be?*

Paul DeVillers: From my perspective as a former Cabinet Minister the one message I would give to introductory business students is to know and understand the roles of business and government as set out in the answers to the previous questions. I believe that knowing these roles and ensuring business and government work cooperatively will lead to success for both. This will avoid the need for some of the discord experienced from civil society trying to protect the rights and wellbeing of the individual when business and government fail to accomplish their roles.

A Practitioners' Perspective: An Interview with Lori MacDonald, Associate Deputy Minister, Immigration, Refugees and Citizenship Canada

Lori MacDonald was appointed Associate Deputy Minister of Immigration, Refugees and Citizenship in August 2018.

Prior to this appointment, Ms. MacDonald served as Assistant Deputy Minister of the Safety and Security Group for Transport Canada. She held a vast array of responsibilities that ensured the safety and security of our transportation system, including the development and oversight of relevant policies, standards, laws, and regulations, as well as the support and facilitation of a sound safety and security culture that also facilitates economic growth.

With 35 years of experience in Public Service, Lori has held a variety of positions within Public Service, including in the Correctional Services of Canada and Public Safety.

Lori has extensive experience at the senior executive level and has developed policy and programs at the local, regional, and national levels of the government. She has championed many projects related to women, Indigenous, and mental health issues. She has extensive experience in operations at all levels of government and has played a leadership role in developing managerial and leadership capacity among teams and managers in the government.

Her affinity for marginalized groups, her passion for progress, and her enthusiastic leadership are evident throughout her career.

Lori holds a diploma in Law and Security Administration from Loyalist College in Belleville and a degree in Criminology with a concentration in Law from Carleton University in Ottawa.

Canadian Business & Society: *From your perspective, how important is political instincts in decision-making?*

Lori MacDonald: The role of public servants is to advise the government on how to best achieve their policy objectives and commitments. While we must be aware of, and responsive to, political developments, the advice we provide must at all times remain impartial and non-partisan in nature. It must be backed up with sound evidence and rigorous analysis, and reflect a diversity of views – including business, civil society, and other stakeholders. All of these elements are critical to the policy development cycle, and the role of the public service in advice and decision-making.

Canadian Business & Society: *Today it is often said that business, government, and civil society must work together synergistically to create sustainable value for Canadians. How do you go about 'dividing the pie' between business, government, and civil society stakeholders?*

Lori MacDonald: At IRCC, we are actively looking to expand on the links between government, business, and civil society, to both advance the government's direction and foster innovation in the policy space. A notable example is the Atlantic Immigration Pilot, which aims to address demographic and labour market challenges in Atlantic Canada by working with employers and settlement agencies to recruit and retain foreign workers and ensure their successful integration in the region. Another example is the Economic Mobility Pathways Project, launched in partnership with two non-governmental organizations, which aims to identify skilled refugees in Africa and the Middle East who can come to Canada as economic immigrants through existing programs. Each of these projects is driven by a desire to innovate, and to experiment with new approaches and new ways of engaging the business and civil society sectors.

Canadian Business & Society: *How important to business success is an understanding of how government works?*

Lori MacDonald: Federal public servants have a responsibility to manage and care for public resources on behalf of the Canadian people and public interest. The policies and programs we advance must be consistent with these expectations, including by demonstrating value for money. Although the business sector may define success differently, the interests of both are served well when they understand their respective roles and priorities. In this fashion, government and business will

Contributed by Lori MacDonald. (C) Kendall Hunt Publishing Company be better placed to identify areas of mutual interest, and to work cooperatively together in meeting the needs of Canadians.

Canadian Business & Society: *From your perspective, if there was one message you would like to give to introductory business students, what would it be?*

Lori MacDonald: I would say that both business and government should acknowledge how much we share in common, and the extent to which we have an opportunity to learn from each other promote our shared interests. The Global Skills Strategy is a great example of what we can achieve when we listen to each other and work to improve public sector program delivery. More can be done. Ultimately, the private and public sectors aim to be client-focused, to create value, to listen to shareholders and stakeholders, and make decisions that ideally have a positive impact on Canada's economy and society. In this light, I encourage you to embrace opportunities to engage with the public service to exchange ideas and to explore innovative approaches that maximize the attainment of our mutual objectives.

End of Chapter Questions

1. Provide some examples of the federal government's exclusive national powers and explain why these powers are exclusive to the federal government.

2. Outline the characteristics of the House of Commons, the Senate, and the Judiciary and discuss their relevance to Canadian business and Canadian civil society.

3. Explain the steps necessary for a federal "bill" to become "law" and discuss why knowledge of this process would be important to Canadian businesses and representatives of Canadian civil society.

4. How does government differ from business? Why is an understanding of these differences important for private sector managers?

5. What are the key challenges of public participation, and how do you suggest these be overcome?

6. Suppose the Northwest Passage opens permanently due to climate change. What issues might arise for the Canadian government and what might be the interests of the business segment?

Application Questions

Referring to the opening new article on the Trans Mountain Expansion, discuss each of the following:

1. In your view, who were the key stakeholders and what were their respective "stakes"?

2. What were the areas of common ground between business and government?

3. How does the TMX exemplify the differences between business and government?

4. How does the TMX exemplify the nature of government activity?

5. Which issues faced by the government today are touched by the TMX?

Research Questions

1. Using the last three censuses conducted by Statistics Canada, report on any changes in the number of seats in the House of Commons by province or territory. In your view, is the census an appropriate means through which to determine the number of seats available or would you suggest a different methodology?

2. Using the Internet, identify and describe the three most important recent pieces of federal and provincial legislation (i.e., three pieces of federal legislation and three pieces of provincial legislation), either passed or in progress, that in your view would have the greatest impact on business and civil society in Canada. In your view why are these pieces of legislation so important and what would the important be?

3. Private capital and expertise can make a significant contribution to building infrastructure projects. The involvement of the private sector in these types of projects typically takes the form of a public-private partnership. Using the Internet and other sources analyze the effectiveness of these "P3s" as private-public partnerships are referred to, citing advantages and disadvantages, and provide your informed opinion on whether P3s would be a good approach for the government to take in building infrastructure projects.

Team Discussion Project

Interview a federal member of Parliament or a provincial member of provincial parliament and ask his/her view on the following:

1. What was the most important piece of legislation they supported during their time as MP or MPP?

2. Who were the key stakeholders and who won? What would you say to the "losing" stakeholders?

CHAPTER 4

The Canadian Civil Society Segment

vector_s/Shutterstock.com

Civil Society in the News

Canada's new food policy aims to improve enforcement[1]

The article published in June 2019 discusses the announcement by the federal government of the new first-ever food policy for Canada. The $134-million budget for the Food Policy for Canada will come from its 2019 budget. Additional funding for the Canadian Food Inspection Agency is intended to support the enforce-

1. Elizabeth Raymer, "Canada's new food policy aims to improve enforcement", Canada Lawyer, June 21, 2019, https://www.canadian-lawyermag.com/news/general/canadas-new-food-policy-aims-to-improve-enforcement/276211, accessed August 7, 2019.

ment of the compliance of labelling and other requirements by food companies. The aim of which is to protect consumers from deception and to protect companies from unfair competition.

The process for developing the policy was rigorous and involved a brand-new multi-stakeholder group to consult with, including civil society groups. The food policy is focused more on civil society groups than on industry. The article notes that Agri-food is an important business for Canadians, and that Canada has the potential to be world leader in this area.

Other Food Policy of Canada initiatives include:

- a new Canada Brand and Buy Canadian promotional campaigns that will aim to increase pride and consumer confidence in Canadian food;
- support for community-led projects such as greenhouses, community freezers and skills training that address food challenges and food insecurity in northern and isolated communities;
- a challenge fund to support the most innovative food waste reduction ideas in food processing, grocery retail and food service;
- work alongside provinces and not-for-profit organizations toward the creation of a National School Food Program.

The full article can be viewed at https://www.canadianlawyermag.com/news/general/canadas-new-food-policy-aims-to-improve-enforcement/276211.

Introduction

The previous chapter explored the Canadian government segment. This chapter introduces and discusses the third segment of the Canadian macro-environment – civil society, arguably the least intuitive and most misunderstood of the three segments. The discussion will frame and contextualize civil society, discuss its importance, introduce social capital, consider the challenges of this segment, feature some selected examples of civil society organizations, and position the segment's importance to business and government.

What Exactly is Civil Society?

Most business students have an intuitive understanding of what is meant by business and government as two major segments of the Canadian domestic macro-environment. The third segment, referred to here as *civil society*, is not as intuitively understood. Indeed selecting the most appropriate nomenclature to define this segment has met with considerable debate among academics. In its simplest form civil society could be considered as any organizations that are independent of business and government and that cannot be classified as part of the business or government segments. This would include voluntary and civic organizations, non-profits and philanthropic organizations, unions, academia, hospitals, and human rights organizations just to suggest a few. Hasenfeld and Gidron depict three different dimensions of civil society: volunteer-run organizations, social movements, and non-profit service organizations, and suggest the development of multipurpose hybrid voluntary organizations.[2] Civil society could also include less formal organizations such as a group of neighbours, members of a bowling team, and co-workers. Certain characteristics of civil society in this context emerge. For example, civil society organizations could be characterized as follows:

- Individuals as members of some construct of a group or informal organization.
- Individuals with common societal interests, purposes and values working together to achieve either something for the individual, something for the group, or something for the broader society – that may or may not align with the prevailing direction of the state.
- Formal organizations that are neither directly coerced by government nor directly affected by the supply-and-demand sorting mechanisms of business, and that are anchored in trust and social obligation sharing a vision of a better society as a result of their efforts.

Given these characteristics and to better focus discussion on civil society as a concept, for our discussion purposes charities, non-profit and volunteer organizations will be used as examples of third-sector organizations from which to study the important contributions and workings of this segment of Canadian society. Canadian non-profit and voluntary organizations generally share some common characteristics. These organizations are typically:

- non-governmental,
- non-profit,
- independent,
- self-regulating, and
- reliant in some measure on the work of volunteers.

According to Statistics Canada, as published in the Cornerstones of Community: Highlights of the National Survey of Nonprofit and Voluntary Organizations, Catalogue no. 61-533-XPE, a range of interests are included in the estimated

---

2. Yeheskel Hasenfeld and Benjamin Gidron, "Understanding Multi-purpose Hybrid Voluntary Organizations: The Contributions of Theories on Civil Society, Social Movements and Non- Profit Organizations," (*Journal of Civil Society*, 1, 2) (September 2005) 97-112.

161,000 such organizations that operated in Canada in 2003, of which more than half were registered charities.[3] Included in this important group are hospitals, universities and colleges, religious organizations, environmental groups, sports organizations and advocacy groups to name just a few. Activities in the areas of health and education dominate the non-profit sector accounting for over 70% of all contributions.[4] Collectively these organizations are important conduits through which ordinary Canadians can engage in activities that make a difference in the quality of Canadian life. Non-profit and voluntary organizations in Canada boasted 139 million members and $112 billion in revenues in 2003 and therefore collectively represented and continue to represent an important economic contribution.[5] Of the revenues approximately one-third were attributed to less than one percent of the organizations comprising hospitals, universities, and colleges leaving $75 billion attributed to the remaining 99 percent of organizations.[6]

In 2013, 82% of Canadians made donations to a charitable organization as compared to 85% in 2004; yet the value of these donations increased from $10.4 billion to $12.8 billion – up 23%.[7] The reasons for this change have been attributed to a particular increase in the amount donated by 'primary donors' who are by definition older now, have higher incomes, and belong to a religious institution.[8] The reasons people give are attributed to social pressure, availability of tax credits, or personal experience or knowing someone who had been personally affected by the cause supported.[9]

In 2017, donations continue to trend downwards. The average donation amount per Canadian, 18 years or older, has decreased from $368 to $346.[10] While those that are 55 or older continue to give the most to charity, donations from this group have also declined due the shrinking demographic. The largest decline occurs in the 45-54 age group where donates rates have dropped 6.4%.[11]

3. Statistics Canada, Cornerstones of Community: Highlights of the National Survey of Nonprofit and Voluntary Organizations, Catalogue no. 61-533-XPE (Ottawa: Minister of Industry, 2005), 8.
4. Statistics Canada, "Non-profit institutions and volunteering: Economic contribution, 2007 to 2017", https://www150.statcan.gc.ca/n1/daily-quotidien/190305/dq190305a-eng.htm, accessed July 17, 2019.
5. Statistics Canada, Cornerstones of Community: Highlights of the National Survey of Nonprofit and Voluntary Organizations, Catalogue no. 61-533-XPE (Ottawa: Minister of Industry, 2005), 10-11.
6. Statistics Canada, Cornerstones of Community: Highlights of the National Survey of Nonprofit and Voluntary Organizations, Catalogue no. 61-533-XPE (Ottawa: Minister of Industry, 2005), 11.
7. Statistics Canada, "Spotlight on Canadians: Results from the General Social Survey Charitable giving by individuals", https://www150.statcan.gc.ca/n1/pub/89-652-x/89-652-x2015008-eng.htm, accessed on July 17, 2019.
8. Statistics Canada, "Spotlight on Canadians: Results from the General Social Survey Charitable giving by individuals", https://www150.statcan.gc.ca/n1/pub/89-652-x/89-652-x2015008-eng.htm, accessed on July 17, 2019.
9. Statistics Canada, "Spotlight on Canadians: Results from the General Social Survey Charitable giving by individuals", https://www150.statcan.gc.ca/n1/pub/89-652-x/89-652-x2015008-eng.htm, accessed on July 17, 2019.
10. "The Giving Report 2018", Canada Helps.org, https://www.canadahelps.org/en/the-giving-report/download-the-report/thank-you/, accessed August 12, 2019.
11. Ibid.

Additionally while the highest income group rate continue to have the highest donation rates of all income groups, lower income families give a higher percentage of their total income.[12] And yet the decline in donation rates from 2006 to 2016 was almost 17 percent in the higher income bracket categories.[13]

This would suggest that a good portion of the organizations in this segment generate low levels of revenue on which they rely to further their cause. Almost half of the revenues of this segment are provided by government, most from provincial governments and most in the form of grants and contributions.

Apart from government as a source of revenue, Canadians donated almost $10.6 billion to charitable and other non-profit organizations in 2010, of which religious, health and social service organizations figured most prominently.[14] In 2017 Canadian donated over a third of their pledges to charities providing social services, with health services and public benefit organization following at 26% and 22%. Almost half (47%) of donations are made in the last two months of the calendar year, with 30% of donations being generated in December alone.[15]

Non-profit institutions (NPI) continue to make a significant contribution to the economic and social well-being of Canadians. In 2007, the value added or gross domestic product (GDP) of the core non- profit sector amounted to $35.6 billion, accounting for 2.5% of the total Canadian economy. This share increases to 7.0% when hospitals, universities, and colleges are included, reaching $100.7 billion in 2007.[16] In contrast, by 2017 charities and non-profits accounted for 8.5% of Canada's GDP.[17]

Non-profit institutions employed 2.4 million persons in 2017.[18] However it is the volunteers that many organizations rely on. More than half of non-profit and voluntary organizations in Canada rely exclusively on volunteers to run the organizations. In 2010, these organizations were bolstered by the efforts of 27 million volunteers collectively producing 2.1 billion hours of volunteer time or the equivalent of approximately 1.1 million full-time jobs.[19] In 2013, 44% of Canadians 15 years

12. Ibid.
13. Ibid.
14. Statistics Canada, Caring Canadians, Involved Canadians: Tables Report, 2010, Catalogue no. 89-649-X -2011001 (Ottawa: Minister of Industry, 2012), 7.
15. "The Giving Report 2018", Canada Helps.org, https://www.canadahelps.org/en/the-giving-report/download-the-report/thank-you/, accessed August 12, 2019.
16. Statistics Canada, Satellite Account of Non-profit Institutions and Volunteering, Catalogue no. (Ottawa: Minister of Industry, 2007), 9-11.
17. Imagine Canada, "Larger percentage of GDP and more employees, but community organizations showing declines", http://imaginecanada.ca/who-we-are/whats-new/news/non-profit-sector-continues-grow, accessed July 17, 2019.
18. Statistics Canada. Table 36-10-0617-01 Employment in non-profit institutions by sub-sector (x 1,000), accessed July 17, 2019.
19. Statistics Canada, Caring Canadians, Involved Canadians: Tables Report, 2010, Catalogue no. 89-649-X -2011001 (Ottawa: Minister of Industry, 2012), 7.

or older volunteered for a charitable or non-profit organization, contributing 1.96 billion hours; representing a slight drop from 2010 (47%).[20] Volunteers most commonly performed coordinating and fundraising activities and were motivated by the desire to make a contribution to the community, to use their skills and experiences, and to work with an organization whose cause had affected them personally.

The civil society segment therefore is as important to Canada's economy as it is to ensuring a high quality of life for Canadians. Yet what is it about this segment that makes it so different from the business and government segments? In the civil society segment the sorting mechanisms of sharing, trust, reciprocity, collaboration, networking and cohesion are the glue that binds the sector together and forms the foundation for coordinated collective action and cooperation; the way things are done in this segment bear no resemblance to the sorting mechanisms of coercion and redistribution or supply and demand found in the government and business segments, respectively. What is found in this segment more than in any other segment that makes it simultaneously unique and complicated? The answer is *social capital*.

Social Capital

Social capital, like the civil society segment itself, is a challenging concept – difficult to define in tangible terms and even more challenging to measure. The dominant definition of social capital emerging from the literature refers to the networks, norms, and understandings that facilitate cooperative activities within and among groups of individuals.[21] Robert Putman describes social capital as referring to connections among individuals – social networks and the norms of reciprocity and trustworthiness that arise from them.[22] Sandra Franke describes social capital as generally associated with social and civic participation and with networks of co-operation and solidarity.[23] It is also worth noting that different types of social capital are found in the literature – bonding versus bridging social capital, for example, as well as different social capital approaches micro, macro, and meso.[24] It is not the intention of this book to present the range of academic positions on social capital or to analyze the many different types of social capital. For the purpose of this text and in the context of its treatment of civil society, social capital is positioned as a

20. "Volunteering in Canada", https://www150.statcan.gc.ca/n1/en/pub/89-652-x/89-652-x2015003-eng.pdf?st=IRu1L_ZG, accessed July 17, 2019.
21. John F Helliwell, "Social Capital, the Economy and Well-Being," (*The Review of Economic Performance and Social Capital Progress*, 2001) 43, accessed May 15, 2013, http://www.csls.ca/repsp/1/03-helliwell.pdf.
22. Robert Putnam, "Social Capital: Measurement and Consequences", (*Canadian Journal of Policy Research* , 2001) 41-51, accessed May 21, 2013, https://www.oecd.org/innovation/research/1825848.pdf.
23. Sandra Franke, "Measurement of Social Capital – Reference Document for Public Policy Research, Development, and Evaluation," *PRI Project: Social Capital as a Public Policy Tool* (September 2005): 1, accessed May 28, 2013, http://publications.gc.ca/collections/Collection/PH4-27-2005E.pdf.
24. Sandra Franke, "Measurement of Social Capital – Reference Document for Public Policy Research, Development, and Evaluation," *PRI Project: Social Capital as a Public Policy Tool*, (September 2005): 1, accessed May 28, 2013, http://publications.gc.ca/collections/Collection/PH4-27-2005E.pdf.

key characteristic of civil society that differentiates it from the operation of the business and government segments. Civil society is both a producer and a user of social capital thematically defined as a form of collective wealth whose strength is in society's social networks and the tendency for members of these networks to do things for each other. As such the characteristics of social capital include networks, norms, reciprocity, trust, collaboration, connection, cooperation, and solidarity.

Reflecting on whether or not social capital is evident in Canadian non-profit, voluntary, and charitable organizations requires a look at the very nature of the work of these organizations. It is safe to say that functioning within Canadian civil society requires collaboration, cooperation, and trust. Notwithstanding the fragmentation of individual organization pursuits, all share similar norms and are working toward a shared belief in improving society for Canadians without the expectation of financial gain. While the focus of civil society thus far in this text has been at the formal organization level, it is important to understand that other forms within civil society also work to improve society and represent, produce, and use social capital: for example, neighbours at a barbeque, a gathering of friends, people in a supermarket line-up, etc. These grassroots organizational forms within civil society display both formal and informal networks, similar norms, a sense of connection, and solidarity. Whereas government and business need social capital to survive, it is the civil society segment that produces more social capital than it uses and from this surplus supplies business and government with the means to measure the pulse of society. Social capital is *not* human capital, but rather is about relationships between people, and as such is measured in the ambiguous science of attitudes and values, with social cohesion as one of the main outcomes.

How Social Capital Forms – One Provocative View

Professor Edward Glaeser of Harvard University, writing in *ISUMA*, presents a provocative perspective on the formation of social capital by suggesting an individual- based economic model of social capital investment. Professor Glaeser defines individual social capital as "the set of social attributes possessed by an individual (charisma, contacts, linguistic skill) that increase the returns to that individual in his or her dealings with others."[25] As such it is individuals and not communities who decide to invest in social capital and the aggregate of community social capital is the total of individual social capital. It is argued that certain conditions exist under which individual social capital will aggregate up to community social capital, some of which are:

- Individuals having longer time horizons in their communities are more likely to invest in social capital

25. Edward Glaeser, "The Formation of Social Capital," (*ISUMA*, Spring 2001) 5, accessed May 28, 2013, http://www.oecd.org/innovation/research/1824983.pdf.

- Individuals having the most education are most likely to invest in social capital
- Community homogeneity increases social capital investment

Social Capital – Measurement and Consequences

According to Robert Putman, the central idea of social capital is that networks and the associated norms of reciprocity have value.[26] Putman's most recent research suggests a revival of the American community and higher levels of social capital. This research offers some important insights. In high social capital states:

- Schools work better
- Kids are better off
- Violent crime is rarer
- People are less quarrelsome
- Health is better
- Tax evasion is lower
- Tolerance is higher
- Civic equality is higher
- Economic equality is higher

It is also interesting to note that, according to Putman's research, being closer to the Canadian border means more social capital.

Social Capital and Civil Society: An Obvious Connection

From the above discussion on social capital it will become obvious how social capital links to the civil society segment. Given the definition of civil society and the definition of social capital the very descriptors of social capital reflect the sorting mechanisms of civil society. As such civil society is both a producer and user of social capital and has been aptly referred to as the social glue that helps unite diverse interests.

Contributions of Civil Society

In an article appearing on CharityVillage.com in March, 2005, Nicole Zummach refers to an Imagine Canada report entitled *Canadian Non-profit and Voluntary Sector in Comparative Perspective*, a part of the Johns Hopkins Comparative Non-profit Sector Project that examines the civil society sector in 37 countries around the world that positions Canada's non-profit sector as the second largest in the world.[27] Canadian

26. Robert Putman, "Social Capital Measurement and Consequences," *ISUMA* (Spring 2001): 1, accessed May 28, 2013, http://www.oecd.org/education/innovation-education/1825848.pdf.
27. Nicole Zummach, "Canada boasts second largest nonprofit sector in the world," *Charity Village* (March 28, 2005), accessed May 28, 2013, http://sectorsource.ca/sites/default/files/resources/files/jhu_report_en.pdf.

non- profit and voluntary organizations employ twelve percent of the country's economically active population and contribute an estimated $75.8 billion (or 8.5%) of Canada's Gross Domestic Product (including the value of volunteer work). The bulk of Canada's nonprofits are service organizations with almost three-quarters engaged in the delivery of education, health, housing, and economic development promotion services. Fifty-one percent of all revenue comes from government and only nine percent comes from philanthropy.

The *2013 Canadian Survey of Giving, Volunteering, and Participating* measures the extent to which Canadians express their community values and pursue their interests through four pro-social behaviours: charitable giving, volunteering through an organization helping others directly, and the extent to which they participate by being members of organizations and associations.[28] The results of this survey provide some insightful findings on the involvement of Canadians and the importance of the civil society segment, for example:

- Over 24 million Canadians aged 15 years and over made a financial donation to a charitable or non-profit organization during the one- year period preceding the survey,
- Total amount donated was $102.8 billion, with the average annual donation valued at $531 per donor,
- Older Canadians give more on average, and
- Women are more likely to give than men; and items donated include cash, good, clothing, toys or household items.[29]

Key Challenges and Issues

Practitioners and academics from all three Canadian domestic macro-economic segments do not always agree on who and what is included in civil society. Yet most would concede that this important segment touches all aspects of society, including social justice, sport, environment, health, faith, the arts, and culture, and would also concede that two uncontested representatives of this segment would be non-profit and voluntary organizations. These two groups will be used as representatives of this segment through which to demonstrate several key issues faced by this segment.

The following recurring key issues are germane to this segment:

1. Segment fragmentation

28. Statistics Canada, *Charitable Giving in Canada*, www.stancan.gc.c.a, https://www150.statcan.gc.ca/n1/en/pub/11-627-m/11-627-m2015006-eng.pdf?st=MOaTl2rb, accessed July 17, 2019.
29. Statistics Canada, *Charitable Giving in Canada*, www.stancan.gc.c.a, https://www150.statcan.gc.ca/n1/en/pub/11-627-m/11-627-m2015006-eng.pdf?st=MOaTl2rb, accessed July 17, 2019.

2. Funding
3. Crowdfunding
4. Attracting and retaining volunteers and strong non-profit board members
5. Measuring outcomes

Segment Fragmentation

The best way to describe what is meant by fragmentation is to consider the composition of this segment. That 161,000 organizations are included in the Canadian civil society segment would tend to suggest that by and large the segment is fragmented, serving a multitude of interests and causes, resulting in difficulty in being heard by government or business, and making it very challenging to influence public policy development. There is at least one voluntary sector organization for every 193 Canadians.[30] Given this, it is difficult to imagine how the segment could organize a coordinated approach through which to have their voices heard collectively and to unite to influence business or government policy. Clearly the larger, more organized members of this segment are in the best position to exert influence as the effect of the missions of these larger organizations can be more effectively positioned on the government agenda. Further, these groups would have a much larger base of managers with wide experience and contacts, many having served in some capacity with either industry or government before becoming involved with the organization. Notwithstanding that all third sector organizations are working in the best interests of society, their individual missions, interests, and goals are frequently so diversified and incongruent with broader government and business interests that even being heard as individual organizations by government or business is unlikely.

Recall one of the main challenges manifest in the government segment: a multitude of stakeholders with a wide array of separate interests. Government generally seeks to put in place public policy that will result in the greatest good for the greatest number, and as important as consultations are to good public policy outcomes, it is impossible for the government to consult with every single stakeholder or stakeholder organization.

Therefore civil society organizations' influence on public policy will be more tangible and pronounced the larger the organization, or the larger the number of organizations united to voice an opinion.

Funding

Civil society, as with the government and business segments, is not without its share of challenges and issues. Hasenfeld and Gidron argue that for civil society organizations to prosper they must be able to mobilize members, garner sufficient

---

30. Statistics Canada, Cornerstones of Community: Highlights of the National Survey of Nonprofit and Voluntary Organizations, Catalogue no. 61-533-XPE (Ottawa: Minister of Industry, 2005), 5.

financial resources, and be recognized as legitimate.[31] Funding remains a major challenge for many organizations of this segment both in terms of increasing pressure on available funds as a result of increasing demand for services, but also due to the administrative reporting burden placed on the organizations by granting authorities. Given that the majority of funds come from government and the majority of *government* funds come from taxpayers it is understandable that government needs to ensure that funds provided are used appropriately and for the purposes provided. In the early 1990s government moved from providing funding to deliver services to providing funding for specific issues, and not providing funding for overhead and administrative costs. Among other things, project- based funding in which overhead costs are not funded results in deteriorating infrastructures – the very infrastructures that are even more necessary under this funding paradigm in order to facilitate meeting the increasing reporting requirements in order to preserve the funding. As well, as government funding becomes increasingly targeted on specific issues or government interests non-profit and volunteer organizations are tempted to follow them, departing from their own long-term purposes and raisons d'être in order to obtain the funding necessary for organizational survival – referred to by some writers as "mission drift".

According to the *Giving Report 2018*, there are 86,000 charities in Canada, of which 91% have ten or fewer paid full-time staff.[32] By comparison just 1% of these charities have more than 200 employees, and it is these charities that receive the bulk of government funding – in 2016 amounting to $150.9 billion.[33] In other words 85% of all government funding goes to only 1% of registered charities.

Funding scandals made public have also precipitated increased scrutiny and control over government monies. The reduced amount of funding available combined with the increased reporting requirements have placed significant administrative burdens on many civil society organizations resulting in them being less able to innovate.

Crowdfunding

"Crowdfunding is a fast growing method of helping, allowing people to instantly feel good about doing so."[34] Data from GoFundMe indicates that in 2017, the company passed 40 million donors who made a total of $4 billion in donations;

31. Yeheskel Hasenfeld and Benjamin Gidron, "Understanding Multi-purpose Hybrid Voluntary Organizations: The Contributions of Theories on Civil Society, Social Movements and Non- Profit Organizations," (*Journal of Civil Society*, 1, 2, September 2005) 97-112, accessed May 28, 2013, http://www.bgu.ac.il/~gidron/publication/Multi_purpose.pdf.

32. "The Giving Report 2018", Canada Helps.org, https://www.canadahelps.org/en/the-giving-report/download-the-report/thank-you/, accessed August 12, 2019.

33. "The Giving Report 2018", Canada Helps.org, https://www.canadahelps.org/en/the-giving-report/download-the-report/thank-you/, accessed August 12, 2019.

34. "The Giving Report 2018", Canada Helps.org, https://www.canadahelps.org/en/the-giving-report/download-the-report/thank-you/, accessed August 12, 2019.

up from 30 million and \$3 billion the eight months prior - whereas the first \$1 billion took five years.[35] Crowdfunding fills a need in Canadians *to do something*; and provides an opportunity for Canadian to rally around good causes, an example of which is the \$15 million that was raised for the families of the tragic Humboldt bus accident in 2013.[36] However there are issue with this method of raising funds as well. So much money was raised for the families in this case, that a non-profit had to be created, and it is reported that there is ongoing legal issues with determining how much money should be disbursed to families and when it should be disbursed. GoFundMe as reportedly collected approximately \$500,000 in payment processing fees alone.[37] So while all for a good cause, donations of this type are often not accompanied by the due diligence that donors often seek, nor is there always the due diligence presence to ensure that accountability.

Attracting and Retaining Volunteers and Strong Non-profit Board Members

Another challenge for this segment is attracting and retaining volunteers. In 2011, 15% of the population was 65 years old or older, and people aged 45 to 64 alone accounted for over one-quarter of Canada's total population.[38] By 2016, those over 65 years amounted to 16.9%.[39]

In 1991, for every person aged 15 to 64, there were 1.8 individuals under 15. By 2001, the ratio was down to 1.47 and by 2011, the ratio was 1.13. More interestingly, the ratio of children and seniors to working-age persons in 2011 was 0.46, down significantly from 0.71 from fifty years ago.[40]

Given these demographic observations it is no surprise that changes in leadership and service delivery can be expected. As the *baby boomers* retire an interesting paradox will develop for this segment of the Canadian domestic macro-environment. Baby boomers typically are defined as those born in the late 1940s through the early 60s, and baby boomers, as has been noted, are generally more inclined and available to do volunteer and charitable work. However, this same group of po-

35. "The Giving Report 2018", Canada Helps.org, https://www.canadahelps.org/en/the-giving-report/download-the-report/thank-you/, accessed August 12, 2019.
36. "The Giving Report 2018", Canada Helps.org, https://www.canadahelps.org/en/the-giving-report/download-the-report/thank-you/, accessed August 12, 2019.
37. "The Giving Report 2018", Canada Helps.org, https://www.canadahelps.org/en/the-giving-report/download-the-report/thank-you/, accessed August 12, 2019.
38. Statistics Canada, "Age Groups and Sex for the Population of Canada, 2011 Census," date modified 2018-07-23, https://www12.statcan.gc.ca/census-recensement/2011/as-sa/98-311-x/98-311-x2011001-eng.cfm, accessed July 17, 2019.
39. Statistics Canada, "Age and Sex Highlight Tables, 2016 Census", https://www12.statcan.gc.ca/census-recensement/2016/dp-pd/hlt-fst/as/Table.cfm?Lang=E&T=11, accessed July 17, 2019.
40. Statistics Canada, "Ratios of broad age groups, 1921-2011 – Canada," date modified 2016-11-23, https://www12.statcan.gc.ca/census-recensement/2011/dp-pd/hlt-fst/as-sa/Pages/highlight.cfm?TabID=1&Lang=E&Asc=1&OrderBy=3&PRCode=01&tableID=23, accessed July 17, 2019.

tential volunteers will also demand more from third-sector services. This segment is represented by considerably more unpaid workers than paid workers, and it is reasonable to suggest that volunteers are the dominant group. Volunteering will change, not only due to the *boomer phenomenon*, but also due to changes in society, motivation, and attitude.

Civil society organizations are also challenged by an increase in the complexity of the issues they address. The changing dynamic of the family, multiculturalism, growing communities, demographics, globalization's effect on the domestic economy, and technology's resulting disenfranchisement of labour-based workers represent only a modest sample of forces in the environment that combine to create complex social problems, the immediate solution to which is both outside the social net provided by government and well beyond the capacity of any single civil society organization to provide. These continuous changes observed in society have led to the emergence of different styles of volunteering. Merrill Associates identify five emerging patterns of volunteerism: employee volunteering, episodic volunteerism, virtual volunteerism, cross- national volunteering and voluntourism.[41]

> *Employee volunteerism* describes the situation in which employee participation is linked with philanthropic dollars, typically through formal and/or informal workplace programs. One of the outcomes of this approach has been the development of shorter-term, project-oriented volunteer activities.

> *Episodic volunteerism* describes the one-time volunteer who performs service of short duration. The outcomes of this approach include, in addition to project- specific volunteer activities, volunteer activities tailored to meld with individual availability, skills, and interests.

> *Virtual volunteerism* occurs through the use of Internet or information and communications technologies to conduct off-site volunteer activities. The outcomes of such an approach are the ability to mobilize a greater number of volunteers supporting the cause as well as an individualized approach to volunteering that can be undertaken from anywhere, anytime.

> *Cross-national volunteering* is the sharing of skills and abilities to undertake volunteer activities that cross national borders. *Doctors Without Borders*, an international medical humanitarian organization is as an example of

---

41. Merrill Associates, "Five emerging patterns of volunteerism," *Charity Village.com* (November 20, 2006), https://charityvillage.com/cms/content/topic/five_emerging_patterns_of_volunteerism#.XS9LJuhKjIU, accessed July 17, 2019.

cross- national volunteering.[42] The outcomes are learning experiences and educational exchange between participants on both sides of the borders.

Voluntourism exemplifies the situation in which volunteers take a volunteer vacation. The outcomes include new and creative partnerships for further volunteer activities around the globe.

Furthermore, what is considered to be "volunteering" by Canadians themselves appears to be changing. The "Recognizing Volunteering in 2017 Summary Report" issued by Volunteer Bénévoles Canada discusses some very interesting developments. While almost 13 million Canadians volunteer and average of 150 hours per year through non-profits, charities and public institutions, how they define volunteering has taken on a new connotation. Social media and technology are influences the interactions between individuals and community organization in a way never before experiences. The concept of *Individual Social Responsibility* (ISR) which is defined as "the continuing commitment to behave ethically and contribute to people's development while improving the quality of life of other individuals, groups, teams as well as society at large" is now driving how people are volunteering, and choosing how to do it.[43] Understanding ISR can help organizations understand the motivations of individuals to give of their time and money, and assist business to strengthen their Corporate Social Responsibility (CSR) programs.

Volunteer Bénévole Canada conducted a study to find out how public perception of volunteering is changing. Key findings were as follows:

- Three in ten Canadians have donated time in the last year, while half have donated money;
- 65% feel that they have a responsibility to their communities, but 71% feel that they are less "connected" to those communities than previous generations;
- 87% feel that volunteering is vital to the wellbeing of society;
- A majority of Canadians feel that the need for volunteering is driven ty inadequate government services;
- Half indicate that they do a lot to help the community in school-related or recreational activities, but they do not consider these activities "volunteering";
- 75% indicate that they have donated used clothing; but only half consider this "volunteering";
- 75% are very willing to volunteer in times of a crisis, even if they do not volunteer on a regular basis.[44]

42. "Doctors Without Borders," accessed May 29, 2013, https://www.doctorswithoutborders.org/, accessed July 17, 2019.
43. "Recognizing Volunteering in 2017 Summary Report", Volunteer Bénévoles Canada, Volunteer.ca, page 4.
44. "Recognizing Volunteering in 2017 Summary Report", Volunteer Bénévoles Canada, Volunteer.ca, page 4.

What is very interesting, and perhaps very telling, is that many of the activities viewed by Canadians as "volunteering" such as reading to patients in a hospices, or serving on a Board of directors of a non-profit, are in fact taken on by individuals.

Obtaining members to serve on volunteer boards of directors is increasingly difficult due to ever-increasing constraints on peoples' time and the continuous struggle of volunteer boards to cope with many of the challenges already mentioned associated with this segment. As with the other segments, technological advances are changing what used to be a predictable pace for volunteers and non-profit organizations. The historical notion of the "long-term" has now been transformed into what was customarily considered as the short-term. Whereas in the past serving on a non-profit board was relaxed and social, anchored around a common desire to progress the cause and in so doing create "good" for society, today non-profits have many of the governance issues associated with for-profits: increasing interest in accountability, responsibility, and stewardship to members; increasing reporting requirements to funders; deadlines for reports; competition with other non-profit organizations for funds; inter and intra-organizational conflict; and activities being featured "in the news". These realities combine to discourage many from participating as members of boards of directors in non-profit and volunteer organizations.

Measuring Outcomes

Another challenge for this segment is measuring outcomes that demonstrate to stakeholders that what they do matters and makes a difference. While work done by this segment is extremely important, the qualitative nature of its work around issues for which no simple solution is possible does not easily lend itself to measurement of progress and results achieved. This challenge is also faced by the government segment.

Developing constructive collaborative arrangements is another challenge for this segment. On the one hand "strength in numbers" creates a stronger voice and greater combined resources – collaboration would therefore be expected to bolster the impact on an issue. On the other hand, collaboration also requires shared governance and mission compromise that could result in mission drift as the collaborators modify their interests to meld with the common cause.

In the larger civil society organizations it is not unusual to find paid workers and volunteer workers side by side. This can lead to a number of interpersonal dynamics challenges. Paid workers might view themselves as more important than voluntary workers, performing more important tasks. Volunteer workers may view themselves as being more dedicated to the cause since they are performing similar duties without remuneration.

Some Organizations Found in the Canadian Civil Society Segment

While participants in this segment are not all formal organizations it is useful to consider some selected organizations in order to portray the depth, breadth, and economic contributions of this important segment of the Canadian domestic macro-environment.

The following organizations have been selected by the author as a random sampling for illustrative purposes and in no way represent an exhaustive list or represent the full range of the contributions of this sector.

The Atkinson Charitable Foundation

The Atkinson Charitable Foundation bears the name of Joseph E. Atkinson, publisher of the *Toronto Star* from 1899 to 1948. The foundation was established in 1942 by Joseph Atkinson and Elmina Elliott, life-long partners in the fight for social and economic justice. Its central principles include a strong, united, and independent Canada; social justice; individual and civil liberties; community and civic engagement; the rights of working people; and the necessary role of government. The Foundation provides approximately $2 million in funding for ongoing and new projects each year.[45]

The Canadian Red Cross

Founded in 1896, the Canadian Red Cross is a volunteer-based humanitarian organization offering international, disaster, safety, and community-based health and social services.

The Red Cross operates over 300 branches with 20,000 volunteers providing services and support to over 2 million Canadians annually. Six thousand Disaster Response volunteers responded to 317 natural disasters in 2014, affecting over 100 million people.

In 2002-2003, with revenues of over $188 million, 6,644 staff, and over 29,000 volunteers, the Canadian Red Cross assisted over 18,000 people in Canada in disaster services, trained over 1 million people in water safety and over 375,000 people in first aid, and recorded over 4.5 million client service hours for homemakers/community health services.[46]

The Red Cross provides mobile food banks, transportation, visitations, and medical apparatus to hundreds of thousands Canadians. Over a million Canadians

---

45. "The Atkinson Charitable Foundation", accessed May 29, 2013, http://www.atkinsonfoundation.ca
46. "Canadian Red Cross," accessed May 29, 2013, https://www.redcross.ca/.

take swimming lessons every year, and 25,000 Water Safety Instructors are certified annually. The Red Cross has been a world leader in first aid training for over fifty years, and services are offered in 19 different languages.[47]

Imagine Canada

Imagine Canada is the result of a union of two of Canada's leading charitable umbrella organizations – the Canadian Centre for Philanthropy, and the Coalition of National Voluntary Organizations. Imagine Canada is a nationally registered charity that looks into and out for Canada's charities and nonprofits. Imagine Canada's mission is "advancing knowledge and relationships to foster effective and sustainable charitable and non-profit organizations."[48]

The Maytree Foundation

The Maytree Foundation is a Canadian charitable foundation established in 1982 focussed on reducing poverty by investing in the development of progressive social policy, leaders who have the capacity to make social change and advance the common good, and accelerating the settlement of immigrants and refugees in large urban centres of immigration. The Foundation operates a series of programs to increase the leadership and management capacity of the nonprofit sector in the Greater Toronto Area: convenes a wide range of people to address complex problems through networking: and offers grants, loans, and scholarships.[49]

Planned Parenthood Ottawa

Founded in 1961 and renamed the Planned Parenthood Association of Ottawa to be a part of the Planned Parenthood Federation of Canada in 1964, Planned Parenthood Ottawa Incorporated became a registered charity in 1971. Throughout its history it has maintained its focus of providing up-to-date, non-judgemental sexual and reproductive health information by offering education, counselling, and referral services to assist people in making informed sexual and reproductive health choices.[50]

United Way Centraide Canada

The United Way Centraide Canada movement was born out of a "community collective" philosophy that began in Denver, Colorado in 1887 and spread to Canada in the 1920s. The mission of the United Way Centraide Canada is to improve

47. The Red Cross, "About the Red Cross", https://www.redcross.ca/about-us/about-the-canadian-red-cross/what-we-do-infographic, accessed July 17, 2019.
48. "Imagine Canada," accessed May 29, 2013, http://www.imaginecanada.ca
49. "Maytree For Leaders For Change," accessed May 29, 2013, https://maytree.com/
50. "The Planned Parenthood Ottawa," accessed July 17, 2019, https://ppottawa.ca/

lives and build community by engaging individuals and mobilizing collective action. The movement consists of:

- 5,863 community programs,
- Serving 31,743,213 people,
- Supported by over one million donors, staff and volunteers
- Raising over $522 million in 2018.

The United Way has 123 volunteer-based offices located in ten provinces and two territories in addition to a national organization, United Way Centraide Canada. The organizations strengthen communities by convening human and social service agencies at the community and neighbourhood level with governments, businesses, and labour; pooling and leveraging resources by building partnerships and collaborations; providing training, learning, and professional development opportunities; and delivering national programs.[51]

---

51. "United Way Centraide Canada," http://www.unitedway.ca/, accessed July 17, 2019.

Chapter Summary

The third segment of the Canadian domestic macro-environment, civil society, despite being equal in importance to the business and government segments and recently having demonstrated the greatest increase in strength in its ability to influence the other segments, remains the most difficult to define and is the least understood. Referred to by an array of labels including non-profit, voluntary, third, independent, commons, and civil society, this segment performs important functions that improve society and add value to both business and government. Its activities are mainly instituted through forms of reciprocal relationships and its sorting mechanisms include networks, norms, trust, and collaboration. These sorting mechanisms describe social capital – the networks, norms, and understandings that facilitate cooperative activities within and among groups of individuals. This segment both produces and consumes social capital. Civil society and social capital are critical for a society's success and provide the glue that binds all segments of the Canadian domestic macro-environment. An understanding of this segment is as critical for business success as it is for the development and implementation of effective government policy.

Volunteers make important contributions to Canada's quality of life and many employers recognize the importance of supporting workers in their voluntary pursuits. However, with the aging of the population, the face of Canada's volunteer segment is changing; the number of potential volunteers is increasing, but so is the number of people who will need volunteer and charitable services. Changing social values combine with advances in information technology to provoke new approaches to volunteering. As society changes so do the expectations of stakeholders, as is evidenced by nonprofit boards of directors facing similar governance issues as for-profit boards – which has the effect of discouraging persons from serving as members of non-profit boards of directors.

A Practitioners' Perspective: An Interview with Heather Norris, President & CEO of the Ottawa Network for Education

Heather is driven to create social change that leads to better lives and healthier communities. Following ten years of management positions in the healthcare industry in Ottawa and Toronto, she's built a reputation as an innovator and change-maker in the non-profit sector. As a leader and advisor invested in community development, she brings skills in operations management, fundraising, government relations, human resources and volunteer management, board governance and public speaking. She has gleaned important lessons and perspectives across the

Contributed by Heather Norris. © Kendall Hunt Publishing Company

public, private and non-profit sectors, which have created a strong foundation for managing complex leadership challenges of modern organizations. Heather holds a Master of Philanthropy and Non-profit Leadership Degree. She is the President & CEO of the Ottawa Network for Education.

Canadian Business & Society: *What motivates you to do what you do?*

Heather Norris: I've gleaned important lessons and perspectives across the public, private and non-profit sectors which have created a strong foundation for managing complex challenges of modern organizations. I'm motivated to use my skills, education and diverse sector experience in a meaningful capacity. The non-profit sector inspires me to support the growth of sustainable and dynamic organizations that create social change and help build healthier and more vibrant communities.

Canadian Business & Society: *In your view, what is your most significant challenge?*

Heather Norris: An ongoing, significant challenge is the lack of sustainable funding coupled with the increased demand for necessary programs and services. These are the programs and services our communities need to remain healthy, vibrant and relevant.

Non-profit organizations should be experts in providing programs and services as well as prevention, but our reality is strategically juggling priorities to scale-up programs to meet increased demand, without having access to the financial resources to do so. You can imagine the frustration across an incredibly impactful sector when you have a successful program and want to do more, but financial limitations constrain the ability to do so.

In Canada, we generally look to government to help solve social issues; however, with short-term project-funding and finite resources in an increasingly competitive environment, organizations are constantly looking for sustainable and innovative financing options. With population growth, shifting demographics, rising costs and increasingly complex issues, the financial gap is widening, and the hunt for financial stability has become an ongoing trend.

Canadian Business & Society: *Do you believe it is important to understand how government and business organizations work to help you accomplish your organization's goals?*

Heather Norris: Absolutely, there are significant cross-sectoral relationships with both government and business organizations that help accomplish our organizational goals; in fact, our organization's survival depends on these relationships. Government and business support (grants, sponsorships and volunteers) are lifelines for our organization.

A key to our success is building relationships with all levels of government; understanding their priorities and informing them on how the work we do can help fulfill their mandates. The same strategy applies in our work with business organizations; understanding their corporate social responsibility and philanthropic initiatives is key to aligning our work to their goals.

No one sector can tackle complex social issues alone. Working to build strong and healthy communities will require continued commitment and cross-sector collaboration with government, business and civil society organizations.

Canadian Business & Society: *From your perspective as an active leader of a civil society organization, if there was one message you would like to give to introductory business students, what would it be?*

Heather Norris: Civil society organizations are an important part of the economic engine of our communities. We are an employer, program/service provider, volunteer recruiter and trainer, influencer of advocacy and policy development, convener and community builder.

Many organizations in civil society grew organically from passionate volunteer-run organizations and evolved into charitable and non-profit service organizations with the professionalism and business acumen of the for-profit sector. Our organizations require leadership and expertise in good governance, marketing and communication, fundraising, event management, stakeholder engagement, human resources, program development, data collection and analysis, business and financial acumen and more, to survive and thrive.

End of Chapter Questions

1. Describe the "civil society" segment. Who is included? What characterizes the sector? What are its dynamics?

2. How important is the civil society sector to the Canadian economy?

3. What are some key challenges for the civil society sector?

4. Describe what benefits the government sector and the business sector might receive when working with the civil society sector, and what the civil society sector might receive in return.

5. What is social capital?

6. How might partnering with civil society sector organizations improve community well-being? Discuss social capital in this context.

7. Given the challenges faced by the civil society segment of the Canadian domestic macro-environment, in your view what could this segment do to reduce its fragmentation and coordinate its efforts?

Application Questions

Referring to the opening news article on Canada's food policy, discuss the following:

1. What do you feel was the involvement of "civil society" in the food policy for Canada?

2. In your view, who are the key stakeholders and what are their "stakes"?

3. Does Canada's food policy generate social capital? Support your position.

4. In your view, what key issues of the civil society segment are addressed by Canada's food policy?

5. In your view, does the implementation of Canada's food policy present any risks to civil society? Explain.

Research Questions

1. Select any two civil society segment organizations of your choice and discuss how the sorting mechanisms of networking, collaboration, trust, and reciprocity are evident.

2. Using the Internet and other sources of information select a non-government organization typically found in this segment and analyze its operations from the perspective of the three key challenges identified in this chapter. Are the key issues identified in this chapter relevant? Are other issues being faced by the organization you have selected?

Team Discussion Project

Heather Norris provided the Practitioner's Perspective at the end of this chapter. Visit the website of the Ottawa Network for Education (ONE) and respond to the following:

1. In your view which of the challenges for civili society identified in this chapter would apply to ONE?

2. Does ONE generate social capital? Explain.

3. What are the key contributions of ONE to Canadian society?

4. How do the activities of ONE align with the goals of business and government?

CHAPTER 5

Stakeholders and Stakeholder Management

Darride/Shutterstock.com

Stakeholders in the News

10,000 Changes: Canada's commitment to rethink plastics[1]

The article published by the Royal Canadian Geographical Society in June 2019 discusses the problem of plastics. The Canadian Geographic and Recycling Council of Ontario have partnered to launch Canada's commitment to rethink plastics through **10,000 Changes**, an innovative plastic engagement program funded by the Government of Canada.

1. Cision, "10,000 Changes: Canada's commitment to rethink plastics", https://www.newswire.ca/news-releases/10-000-changes-canada-s-commitment-to-rethink-plastics-862428752.html, accessed July 17, 2019.

10,000 Changes will empower Canadians to commit to plastic waste reduction solutions and move towards a zero plastic waste solution. Over the next year, **10,000 Changes** will provide resources to help shift behaviour through engagement, and tools needed to make informed decisions about plastics. The partnership between Canadian Geographic and the Recycling Council of Ontario has been funded through Environment and Climate Change Canada.

The full article can be viewed at https://www.newswire.ca/news-releases/10-000-changes-canada-s-commitment-to-rethink-plastics-862428752.html.

Introduction

Earlier chapters introduced each of the three key segments of the Canadian domestic macro environment. Throughout these discussions reference was frequently made to stakeholders – generally those persons or groups within each segment that have an interest in how representatives of the segment operate, and how the actions of these segment representatives affect them.

However, considering "stakeholders" in the way described suggests certain simplicity in terms of identifying stakeholders, determining their interest, and managing them.

Stakeholder identification and management is in reality much more complex, as this chapter will present.

What is a Stakeholder?

There are many ways to define a stakeholder. In its simplest form a stakeholder is anyone or any group with a perceived stake in an organization's activities. The concept of stakeholder can also be extended to include comparatively inanimate "objects" such as the environment as well as "non human" stakeholders such as animals (or possibly uncle Louis). This general definition can apply to business, government, and civil society but the stakeholders and their perceived interests will not necessarily be the same for each segment. Typical stakeholders can be intuitively proposed for each of these segments.

Segment	Typical Stakeholders
Business	shareholders (if a corporation), employees, suppliers, unions (if a unionized company), creditors, government, civil society
Government	voters, politicians, suppliers of goods and services to government, business in general, civil society in general, foreign governments
Civil Society	volunteers, charities, communities, disenfranchised individuals, social cause groups, government, business

While stakeholders and their perceived stakes certainly must be considered, there are a number of realities concerning stakeholders that apply regardless of what segment is under consideration.

1. All stakeholders are not created equal
2. There will be stakeholder winners and losers – it is simply not possible to satisfy "all of the stakeholders all of the time"
3. All stakeholders do not always understand their *stakes* (hence the earlier reference to stakeholders' perceived stakes)
4. Ignoring stakeholders is not a viable option
5. Stakeholders can often influence other stakeholders
6. Identifying, analyzing, and managing stakeholders is time consuming and difficult
7. Managing stakeholders involves costs – it is not free, but as other writers have noted, it is cheaper than not managing them!
8. Stakeholders and their perceived stakes are not static, but rather can change over time and can change *quickly*.
9. Stakeholders can have a positive and negative effect on business's "bottom line, government and political "bottom lines," and civil society's "bottom line"
10. Stakeholders can emerge from anywhere and at any time – frequently predictable, but just as often not predictable

The number of available methods for identifying stakeholders is endless, and given the realities that are portrayed above, the management of stakeholders involves considerable challenges. For example:

1. Who are the organization's stakeholders?
2. Of these stakeholders, who are the organization's most important stakeholders and what criteria are used to determine which stakeholders are more important than perhaps other stakeholders?
3. For those stakeholders not currently classified by the organization as the most important, to what extent do they have the capacity to become important?
4. To what extent can stakeholders affect the organization, either positively or negatively?

5. To what extent should the organization invest in managing stakeholders, i.e. what is the "risk-return-trade-off" ratio that is acceptable to the organization?

Two Opposing Views Concerning Stakeholder Management

Despite the importance of stakeholders and stakeholder management there have been opposing views presented over the years. These views are most intuitively understood in the context of business, and the discussion that follows is anchored in the business segment of the Canadian domestic macro environment.

According to Charles Handy, business's purpose goes beyond simple profit maximization:

> *The purpose of a business…is not to make a profit, full stop. It is to make a profit so that the business can do something more or better. That "something" becomes the real justification for the business…It is a moral issue.*[2]

In contrast Milton Friedman has a different view:

> *…there is one and only one social responsibility of business–to use its resources and engage in activities designed to increase its profits so long as it stays within the rules of the game, which is to say, engages in open and free competition without deception or fraud.*[3]

These two viewpoints exemplify what is frequently referred to as 1) the *stakeholder viewpoint*, and 2) the *shareholder viewpoint* of the business firm respectively.

The stakeholder view is anchored in social institution theory that positions business as a public institution – an institution whose very existence is provided by society through the prevailing laws that reflect the expectations, beliefs, and operation of that society. In other words, legal statutes evolve over time from "judgements" of the actions of society members that reflect the beliefs of society. A company exists to satisfy needs and wants of society and that same society, through its laws, provides the legal authority for the company to exist. Supporters of this view would argue:

- Business is a "social institution", sanctioned by the society in which it operates and is not the sole dominion of business owners; and,

---

2. Charles Handy, "What is Business For?" *Harvard Business Review*, Vol. 80, No.12 (2002): 49- 55.
3. Milton Friedman, "The Social Responsibility of Business is to Increase Its Profits," *The New York Times Magazine*, September 13, 1970.

- Business has caused a number of social problems that otherwise may not have occurred, and as such has a responsibility to fix these problems.

Beyond the pure social institution theme, supporters of the stakeholder view would argue further the following additional benefits:

- More secure longer-term profits can result; not only in terms of risk mitigation, but also given the important contributions stakeholders can make to enhance the effectiveness and the efficiency of the company.
- Organizational reputation can be enhanced resulting in the recruitment and retention of high-calibre staff.
- Market position and competitiveness can be improved through mitigating the potential negative actions of stakeholders as well as using their input to improve organizational operations
- An enhanced ability to attract and build effective and efficient supply chain relationships and address change
- Improved relationships with regulators -- demonstrating social responsibility could dissuade regulators from imposing certain actions on the company.[4]

The shareholder viewpoint is distinctively opposite, stating that a business exists to make money and the greatest business efficiency is achieved through maximizing the wealth of shareholders. Anchored in property rights theory that the corporation is owned by shareholders, this view supports a very simple and clear premise of business accountability that management is accountable to shareholders. The greater the profits the greater the amount of taxes paid to government and therefore the more funds available to government to deal with social issues. Several arguments in support of this view have been advanced, for example:

- Business is not equipped to deal with social issues – business is most efficient and effective when it does what it was originally intended to do;
- Costs of social responsibility must be passed on, either in the form of reduced return on investment to shareholders, and/or ultimately to consumers through a price that reflects these additional costs, compromising business's ability to remain competitive;
- Business is not government - its managers and shareholders are not elected by the voting public and as such cannot be held accountable for its social activities – if voters do not like what government is doing for the public good, they can vote out the government, they cannot vote out a business; and

---

4. Paul Hohnen and Jason Potts, "Corporate Social Responsibility: An Implementation Guide for Canadian Business," *International Institute for Sustainable Development* (2007), https://www.iisd.org/library/corporate-social-responsibility-implementation-guide-business, accessed July 17, 2019.

- Many large multinational companies generate more revenues than some developing countries – adding social responsibility decisions to these powerful organizations would ultimately dilute the capacity of governments to govern, giving business too much power.

The reality of today is that stakeholders cannot be ignored to concentrate on the profit motive. Many stakeholders have legitimate stakes and can exert significant influence on companies and organizations in all segments. The need for stakeholder identification, analysis, and management exists because no one individual or group holds all the power -- a condition known as pluralism.

Pluralism

Canada is a pluralistic society. In the words of Joseph W. McGuire, a pluralistic society is "one in which there is wide decentralization and diversity of power concentration."[5] Pluralism therefore implies the existence of many stakeholders.

A pluralistic society offers both strengths and weaknesses that taken together underline the complexity of both identifying and dealing with stakeholders.[6]

Strengths	Weaknesses
• Prevents concentration of power • Maximizes freedom • Disperses individual allegiances • Creates diversified loyalties • Provides safeguards	• Encourages pursuit of self-interest • Proliferates organizations with similar goals • Forces conflicts • Promotes inefficiency

Given Canada's pluralistic society and the need for a stakeholder approach, a logical starting point toward understanding stakeholder management would be to explore how stakeholders are identified. Note that identifying stakeholders is only the beginning – this identification must be followed by some form of analysis in which to determine the most important stakeholders.

5. Joseph W. McGuire, *Business and Society* (New York: McGraw-Hill, 1963), 130.
6. Len Karakowsky, Archie B. Carroll and Ann K. Buchholz, *Business and Society: Ethics and Stakeholder Management*, First Canadian Edition (Thomson-Nelson, 2005).

Identifying Stakeholders

There are several approaches to identifying stakeholders. The simplest approach would be to identify any individual, group, organization, or inanimate objects that have a stake in the organization's operations. From this list, the stakeholders with the least amount of interest and/or the least capacity to influence the organization (positively or negatively) can be eliminated in order that the organization concentrate its effort of working with stakeholders on those who have legitimate claims. At first glance this approach is intuitively appealing. Consider the application of this approach in the following scenario:

> *Mike Martel was President and Chief Executive Officer of Mike's Previously Enjoyed Automobiles Inc. (MPEA Inc.) located in Arnprior, Ontario. His corporation is private and owned by him and five other family shareholders. Mike's debt instruments and banking activities are managed through the local bank. MPEA has in its employ a sales staff of ten people, a service staff of five mechanics, a service advisor, and an administrative staff of three. All his staff lived in Arnprior. MPEA's automobile service centre and sales showroom were on Madawaska Drive on land leased from the municipality. The business is a regular supporter of local charity as well as golf tournaments at local golf courses. Mike employs a number of students from Arnprior Secondary School during the summer months.[7]*

A list of MPEA Inc. stakeholders could include the following:

Stakeholders	Stake
Mike and his family shareholders	return on investment, profit
Employees	source of income
Customers	source of automobiles, service on those automobiles
The local bank	profitability of the corporation; security of debt instruments
Suppliers/other businesses	source of revenue
Competition	MPEA Inc. customers
Local charities/civil society	source of financial support
Local golf courses	source of revenue
Arnprior Secondary School and students	source of student employment
Government	source of tax revenue

---

7. Note: The people and companies portrayed in this case are fictitious. Any resemblance to real persons, companies, or organizations is purely coincidental.

This list provokes a number of questions:

1. Which of these stakeholders are most important to the survival of the company?
2. Which of these stakeholders has the greatest capacity to influence the company (positively or negatively)?
3. Which stakeholders need to be kept "the most happy" with the conduct and operations of the company?

Of course answers to these questions are not always easy and the most intuitive of responses is capable of generating great debate. However, for the purposes of illustration, suppose Mike arranged each of the above shareholders on a continuum with a brief rationale, as follows:

TABLE 9

MPEA Inc. Stakeholder Analysis

	Least Important	Less Important	Important	Most Important
Most Important				**Employees** – generate the revenue
Important			**The local bank** – provides credit and other services (payroll) – not most important because the bank has substitutes	**Suppliers** – provide the raw material inputs
\Less Important		**Arnprior Secondary School and students** – cannot be viewed as least important because these students' parents could be either existing or potential customers, the students are potential customers as well as a source of employees	**Mike and his family of shareholders** – this would likely be a private corporation for which share transfer is restricted; if a public corporation the shareholders could be viewed as most important due to the ease with which shareholders could sell their shares in search of higher investment returns	**Government** – taxes need to be paid to avoid government interest in the business (e.g. a tax audit)
\Least Important	Local charities – cannot be viewed as least important because they contribute to positive company reputation	**Local golf courses** – cannot be viewed as least important because their membership likely includes considerable local residents who patronize MPEA Inc. and involvement in the golf course activities likely generates sales	**Competition** – can present purchase alternatives to existing customers	**Customers** – purchase the product and are the source of revenue
	Least Important	**Less Important**	**Important**	**Most Important**

Note that even with this simple example, it is very difficult to identify a stakeholder or stakeholder group who is *not important* or in this case *least important*. As previously noted, however, all stakeholders' stakes and demands cannot be met, and so management must be able to identify the most important stakeholders and, their "stakes," and then develop an approach to "manage" these stakeholders in order that their input provides value to the organization.

Managing stakeholders and stakeholder expectations is a critical responsibility of management. A general approach can be described as consisting of four distinct steps:

Step 1.   Identify the organization's stakeholders

Step 2.   Determine each stakeholder's unique interests or concerns

Step 3.   Decide how critical each stakeholder is to the organization

Step 4.   Determine how to manage the different stakeholder relationships.[8]

In practical terms however, the management of stakeholders is rather more complex than what the above approach might suggest. For example, *how* does an organization determine who are its stakeholders, exactly *what* are their unique interests and concerns and, the *importance* of each stakeholder to the organization's sustainability, and which *relationships* actually exist both between the organization and the stakeholder, as well as *between* stakeholders?

Key Stakeholders

An initial list of stakeholders is only a starting point from which to conduct a more in- depth analysis. Not all stakeholders are created equal in terms of their importance to a company or organization. The challenge at this point is to identify, from the list of stakeholders, those who are *key* to the company. In this context "key" refers to a stakeholder's ability to exert and sustain a positive or negative effect on the company.

Once stakeholders have been identified, Robert Sexty proposes that management will want to consider:

1.   What are the stakeholders' stakes?
2.   What opportunities and challenges do stakeholders represent?

---

8. J.S. Harrison and C.H. St. John, "Managing and Partnering With External Stakeholders," *Academy of Management Executive* (May 1996): 46-60.

3. What economic, legal, ethical, and philanthropic responsibilities does the firm have in relation to stakeholders?

4. What strategies and actions should a firm take to manage stakeholders' opportunities and challenges?[9]

In identifying key stakeholders, many approaches have been advanced in the literature including stakeholder mapping and stakeholder attributes.

Stakeholder Mapping

Stakeholder mapping represents an approach through which to classify stakeholders according to their attributes. Although several matrix mapping approaches have been advanced in the literature, one that is most intuitive is mapping stakeholders according to their level of power to influence the company and the extent to which they are likely to show an interest in the activities of the company.[10] Stakeholders can be classified in any of four ways - those with:

1. a high level of power and a high level of interest;
2. a high level of power and a low level of interest;
3. a high level of interest and a low level of power; and
4. a low level of interest and a low level of power.

Stakeholders with high interest and high power would be considered "key" stakeholders. Using this approach, a mapping of the MPEA Inc. stakeholders identified above results in the following:

	Low Interest	High Interest
Low Power		Local charities Local golf courses Arnprior secondary school and students
High Power	Government (provided taxes are paid and laws are respected)	Employees Suppliers Customers Local bank Competition Mike and family shareholders

9. Robert W. Sexty, *Canadian Business and Society, Ethics and Responsibilities*, 2nd Edition, (Toronto: McGraw Hill Ryerson, 2011), 70-71.

10. A. Mendelow, *Proceedings of 2nd International Conference on Information Systems*, Cambridge, MA, 1981 by Gerry Johnson and Kevan Scholes, *Exploring Corporate Strategy: Text and Cases*, Third Edition (London: Prentice Hall International, 1993), 176-177.

From this illustration three important observations can be made:

1. There are many perspectives possible in determining *which* stakeholders are classified *where* and this can be complex and time-consuming;
2. Defining stakeholders with low interest and low power is often difficult; and
3. The mapping exercise becomes increasingly difficult as the company or organization increases in size or complexity.

Following high power and high interest stakeholders, the next most important stakeholder group is those having high power and low interest, because if their interest increases they have the power to exert influence on the company, or in other words, to migrate to key stakeholder status. A critical part of the analysis must consider the circumstances under which this group could become "key" and what is the likelihood of these circumstances developing in the time period covered by this stakeholder mapping.

Stakeholder Attributes

Perhaps one of the best models of stakeholder identification has been advanced by Mitchell, Agle, and Wood.[11] This model proposes that the extent of management priority given to stakeholder claims depends on the extent to which a stakeholder or stakeholder group possesses three key attributes: *power, legitimacy*, and *urgency*.

> *Power* refers to a stakeholder's ability to provoke an outcome that may not otherwise occur. According to the model, a stakeholder has power "to the extent it has or can gain access to coercive, utilitarian, or normative means to impose its will…"[12]

> *Legitimacy* refers to the perceived validity of a stakeholder's stake.

> *Urgency* refers to the timeliness with which the business must address the stakeholder's claim, or more specifically when "…a claim is of a time-sensitive nature and when that claim is important or critical to the stakeholder."[13]

According to the model any party that possesses at least one of the three attributes is a stakeholder. The priority given to the stakeholder will depend upon the number of attributes the stakeholder possesses.

> A *latent stakeholder* possesses only one of the three attributes and would demonstrate a low salience (or priority) to the company.

11. R. Mitchell, B. Agle, & D. Wood, "Toward a Theory of Stakeholder Identification and Salience: Defining the Principle of Who and What Really Counts," *Academy of Management Review 22* (1997), (4): 853-886.
12. Mitchell, 855.
13. Mitchell, 867.

A stakeholder possessing two attributes would be perceived by management as an *expectant stakeholder* demonstrating a moderate salience.

A stakeholder possessing all three attributes would demonstrate high salience and would be viewed as a *definitive stakeholder*.

The greatest priority would be given to the definitive stakeholder. The model further classifies stakeholders as either *latent* or *expectant*, emphasizing that the stakeholder's classification can change as the situation changes – in other words, a stakeholder's urgency, power or legitimacy does not necessarily remain static.[14]

Typology	Rank	Attribute	Attribute Description
Latent stakeholders	1	Dormant	Possessing power but no legitimacy or urgency
	2	Discretionary	Legitimate but powerless to influence and no urgency
	3	Demanding	Possessing urgency, but no power or legitimacy
Expectant stakeholders	4	Dominant	Having power and legitimacy
	5	Dangerous	Having legitimacy and urgency
	6	Dependent	Having urgency and power, but no legitimacy
Definitive	7		As noted above
Non-stakeholder	8		Having no power, legitimacy or urgency

This approach suggests that management's priority should be given to stakeholders with two or three attributes such as classifications 4, 5, 6 and 7 in the figure below.

FIGURE 10

Stakeholder Typology: One, Two or Three attributes present.

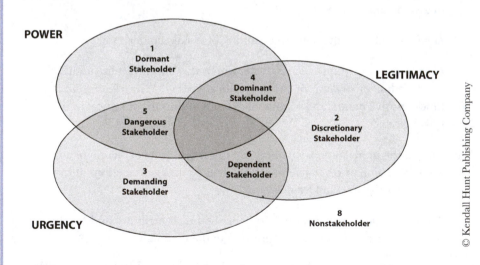

© Kendall Hunt Publishing Company

---

14. Brad L. Rawlins, "Prioritizing Stakeholders for Public Relations," *Institute for Public Relations* (2006).

For MPEA Inc., stakeholders could be classified as follows:

Definitive stakeholders would be employees, suppliers, and customers.

Expectant stakeholders would be the local bank, government, competition, and Mike and family shareholders – all of whom would be classified as dominant stakeholders.

Latent stakeholders would be local charities, local golf courses, and Arnprior Secondary School and students – all of whom would be classified as discretionary stakeholders.

Stakeholder	Power	Legitimacy	Urgency	Classification
Employees	X	X	X	
Suppliers	X	X	X	Definitive
Customers	X	X	X	
Local bank	X	X		
Government	X	X		
Competition	X	X		Expectant
Mike & family shareholders	X	X		
Local charities		X		
Local golf courses		X		Latent
Arnprior Secondary School and students		X		

Stakeholder Capacity

Stakeholder identification is a complex process, and difficult to do well. The literature abounds with many suggested approaches. However, one common theme appears to be *capacity*; that is, the capacity for a stakeholder to exert positive or negative influence on an organization. There is a tendency to interpret many stakeholder models as a means to identify and deal with those stakeholders who could adversely affect the organization.

However, it is essential to appreciate that working with other stakeholders can often provide considerable value to the organization by offering important insights and information that can greatly assist the organization.

The author proposes a *stakeholder capacity* model – an approach to identifying stakeholders in terms of their capacity to influence the organization and the association of this capacity with the level of risk the organization's senior management has determined it is willing to assume. The appeal of determining "capacity" parallels many existing models, including those presented earlier. For example, a definitive stakeholder has great capacity to influence. Similarly a stakeholder with high power and high interest also has great capacity to influence.

The second aspect proposed in the stakeholder capacity model is *risk* and is at best implied in many models. Yet the management of risk is essential to every organization. Risk profiles are often developed that identify risk events from which senior management decides which risks are critical and the extent to which risks will be tolerated. Incapacity, inability, or general unwillingness to explicitly mitigate certain known risks means that these risks will be tolerated by the organization – in other words, they will assume the risk of occurrence and the associated fallout should these risks materialize.

As with stakeholders, all risks are not created equal, and senior management will never be capable of covering all risks all of the time. The correlation of risk to stakeholder management is directly related to stakeholder capacity. In simple terms stakeholders present risk to the organization. The risk of a stakeholder adversely affecting the organization and/or the reduction of risk to the organization by stakeholder actions depends on the capacity of the stakeholder to exert influence.

The stakeholder capacity approach consists of the following steps:

1. Develop a list of any individuals, groups of individuals, organizations, or inanimate objects that logically could influence the organization and its operations in some way – this becomes the initial stakeholder list.
2. Rate each stakeholder identified on a scale of Low, Medium, and High in terms of their capacity to affect the organization positively and/or negatively in each of the following five key areas of influence: public reputation, other stakeholders, supply chain members, financial condition areas; and the ability to sustain supportive or unsupportive activities. For illustration purposes, assume that senior management at MPEA Inc. has conducted sufficient analysis and has agreed with the ratings on each of the stakeholders identified. Consider the local bank:

Stakeholder: Local Bank	Positively (high/medium/low)	Negatively (high/medium/low)
Capacity of the stakeholder to positively or negatively:		
influence public reputation	L	L
influence other stakeholders	L	L
influence supply chain members	M	M
influence financial condition	M	M
sustain supportive or unsupportive activities	M	H

3. Assign a numerical equivalent to Low, Medium, and High to quantify the ratings; for example, Low = 1, Medium = 2, and High = 3. It should be noted that how each of these capacities are rated depends on senior management. For example in the case of a competitor stakeholder, its capacity to influence supply chain members and other stakeholders depends on many factors: its financial strength, depth and breadth of advertising, whether it uses the same supply chain members and the nature of supply chain agreements and arrangements. Only the organization's senior management, after analyzing as much information as possible concerning the stakeholder, can determine which rating to assign to each capacity. For the local bank:

Stakeholder: Local Bank	Positively (high/medium/low)		Negatively (high/medium/low)	
Capacity of the stakeholder to positively or negatively:				
influence public reputation	L	1	L	1
influence other stakeholders	L	1	L	1
influence supply chain members	M	2	M	2
influence financial condition	M	2	M	2
sustain supportive or unsupportive activities	M	2	H	3

4. Compute the overall score for each stakeholder. For the local bank:

Stakeholder: Local Bank	Positively (high/medium/low)		Negatively (high/medium/low)	
Capacity of the stakeholder to positively or negatively:				
influence public reputation	L	1	L	1
influence other stakeholders	L	1	L	1
influence supply chain members	M	2	M	2
influence financial condition	M	2	M	2
sustain supportive or unsupportive activities	M	2	H	3

SCORE	POSITIVE CAPACITY		NEGATIVE CAPACITY	TOTAL CAPACITY
High	0		3	3
Medium	6		4	10
Low	2		2	4
TOTAL	8		9	17

5. The next step is to compare each stakeholder's overall capacity score with the organization's risk-informed stakeholder relevance intervals (SRIs) pre- determined by the organization's senior management team commensurate with its risk tolerance level.

To illustrate, assume that in determining these SRIs, senior MPEA Inc. management, in conjunction with its corporate risk profile, has developed the following:

Stakeholder Relevance Interval (SRI)	Type of Stakeholder
Capacity Score (CS) $\geq$ 20	Significant
20 < CS $\square$ 15	Acknowledged
CS < 15	Minor

With definition of SRI established by MPEA's management, we can categorize the MPEA Local bank as an *acknowledged* stakeholder.

To further illustrate this model, consider the application of this approach to a second stakeholder of MPEA Inc., a competitor:

Stakeholder: Competitor	Positively (high/medium/low)		Negatively (high/medium/low)	
Capacity of the stakeholder to positively or negatively:				
influence public reputation	L	1	M	2
influence other stakeholders	L	1	M	2
influence supply chain members	L	1	L	1
influence financial condition	L	1	M	2
sustain supportive or unsupportive activities	L	1	L	1

SCORE	POSITIVE CAPACITY	NEGATIVE CAPACITY	TOTAL CAPACITY
High	0	0	0
Medium	0	6	6
Low	5	2	7
TOTAL	5	8	13
TYPE (based SRI thresholds)			Minor

As with the capacity rating, the SRIs can be adjusted by senior management. From the chart above and the resulting CS ratings for each of the stakeholders, a few observations can be made:

- The local bank is an *acknowledged* stakeholder, and the competitor is a *minor* stakeholder;
- The competitor has a greater "negative" capacity than a "positive" capacity (which is to be expected); and
- The local bank has almost equal negative and positive capacity.

6. The next step is to determine how each type of stakeholder will be managed —the subject of the next section.

Managing Stakeholder Relationships

Once stakeholders have been identified and classified it is necessary to determine how each stakeholder or stakeholder group will be managed. *Stakeholder management* has been described as "…a way of organizing the firm so that it can be responsive to the concerns of its stakeholders precisely because those stakeholders can affect the plans and activities of the firm."[15] It is necessary for management to recognize the opportunities to develop productive working relationships with stakeholders, as well as to recognize the challenges and develop appropriate actions for how the business will contend with challenges presented by stakeholders.

The approach to stakeholder management will vary between organizations and various authors have proposed nomenclature to describe the different approaches that are generally commensurate with the perceived level of the stakeholder's importance to the organization. For example, Savage proposes that where a stake-

---

15. Bryan W. Husted, "Organizational Justice and the Management of Stakeholder Relations," *Journal of Business Ethics* (1998), 17: 647.

holder's potential for threat to, and cooperation with, the organization is high, collaborating with the stakeholder is the preferred approach. In contrast marginal stakeholders, those with low potential for threat to, and cooperation with, the organization should be monitored.[16] Mitchell, Agle and Wood recommend that management immediately address the concerns of definitive stakeholders as these stakeholders possess all three attributes of power, urgency, and legitimacy.[17]

Building on the author's stakeholder capacity approach, recall the three emerging types of stakeholders – significant, acknowledged, and minor. A *significant* stakeholder has *extensive* capacity to influence the organization and can be expected to be motivated to do so. This type of stakeholder generally exemplifies the key stakeholder, the definitive stakeholder, the dominant stakeholder, and the core stakeholder of other stakeholder models. An *acknowledged* stakeholder is one who has *substantial* capacity to influence the organization but is less motivated to do so. A *minor* stakeholder has *little* capacity to influence the organization regardless of its level of motivation.

Given these definitions the majority of management's time that is dedicated to stakeholder relations and stakeholder management should be given to important stakeholders, some time should be devoted to acknowledged stakeholders, and the least amount of time given to marginal stakeholders. The management approach by type of stakeholder might appear as follows:

Stakeholder Type	Management Approach
Significant	*Partner* – work closely with the stakeholder to determine win-win scenarios in the areas of the stakeholder's interest.
Acknowledged	*Dialogue* – communicate regularly, work to better understand the stakeholders' interests, keep them aware in a general sense of what the organization is doing and how it affects them.
Minor	*Passive Observation* – no direct engagement unless the stakeholder type changes in its capacity to influence.

In the case of MPEA Inc. the local bank, as an acknowledged stakeholder, should be kept informed of the company's progress. The company should also keep abreast of the bank's expectations of the company as well as any emerging trends such as, for example, planned increases in interest rates.

---

16. Grant T. Savage et al. "Strategies for Assessing and Managing Organizational Stakeholders," *Academy of Management Executive*, 5(2) (1991): 65.
17. R. Mitchell, B. Agle, & D. Wood, "Toward a Theory of Stakeholder Identification and Salience: Defining the Principle of Who and What Really Counts," A*cademy of Management Review* 22 (1997), (4): 853-886.

As previously noted there are many possible approaches to the management of stakeholders. One approach advanced by M. Joseph Sirgy in exploring the manufacturing industry is perhaps applicable to all industries and builds on the relationship marketing concept suggesting that three major groupings of stakeholders exist, requiring different relationship management strategies: *external stakeholders, internal stakeholders,* and *distal stakeholders.*[18]

Internal stakeholders result from the internal division of labour and would include among others, executive staff, the board of directors, and the various internal organizational departments and their respective managers.

External stakeholders are those with which the firm exchanges resources and would be exemplified by employees, shareholders, lending institutions, suppliers, the local community, and the environment.

Distal stakeholders exert indirect influence on the business's survival and growth and would include competitors, advocacy groups, government agencies, labour unions, and trade associations to name a few.

The model suggests distinguishing among organizational stakeholders by assigning certain internal stakeholders to serve external stakeholders (such as the CEO serving the shareholders), to support other internal stakeholders (such as the CEO supporting the board of directors), and to influence the attitude of distal stakeholders (such as the CEO influencing industry leaders, auditors, and consumer advocacy groups).[19] Thus according to this model, the management of all stakeholders is the responsibility of internal stakeholders.

A further model is advanced by Kenneth Goodpaster who proposes three approaches to stakeholder management: *strategic, multifiduciary,* and *synthesis.*[20]

The *strategic approach* takes stakeholders into account in order to avoid their adverse effect on organizational activities.

The *multifiduciary approach* suggests that managers have a fiduciary duty to stakeholders along the lines of a corporate director's fiduciary responsibility: to act honestly and in good faith with a view to the best interests of the stakeholder, putting the stakeholder on more-or-less the same level as the shareholder.

18. M. Joseph Sirgy, "Measuring Corporate Performance by Building on the Stakeholders Model of Business Ethics," *Journal of Business Ethics* (2002), 35: 143-162.
19. M. Joseph Sirgy, "Measuring Corporate Performance by Building on the Stakeholders Model of Business Ethics," *Journal of Business Ethics* (2002), 35: 143-162.
20. Kenneth E. Goodpaster, "Business Ethics and Stakeholder Analysis," *Business Ethics Quarterly* Vol. 1, No.1, January (1991): 53-73.

The *synthesis approach* "synthesizes" the strategic and multifiduciary approaches, balancing management's moral obligation to stakeholders with responsibility, but not *fiduciary* responsibility.

Multi-Stakeholder Dialogue

Multi-stakeholder dialogue can be described as managers deliberately communicating with the firm's stakeholders in order to better understand and appreciate their interests and their stakes. It has been suggested that the greatest meaningful dialogue will result when both management and the stakeholders understand how each other perceives the risks associated with the firm's potential action.[21] Multi-stakeholder dialogue offers several advantages, among them:

- The mobilization of specific expertise held by stakeholders;
- Improved awareness on the part of both the company and its stakeholders;
- The establishment of new networks; and,
- The establishment and/or strengthening of strategic partnerships.[22]

Several approaches to multi-stakeholder dialogue are possible, of which consensus building is the most intuitive. Consensus building necessarily requires that both parties understand the issue as well as how the other perceives the risk. Deliberation is a viable alternative in conducting multi-stakeholder dialogue and refers to "a process of argumentation and communication in which the participants engage in an open process in which they exchange opinions and viewpoints, weigh and balance arguments, and offer reflections and associations."[23] To engage stakeholders in dialogue through deliberation, a variety of methods can be used, including:

- value-focussed thinking based on values not alternatives;
- methodology through which patterns of belief are uncovered as well as prevailing views; and,
- semantic differential that is intended to measure attitudes.[24]

During dialogue with stakeholders it is essential to be sensitive to cultural differences that might manifest in verbal and non-verbal communications. It is also advised to report the deliberations and results of such dialogues as "reports of dialogic processes and outcomes allow checks or controls to determine whether representative

---

21. David L. Schwarzkopf, "Stakeholder Perspectives and Business Risk Perception," *Journal of Business Ethics*, 64 (2006): 327-342.

22. Marlene van de Kerkhof, "Making a difference: On the constraints of consensus building and the relevance of deliberation in stakeholder dialogues," *Poly Sci*, 39 (2006): 279-280.

23. Marlene van de Kerkhof, "Making a difference: On the constraints of consensus building and the relevance of deliberation in stakeholder dialogues," *Poly Sci*, 39 (2006): 279-280.

24. Marlene van de Kerkhof, "Making a difference: On the constraints of consensus building and the relevance of deliberation in stakeholder dialogues," *Poly Sci*, 39 (2006): 279-280.

perspectives have been included and enable other non-participating stakeholders to be informed of key exchanges that took place."[25]

Notwithstanding the potential positive outcomes of multi- stakeholder dialogue, some cautionary notes are offered. First, too many voices could lead to inaction or fragmentation inside the organization, and second, high expectations for the achievement of learning and relationship building could lead to disappointment when planned outcomes are not achieved.

Multi-stakeholder recognition and management

Ignoring stakeholders is clearly not an option. As Daboub and Calton point out: "The evolution of organization structure seems to have gone from the vertically integrated functional structure, to the multidivisional form, to the matrix, to the network, and finally to the … cellular form,"[26] this latter form representing a living, adaptive organization that goes beyond the network structures.[27] To create a sustainable competitive advantage in an environment characterized by short product shelf life, supply chain management of value-added, endless and severe competition, instantaneous communication, increased visibility, a more informed and product/service-savvy society, and dwindling margins, sustaining complex stakeholder relationships will be critical. No longer does management have exclusive dominion over the decision-making process and the governance of companies – value creation requires a knowledge contribution from everyone both inside and outside the company. Collaboration, partnerships, and networks anchored in trust, reciprocity, and common norms – indeed the very sorting mechanisms of civil society – as well as social capital, defined by The World Bank as referring to "the institutions, relationships, and norms that shape the quality and quantity of a society's social interactions," is required for success in the prevailing business macro-environment.[28]

25. Stephen L. Payne and Jerry M. Calton, "Exploring Research Potentials and Applications for Multi-stakeholder Learning Dialogues," *Journal of Business Ethics*, 55 (2004): 75.

26. Anthony J. Daboub and Jerry M. Calton, "Stakeholder Learning Dialogues: How to Preserve Ethical Responsibility in Networks,"*Journal of Business Ethics* 41 (2002): 89.

27. R.E. Miles, C.C. Snow, J.A. Matthews, G., Miles, and H.J. Coleman Jr. "Organizing in the Knowledge Age: Anticipating the Cellular Form,"*Academy of Management Executive* 11 (4) (November 1997): 7-20.

28. "What is Social Capital?" The World Bank, accessed June 16, 2013, https://www.worldbank.org/en/webarchives/archive?url=httpzzxxweb.worldbank.org/archive/website01360/WEB/0__MEN-2.HTM&mdk=23354653.

Chapter Summary

Canada's pluralistic nature means that power is disbursed among many "stake-holders." A stakeholder can be any person or any group with a perceived stake in an organization's activities. However, all stakeholders are not created equal. Some stakeholders are particularly important to an organization in terms of their capacity to exert positive and/or negative influence. Other stakeholders may have considerably less capacity to influence the organization. Accordingly an organization needs to analyze its stakeholders and to "classify" them in terms of legitimacy, power, interest, and capacity to influence, and determine how each type of stakeholder should be managed.

Several approaches can be used in identifying and analyzing stakeholders from the relatively unsophisticated intuitive list to the more complex model advanced by Mitchell, Agle, and Wood. Once stakeholders are identified, their stakes understood, and their capacity to influence the organization determined, the next step is deciding how to manage them. This can also range from a simple, intuitive approach to a more complicated approach. The reality is that stakeholder management is complex, time consuming, expensive, and necessary. Ignoring stakeholders is not an intelligent option. In the prevailing globalized economy a multi-stakeholder approach is critical in order to develop and sustain a competitive advantage for business. Government and organizations within the Civil Society segment must also be mindful of their stakeholders in order to better manage their affairs and achieve targeted outcomes and desired results.

End of Chapter Questions

1. Define a stakeholder and discuss the issues surrounding stakeholder management.

2. Discuss the two opposing views concerning stakeholder management, exemplified by Charles Handy and Milton Friedman, respectively. Which approach do you believe is most relevant in the 21st century?

3. Compare and contrast the Stakeholder Capacity Model proposed by the author with other models presented in this chapter.

4. What is multi-stakeholder dialogue? Identify the benefits and shortcomings of such an approach to stakeholder management.

Application Questions

Returning to the opening news article, discuss each of the following:

1. Using the Stakeholder Capacity Model, identify the key stakeholders in the 10,000 Challenges initiative and indicate how they should be managed.

2. The catalyst for removing plastics from use is concern for the environment. In your view, how would the positions of Handy and Friedman enter into in this matter?

3. Is pluralism relevant in the 10,000 Challenges initiative?

4. In your view would there be any disenfranchised stakeholders in the 10,000 Challenges initiative?

Research Questions

1. Using the Internet and other on-line resources, including academic journals, determine whether other models of stakeholder identification and management exist. Compare and contrast your findings with both the Mitchel, Agle and Wood model and the Stakeholder Capacity Model presented in this chapter. In your view, which model best provides a comprehensive understanding of the stakeholders involved in the 10,000 Challenges initiative?

Team Discussion Project

Pick any organization of your choice. Provide a complete stakeholder analysis for this organization.

CHAPTER 6

Globalization and Multiculturalism

Vasin Lee/Shutterstock.com

Globalization & Multiculturalism in the News

The World Still Believes in Globalization[1]

The article published in June discusses the 2019 Best Countries Survey Report conducted by US News.

While the recent summit of the Group of 20 nations held in Osaka, Japan permitted world leaders to discuss eight major themes, including energy and the environment,

---

1. USNews, "The World Still Believes in Globalization", https://www.usnews.com/news/best-countries/articles/2019-06-27/global-survey-shows-most-people-believe-in-globalization, accessed July 17, 2019.

women's empowerment, innovation, and trade and investment, the "Best Countries Survey" indicates that the majority of people surveyed continue to support the concept of globalization.

The Best Countries report is based on a survey of more than 20,000 people in 36 countries. Some of the findings include:

- More than 70% of people surveyed said they agreed to some extent that globalization is important and a positive goal to strive toward.
- Women around the world are more likely to agree with the importance of globalization than men. More than 79% of women said that globalization is important and a positive goal to strive toward. About 76% of male respondents agreed with the statement.
- The younger generation is also the most likely to support globalization. More than 80% of those age 18-24 and 25-35 surveyed in the study said they agreed with the statement to various extents; more that 77% of those 36-45 agreed with the same statement, while the lowest values were reported for people older than 55.
- Kenya is the country that showed the strongest support for globalization, with more than 60% of those surveyed in Kenya saying they strongly agreed with the statement on the concept. More than 21% agreed moderately, while 10.8 agreed slightly.
- While the country that reported the highest levels of strong disapproval toward globalization is France, where more than 9% of those interviewed said they strongly disagreed with the statement.

The full article can be viewed at https://www.usnews.com/news/best-countries/articles/2019-06-27/global-survey-shows-most-people-believe-in-globalization.

Introduction

Globalization and multiculturalism are two important and interconnected issues that affect each segment of the Canadian domestic macro-environment. Today's world is a place of intermingling differences – a place where business, government, and civil society cannot always be understood using one's own country or culture as the basis; where our business and political practices are neither uniformly accepted nor always effective; a place where differences need to be understood and accepted; and where these differences, once understood, can bring added value to business, government, and civil society.

In early 2016 21.9% of the Canadian population reported that they were or had been immigrants to Canada, as compared to the 22.3% recorded in the 1921 Census.[2] While almost half of the foreign-born population is from Asia, for the first time Africa is not the second largest source of recent immigrants.[3] Overall respondents reported over 250 ethnicities.[4] To work in a globalized environment does not necessarily require a physical move to another country! However, to develop and maintain a sustainable competitive advantage many companies will need to service foreign markets and deal with foreign governments and foreign civil society issues. To do so will require knowledge of globalization and multi-cultural sensitivity. Not only businesses are affected. To exercise its role of creating an environment conducive to effective and efficient business operations, it is essential that government moves beyond parochial domesticity and works with other governments around the world to ensure the international competitiveness of Canadian businesses and to learn from the drivers of international social movements. Globalization has brought international focus to many issues supported by civil society throughout the world.

This chapter will explore the concept of globalization and the importance of multicultural understanding.

Globalization

What is globalization?

Globalization has come to mean many things to many people. Over the years writers have described globalization in terms of the interconnectivity of nations, the melding of political spaces, and the creation of a borderless world. Jan Aart Scholte has suggested five different views of globalization:

1.   cross-border relations between countries;
2.   the removal of government restrictions in the creation of an open, borderless world economy;
3.   universalizing experiences and objects;
4.   the replacement of pre-existing cultures with the social structures of modernity; and,
5.   the reconfiguration of geography such that social space is no longer mapped in terms of territorial places, distance and borders.[5]

---

2. Statistics Canada, "Immigration and ethnocultural diversity: Key results from the 2016 Census", https://www150.statcan.gc.ca/n1/daily-quotidien/171025/dq171025b-eng.htm, accessed July 17, 2019.
3. Ibid.
4. Ibid.
5. J.A. Scholte, *Globalization: A Critical Introduction* (London: Palgrave Macmillan, 2000).

Held, McGrew, Goldlatt and Perraton propose that globalization can be thought of as "...the widening, deepening and speeding up of worldwide interconnectedness in all aspects of contemporary social life...,"[6] and Richard Haass' perspective on globalization is "...the totality and velocity of connections and interactions – be they economic, political, social, cultural – that are sometimes beyond the control or even knowledge of governments or other authorities...[globalization is] a multifaceted and transnational phenomenon."[7]

Many definitions of globalization have an inherent business theme to them. If one were to consider globalization on the margins of social institution theory, one might propose the following:

- business exists because society explicitly sanctions its existence through law;
- business exists to satisfy the wants and needs of society – if society did not want the products and services business would not produce them;
- business's offerings to satisfying society's wants and needs must be affordable, and in order to keep products and services affordable, business must either raise prices and/or reduce production costs while constantly increasing quality to remain competitive;
- the wants and needs of society are growing in complexity making it difficult if not impossible for any single firm to develop product offerings entirely by itself – specialization is necessary at both the level of raw material input as well as knowledge - such specialization requiring businesses to collaborate with international suppliers;
- such collaboration results in lower input costs, making society's wants and needs affordable and also resulting in knowledge transfer of business, government, and civil society practices in other countries; or,
- the products and services provided by business are demanded by society because these products and services will increase the quality of life of society in some way.

Pursuing this line of thought produces another definition of globalization proposed by the author:

> *Globalization is multinational collaboration in the creation of business, political, and social wealth by maximizing the unique knowledge contributions of nations and cultures worldwide in developing a better living standard for all nations.*

---

6. David Held, Anthony McGrew, David Goldblatt and Jonathan Perraton, *Global Transformations* (US: Standford University Press, 1999), accessed June 16, 2013, http://www.polity.co.uk/global/.
7. Richard N Haass, "Policymakers and the Intelligence Community in this Global Era," (Remarks to CIA Strategic Assessments Group Annual Conference: The United States in the Third World Century, Department of State, U.S., 2011).

Of course many theorists would argue that this proposed definition is rather utopian and leads a reader to the conclusion that globalization is a great thing for all nations. Indeed there are arguments "for" and "against" globalization as presented in the next section.

Globalization—Is it Good or Bad?

As with most complex issues globalization has both its supporters and its critics. It would be impossible to consider every argument in depth within the space of this section; however, it is instructive to present a reasonably balanced view of some of the more common points made in the literature by those who support globalization and the points raised by those who reject globalization. Arguments in *support* of globalization include:

1. *Globalization increases prosperity and opportunity of all participating countries*

   In the case of developed countries, globalization facilitates the development of affordable products and services to meet the needs and wants of society through lowering the costs of inputs and maintaining a pricing structure through increasing sales to new non-domestic markets. For developing countries, globalization results in the reduction of poverty through the creation of jobs that would have otherwise not materialized resulting in higher standards of living.

2. *Globalization leads to greater market efficiency*

   Globalization facilitates greater output with fewer inputs resulting in increased market efficiency that in turn allows for lower prices which, assuming equal or higher product quality, results in more demand generating jobs and increasing the standard of living for both developed and developing countries.

3. *Globalization will result in a cleaner world environment*

   As developing countries become richer their standards of living will increase and constituents will eventually demand a higher level of standards and environmental responsibility from business.

4. *Globalization will increase competition that will in turn result in higher quality goods and services*

   Globalization will increase competition – in order to maintain a sustainable competitive advantage companies will strive to develop products and services of increasing quality. This raises the quality of life of consumers.

5. *Globalization facilitates knowledge transfer*

   Globalization results in the transfer of knowledge relating to technology, manufacturing, culture, and managerial practices and promotes collaboration
   among countries and organizations.

There are also many arguments *against* globalization:

1. *Globalization increases the wealth of giant multinational corporations by exploiting developing countries*

   A sobering thought is that the income of many giant multinational corporations exceeds the GDP of some of the developing countries in which they
   work. To what extent can these countries impose on these giant companies?
   How can a small under-developed country force these large companies to operate in an environmentally responsible way? What if the company pulls out
   of the country? Notwithstanding the wage rate offered to "host" workers being
   greater than the worker's domestic alternative, does this higher wage rate actually make a difference? In many cases workers cannot afford to purchase the
   product they are making, despite deep company discounts available to them.
   The only winner in this is the giant multinational corporation that gets richer
   on the backs of developing countries who get poorer.

2. *Globalization is degrading the natural environment*

   As multinational corporations strive to develop affordable products and services to supply the needs and wants of consumers, respecting environmental
   laws in developing countries would contribute to higher input costs and therefore higher selling prices. To keep prices low, input costs must be reduced
   and manufacturing products in countries where environmental laws are either
   slack or not enforced accomplishes this but at the risk to the environment.

3. *Under globalization big corporations are the most powerful players in developing countries*

   The power wielded by large multinational corporations can compromise a
   developing country's ability to govern itself since the government is powerless
   to influence the company and yields to its demands.

4. *Globalization will homogenize all cultures*

   Globalization will result in the homogenization of cultures resulting one single, materialistic "globalized culture."

5. *Globalization provokes the development of problems that cannot be solved by single nations — over-fishing and global warming provide some examples*

As large transnational companies set up shop in undeveloped countries and manufacture without regard to leading-edge sustainable development practices they will make greater contributions to environmental problems that affect the world and are not under the purview of any one nation to resolve. As well, despite governments' best efforts to agree to measures such as allowable catch quotas for marine species, for example, enforcement at the level of the company is difficult given the practices of some companies. For example flying "flags of convenience" on commercial fishing vessels that "conveniently" identify a vessel as being owned by a company resident in a country either not part of the international agreement or as a falsely identified legal fisher of the ocean zone.

There are many additional arguments that can be advanced either in support of or against globalization. The purpose of the foregoing was not to create a view that globalization is necessarily good or necessarily bad, but rather to present some of the more common arguments in presenting both sides of a continuing debate.

Globalization's Impact on Each Segment of the Canadian Domestic Macro-environment

Globalization has tangible effects on each segment of the Canadian domestic macro- environment. This section will consider some of the more important ways business, government, and civil society have been affected by globalization.

Globalization and the Business Segment

Many of the effects of globalization on business are intuitive. As information and communications technologies facilitate the conduct of business anywhere in the world, managing business has become more complex and must take into account different customs, cultures, business and management practices, laws, approaches to and expectations of social responsibility, and different governments.

Globalization offers new markets to business both for selling products and services as well as for sources of investment capital. It has also increased the level of competition as well as the pressure on product and service quality, the need to constantly innovate, and the capacity to commercialize this innovation. Business is no longer affected by time zones, and the pressure to constantly increase efficiency for sustained profitability results in increasingly short product and service lifecycles and collaborative relationships with members of the supply chain.

Cultural differences with respect to the definition and treatment of intellectual property and the management of intangibles will place greater demand on business to develop different management paradigms that balance shareholder and stakeholder interests.

To be successful in the global economy, Canadian businesses and business managers need to develop what is referred to as a *global mindset*. A company with a global mindset "...understands that the world of business is changing rapidly and that the world is more interdependent in business transactions."[8] A manager with a global mindset operates "...with a state of mind that is manifested as an orientation toward the outside ... and which seeks to reconcile the global with the local and mediate between the familiar and the foreign"[9] and in addition has "...a willingness to explore and learn from alternative systems of meaning held by others."[10] In other words businesses and managers with a global mindset recognize the interconnectivity of business transactions at a variety of levels, as well as the need to be culturally sensitive, continuous learners in order to bring best global practices to bear on domestic practices with a view to more efficient and effective value creation.

Conducting business globally of course is fundamentally an end-state in company growth strategies. Companies do not start out global but typically emerge through a number of stages ranging from the risk-taking entrepreneurial innovative spirit serving domestic markets, to serving perhaps the domestic market and one additional country, to serving many countries, and eventually to full-scale globalized operations. Having a global mindset will greatly assist in this evolution process and is necessary to develop a sustainable competitive advantage.

Globalization and the Government Segment

Inasmuch as Canadian businesses are impacted by globalization, the government is equally affected. If one of government's roles is to ensure an environment in which business can be most efficient and effective in order to create jobs and increase the standard of living for society it follows that, to do so, the government will need to be involved globally - in particular with trading nations and international fora such as the World Trade Organization through which world trade is governed. Such involvement complicates governing since for international trade to be effective a balanced approach to trade is required. To be perceived as a global trading partner, a government may have to negotiate market access through the elimination of traditional pro-

---

8. John B Cullen and K. Praveen Parboteeah, *Multinational Management A Strategic Approach*, 6the Edition (Ohio: South-Western Cengage Learning, 2014), 23.
9. Orly Levy et al, "What We Talk About When We Talk About 'Global Mindset': Managerial Cognition in Multinational Corporations," *Journal of International Business* Studies 39, no. 1 (2008): 82.
10. Orly Levy et al, "What We Talk About When We Talk About 'Global Mindset': Managerial Cognition in Multinational Corporations," *Journal of International Business* Studies 39, no. 1 (2008): 82.

tectionist measures such as tariffs and quotas – the result of which may be less favourable treatment of domestic businesses. The political challenge becomes satisfying the expectations of small non- international businesses, key players in contributing to the Canadian GDP, in an economy that is primarily globalized.

For the government the challenges of governing are becoming increasingly complex. Far from being able to focus solely on its own nation and its economic and social issues, government must now focus on and respond to issues occurring in other countries, not only due to their possible impact at home but also because society expects its government to deal with global social issues. Government is also expected to solve problems for which no viable solution readily exists such as off-shoring and near-shoring of jobs, humanitarian practices that are different and culturally-based, and instilling democratic values in countries under oppressive regimes.

As with business, government action (or inaction) now falls under a very transparent and international public microscope and this has resulted in the creation of many stakeholders beyond domestic voters. This increased "international" transparency of government combines with the broad sharing of instantaneous information among these stakeholders to create new policy issues for which constituents will expect a solution for problems that do not fall under the purview of any single government – climate change, the melting of the polar cap, and overfishing provide some examples.

Globalization and the Civil Society Segment

Globalization has had many effects on civil society. Advances in information and communication technologies driven by globalization provide opportunities for civil society to obtain more information, disseminate information, and raise public awareness internationally on their cause and obtain resources from global sources. Globalization may facilitate new practices that "may transform dysfunctional traditional groups into more productive ones."[11] Globalization facilitates civil society finding partners and partnering with those who have kindred interests as well as providing channels through which to share social innovation with stronger and more informed networks.

Globalization is also facilitating new and important roles for civil society, such as international conflict mediators, and providing the need for governments to consult with third segment representatives as they develop the positions and policies in their deliberations with member countries in globalization institutions.

Globalization is complicated territory with important implications for all segments of Canada's domestic macro-environment. As the evolution toward a global village

---

11. Marzia Fontana and Yukitsuga Yanoma, "Democracy and Civil Society," International Food Policy Research Institute (2001), accessed June 16, 2013, http://ebrary.ifpri.org/cdm/ref/collection/p15738coll2/id/128102.

continues there is a need to become culturally sensitive. The next section will consider culture and cross-cultural issues.

Culture

Culture has been described in many ways:

> *"the sum total of the ways of life of a people; includes norms, learned behavior patterns, attitudes, and artifacts; also involves traditions, habits or customs; how people behave, feel and interact; the means by which they order and interpret the world; ways of perceiving, relating and interpreting events based on established social norms; a system of standards for perceiving, believing, evaluating, and acting."*[12]

> *"the customary beliefs, social forms, and material traits of a racial, religious, or social group; also: the characteristic features of everyday existence (as diversions or a way of life) shared by people in a place or time"*[13]

From these definitions can be extracted some important points:

1. culture is learned and forms the basis for interpretation;
2. identity is based in culture;
3. culture and diversity are not mutually exclusive;
4. there is no right and wrong culture and judgement as to right or wrong cannot be based solely on the perspective of one's own culture;
5. cultural diversity is a fact of life in today's society and one needs to develop cultural sensitivity for peak performance;
6. culture will have a powerful influence on all segments of the Canadian domestic macro-environment; and,
7. North American management principles will not be uniformly applicable across the globe.

Given these observations, insensitivity toward different cultures can have serious consequences. Professor Geert Hofstede who has researched extensively on the subject of national culture puts it this way:

> *Culture is more often a source of conflict than of synergy. Cultural differences are a nuisance at best and often a disaster.*[14]

---

12. "EFL teaching terminology," International Teacher Training Organization, https://www.teflcertificate-courses.com/about-tefl.php, accessed July 17, 2019.
13. "Merriam-Webster, An Encyclopedia Britannica Company," accessed June 16, 2013, http://www.merriam-webster.com/dictionary/culture.
14. "National cultural dimensions," The Hofstede Centre, https://www.hofstede-insights.com/models/national-culture/, accessed July 17, 2019.

Yet in the global village success will depend on collaboration, partnering, trust, and social capital, so regardless of how much of a nuisance culture may be, ignoring cultural differences is not an option.

Theories of Culture

Many writers have explored the culture domain. Tony Morden categorizes models of national culture as consisting of historical social models, single dimension models, and multiple dimension models.[15] The approaches range from considering culture from the perspective of context, time, and trust through more complicated models such as Professor Geert Hofstede's five dimensions of culture and Fons Trompenaars' seven dimension model. These latter two models provide significant insight into cultural differences and will be explored below.

Hofstede's Dimensions of Culture

Geert Hofstede analyzed cultures based on six dimensions.[16] *Power distance*, the first dimension, measures the extent to which less powerful members of society expect and accept that power is distributed unequally. "The fundamental issue here is how society handles inequalities among people." Malaysia and Slovakia have the highest power distance rating and would represent those countries most accepting of the unequal distribution of power.[17]

The second dimension is *individualism vs. collectivism*, which refers to the extent to which the individual person is more important than the groups to which they belong. For example in highly individual societies the ties between individuals are loose whereas in highly collectivist societies individuals are more concerned with the well-being of the group. The United States ranks as the most individualist country, followed by Australia and the United Kingdom.[18]

Masculinity vs. femininity refers to the distribution of roles between the genders and is the third of Hofstede's cultural dimensions. Societies that are dominantly masculine are assertive and competitive, whereas feminist societies are dominantly modest and caring. The most masculine countries are Slovakia and Japan; the most feminist countries are Sweden and Norway.[19]

The fourth dimension is *uncertainty avoidance* and is a measure of the extent to which a society tolerates uncertainty and ambiguity. Societies with a low tolerance for un-

---

15. Tony Morden, "Models of National Culture – A Management Review," *Cross Cultural Management*, Vol. 6, No. 1(1999).
16. "National cultural dimensions," The Hofstede Centre, https://www.hofstede-insights.com/models/national-culture/, accessed July 17, 2019.
17. Ibid.
18. Ibid.
19. Ibid.

certainty will display a high ranking for uncertainty avoidance and will demonstrate intolerance for opinions that differ from what they are accustomed to encountering. Greece demonstrates the highest level of intolerance for uncertainty, followed by Portugal and Guatemala.[20]

The fifth dimension is *long-term orientation vs. short-term orientation* and is a measure of the extent to which a culture is future-oriented, patient and persevering. Hofstede identifies the values of thriftiness and perseverance as being associated with a long-term orientation, and the values of respect for tradition, fulfilling social obligations, and protecting one's "face" as being those associated with a short-term orientation.[21] East Asian countries including China, Hong Kong, and Taiwan demonstrate the highest score with regard to long-term orientations.[22]

The final and sixth dimension is indulgence vs. restraint and refers to the extent to which a society regulates social norms and supresses gratification.

From the descriptions above it is obvious that interacting with different cultures will present numerous challenges and will require different management approaches.

TABLE 10

Hofstede's Cultural Dimension for Canada and Selected Countries

Incentives that are effective motivators in individualist countries will not be effective in collectivist countries. Aggressiveness in negotiations will not be effective in feministic countries. For effective cross-cultural interaction it is essential to understand the cultural dimensions of countries and societies. The table below provides a comparison of Canada with some selected countries using Hofstede's six dimensions.

Hofstede's Cultural Dimensions for Canada vs. Selected Countries						
Country	Power Distance	Individualism	Masculinity	Uncertainty Avoidance	Long Term Orientation	Indulgence
Canada	39	80	52	48	36	68
China	80	20	66	30	87	24
Japan	54	46	95	92	88	42
Norway	31	69	8	50	35	55
Singapore	74	20	48	8	72	46
United Kingdom	35	89	66	35	51	69
United States	40	91	62	46	26	68

The reference for this table is Information derived from "Hofstedes' Insights Compare Countries" tool, https://www.hofstede-insights.com/product/compare-countries/, accessed July 17.2019.

---

20. Ibid.
21. Ibid.
22. Ibid.

Trompenaars Fundamental Dimensions of Culture

According to Trompenaars' every culture shares three universal problems: relationships with others; the relationship with time; and the relationship with nature.[23] From these three universal problems can be derived seven fundamental dimensions of culture as seen in the figure below.

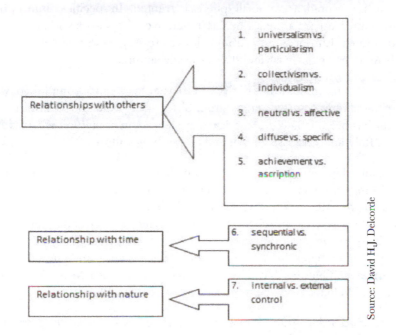

Source: David H.J. Delcorde

FIGURE 11

Trompenaars' Fundamental Dimensions of Culture

In *universalistic* cultures, rules, codes, and values take precedence over relationships whereas in *particularistic* cultures friendship and relationships are seen as more important. North Americans, Germans, and Northern Europeans are seen as individualistic cultures, whereas Koreans, Venezuelans, and the French are seen as particularistic cultures.

In *collectivist* cultures, "we" is more important than "I," whereas in *individualistic* cultures individuals are more self-oriented. Singaporeans, Nigerians, and Chinese are viewed as collectivist cultures, whereas North Americans and the British are seen as individualistic cultures.

In *neutral* cultures, human relations are dominated by reason, whereas in *affective* cultures human relations are dominated by emotion. In affective cultures it is acceptable to openly display feelings and emotions.

23. Fons Trompenaars, "Cross-cultural management [video-recording]: the human side to international management," (Brussels: Video Management, 1993).

Specific cultures are analysts – the whole is the sum of its parts. The public sphere of specific cultures is significantly larger than the private sphere. It is easy to be accepted into the public sphere but extremely challenging to get into the private sphere. *Diffuse* cultures are integrators. Integrators view the parts in perspective of the whole. The public sphere of diffuse cultures is very small while the private sphere is very large. While it is difficult for outsiders to be accepted in either sphere, once one is accepted, access to all spheres is granted. In specific cultures work and private matters are separated, whereas in diffuse cultures work and private matters are integrated. European and Asian cultures are seen as diffuse cultures whereas North American culture is viewed as a specific culture.

In *achievement* cultures, status is derived from what has been accomplished, whereas in *ascribed* cultures status is derived from birth, age, gender, or wealth irrespective of what has been achieved. America is an achievement culture, whereas France, Greece, Italy, and East Asia are viewed as ascribing cultures.

The relationship with *time* is exemplified by the difference between cultural views toward time, more specifically whether the culture's view on time is seen as sequential or synchronic. The "time is money" view exemplifies a *sequential* approach to time where staying on schedule is essential and time commitments are taken seriously. A *synchronic* culture sees time as flexible and intangible with time commitments not being essential; in synchronic cultures past, present, and future are all interrelated. Cultures that view time sequentially include North Americans, the British, and Italians. Asian cultures see time synchronically.

Cultures' relationships with *nature* is viewed through two approaches. *Internalistic* cultures believe they control nature and do not subscribe to the notions of luck or predestination. In contrast *externalists* believe that mankind should operate in harmony with nature and do not believe they can shape their own destinations. North Americans exemplify an internalistic culture and Asian cultures exemplify externalistic cultures.

Exploring cultural differences using the Hofstede and Trompenaars models provides insight into how diverse cultures actually are as well as how culture complicates management. The complexities attributed to cultural differences affect all segments of the Canadian macro-environment.

Culture's Effect on Business in Canada

Against the backdrop of globalization, culture has a significant impact on business. For Canadian business to thrive in foreign countries an understanding of culture in host countries is essential to avoid misunderstandings that could compromise the future of the firm. While the picture of a business operating in a foreign country provides an intuitive basis from which to appreciate the effect and importance of multiculturalism, the impact can also be felt domestically. To be competitive Canadian business needs to attract the best talent and expertise. This is not always available in Canada and may need to be sourced from persons from diverse cultural backgrounds. This results in cross-cultural work teams inside a given company that can reasonably be expected to collaborate with another strategic partnering firm who has obtained their human resources assets in the same way. The end result is the intermingling of individuals from a wide range of cultural backgrounds. This intermingling demands well- developed intercultural sensitivity at the level of the employee and the level of the manager to ensure the creation of knowledge and innovation to sustain a competitive advantage that is not compromised by unintentional culturally-related misunderstandings. The recognition that Canadian management techniques may not always produce expected results when applied to different cultures is also necessary.

Culture's Effect on Government in Canada

Canada represents a multicultural society within a bilingual framework that has acknowledged multiculturalism as a fundamental characteristic of Canadian society through the 1988 *Canadian Multiculturalism Act*.[24] With approximately 200,000 immigrants per year from all parts of the world, Canada's 36 million people "reflect a cultural, ethnic and linguistic makeup found nowhere else on earth."[25] With this degree of cultural richness it is reasonable to suggest that the stakeholder issues faced by government are numerous and diverse. As well, elected officials at all levels of government in Canada are drawn from diverse cultural backgrounds. Cultural diversity in Canada may also increase the complexity of public policy issues and impact the directions taken by Canada in international fora.

Culture's Effect on Canadian Civil Society

From diverse cultures will emerge diverse civil society issues that could complicate the formation and use of social capital and further fragment the civil society segment. In other words, ethnic diversity could affect civil society *compositionally* – some groups being more civic than others, and *contextually* – as a place becomes more heterogeneous, this shift could result in the older, dominant groups becoming less civically engaged.[26] At the same time, however, cultural diversity can bring a certain richness to civil society by promulgating different ways of looking at problems and facilitating greater networking capacity.

24. Sarah Wayland, "Immigration, Multiculturalism and National Identity in Canada," . *International Journal on Group Rights* 5 (1997): 33-58.

25. "Genealogy and Family History," Library and Archives Canada, http://www.bac-lac.gc.ca/eng/discover/Pages/ethno-cultural-groups.aspx, accessed July 17, 2019.

26. Richard Johnston and Stuart Soroka, "Social Capital in a Multicultural Society: The Case of Canada," *Social Capital and Participation in Everyday Life,* edited by Paul Dekker and Eric M. Uslaner (London: Routledge, 2001), 26

Chapter Summary

Globalization and multiculturalism are two related and important issues that affect all segments of the Canadian domestic macro-environment. Globalization generally refers to the merging of previously domestic spaces and issues into one multifaceted and interconnected transnational global village. Driven by market, cost, competition, government, and technology, globalization has both its supporters and non-supporters. Supporters advance arguments of wealth maximization for all, an increase in civil liberties, higher standards of living, a cleaner world environment, higher standards, and better international behaviour. Non-supporters contend that globalization will result in a wider gap between the haves and the have-nots, be detrimental to the environment, reduce standards, homogenize all cultures, diminish governments' ability to govern, and place too much power in the hands of big business. There are many institutions of globalization, among which are included the World Trade Organization, the Organization for Economic Cooperation and Development, the World Bank Group, the International Labour Organisation, the United Nations Environmental Programme and the United Nations Commission on Human Rights. Globalization has a number of effects on all segments of the Canadian domestic macro-environment.

Culture can be thought of as a set of shared norms and values that together form a sense of identity. Cultural diversity is reality and all three macro-environmental segments will need to become increasingly culturally sensitive to remain effective and relevant. Geert Hofstede and Fons Trompenaars propose a number of dimensions from which culture can be described and both models provide very useful bases from which to learn cultural differences and how to use this knowledge for effective intercultural relations.

End of Chapter Questions

1. What is globalization?

2. Discuss the arguments for and against globalization. In your view is globalization good for Canada?

3. Describe how globalization affects each segment of the Canadian domestic macro- environment.

4. Define culture and compare and contrast Hofstede's six dimensions of culture with Trompenaars' seven dimensions.

5. With reference to Table 10.1 in this chapter, describe how Canada differs from the United States and China. What might explain these differences? How might these differences affect management?

Application Questions

Returning to the opening news article discuss each of the following:

1. To what extent has countries' challenges of the long-held beliefs of the Group of 20 Nations been influenced by the impact of globalization? Do these 'challenges' reflect a growing propensity toward supporting globalization or a recognition of some of the disadvantages of globalization?

2. Globalization is supported most by the younger generations. In your view what might explain this comparatively pervasive support?

3. In your view, to what extent does culture impact positions put forward by member countries of the Group of 20 Nations?

Research Questions

1. Using the Internet and other sources select any foreign country of your choice and, using both Hofstede's and Trompenaars' models, analyze how your selected country differs from Canada.

2. Using the Internet and other sources, develop a cultural profile for Canada – does Canada in fact have a distinguishable national culture?

Team Discussion Project

Other than Canada and the United States of America identify three country members of the Group of 20 Nations and develop a national cultural profile for each country. Given these cultural profiles, what might be each country's position concerning the eight major themes of the summit?

CHAPTER 7

Ethics

Olivier Le Moal/Shutterstock.com

Ethics Issues in the News

UN official criticizes Canadian delays setting up corporate ethics watchdog[1]

The article published in April 2019 noted with criticism the length of time it took International Trade Minister Jim Carr took 15 months to appoint a new ombudsperson.

The article noted that Canada is falling behind other countries such as France, Germany, Switzerland and Australia in enacting laws to improve the conduct of their companies operating abroad, and that the Minis-

1. CBC News, "UN official criticizes Canadian delays setting up corporate ethics watchdog", https://www.cbc.ca/news/politics/un-watchdog-carr-corporate-ethics-1.5116399, accessed July 17, 2019.

ter's decision to announce a further legal review also drew condemnation from rights groups.

Canada's reputation is at stake

The government promised to create the position as part of their 2015 campaign platform, and announced the details of the new office in January 2018. The reform effort has been spearheaded by Liberal MP John McKay, who introduced a private member's bill on corporate social responsibility for Canadian resource and energy firms in 2010.

The full article can be viewed at https://www.cbc.ca/news/politics/un-watch-dog-carr-corporate-ethics-1.5116399.

Introduction

Ethics is a complex but important subject that at its most intuitive level concerns differentiating between what is bad, what is good, what is right and what is wrong, and to borrow from Hosmer, doing what is right, just, and fair.[2] Ethics and ethical conduct are frequently featured in the domain of "business ethics" in which the perceived ethical floundering of companies receives widespread and timely media coverage. In the same way that the stakeholder concept forms the foundation for corporate social responsibility, corporate social responsibility itself is grounded in stakeholders' perceptions of the ethical actions and decisions of business. However ethical theory and ethical conduct are not unique to the domain of the business segment and it would be both misleading and an oversimplification to restrict a discussion of ethics to the business segment, as ethical theory and ethical issues are also found in both the government and civil society segments of the macro-environment.

Ethics

The word *ethics* is derived from the Greek *ethikos* and *ethos* which relates to "the distinguishing character, sentiment, moral nature, or guiding beliefs of a person, group or institution."[3] Some definitions present ethics as being concerned with

---

2. LaRue Tone Hosmer, *The Ethics of Management*, Fifth Edition (Canada: McGraw-Hill Irwin, 2006).
3. "ethos," Merriam-Webster, An Encyclopedia Britannica Company, accessed June 18, 2013, https://www.merriam-webster.com/dictionary/ethos.

evaluating human action,[4] or as principles or assumptions underpinning appropriate conduct.[5] While at the outset doing what is right, just, and fair would appear to be intuitive and straight-forward, the supporting theory and practice are not. It is relatively easy to discern right and wrong behaviour within one's own culture and therefore the correct and ethical choice between an action that is good and an action that is bad is obvious. But what happens when a choice must be made between two *good* actions? If choosing the good action is ethical, which good action is the most ethical? This exemplifies what some writers refer to as the ethical dilemma.

Ethics is a complex area and has been considered extensively in the literature. Notwithstanding the *right* and *wrong* flavour from which much discussion originates, the complexity of ethics can be demonstrated through the following:

- What is right and what is wrong is culturally bound and not always transferable across nations or within subcultures
- Personal or individual morals and values may be different from organizational morals and values and this must be reconciled
- While businesses and organizations must conduct operations in an ethical manner, being ethical is not free, but it is cheaper than being unethical
- Ethical conduct is similar to stakeholder management insofar as, regardless of the effort to be ethical, there will be winners and losers
- What is the appropriate amount of ethics? If an organization meets the minimum legal standard is that organization ethical or merely "not unethical"?
- What exactly is ethics and do all stakeholders agree?
- How does an organization make publicly *defensible* ethical decisions?

A brief review of ethics in the news provides an interesting sampling of the issues that are perceived to be ethical in construct. These ethical issues include consumer credit, the environment, financial misreporting, toxin-free products, social media, bribes, tobacco and hazardous products that are legal, food and drug ingredients, labour practices, and extended warranties – to name just a few.

The intention of this chapter is to provide readers with an overview of ethics. It does not purport to present a full treatment of ethics. Indeed entire courses are offered in this important area. A key message to readers is that, notwithstanding the complexities surrounding ethics and ethical conduct, organizations must operate in an ethical manner.

---

4. "Glossary of Historical terms," WebChron – The Web Chronology Project, accessed June 18, 2013, http://www.thenagain.info/WebChron/Glossary/Glossary.html
5. John G. Beech, John Beech, Simon Chandwick, "The Business of Sport Management," Pearson Education, 2004.

This chapter's consideration of ethics will start with a description of ethical influences and the main branches of ethics theory. This will be followed by a discussion of business ethics and managerial ethics, ethical government, and ethical civil society organizations in response to three key questions: What is an ethical business? What is ethical government? What is an ethical civil society organization? The chapter will conclude with a discussion and a model on how to make defensible ethical decisions, and factors that encourage ethical decision-making.

Ethical Influences

Discussions about ethics and ethical conduct are frequently found in the realm of organizations and it is common to read about the ethical conduct of business, government, and civil society organizations. However all organizations are composed of people and these people are responsible for the operation and the conduct of the organization, not this inanimate object called an organization operating on its own without human intervention. It follows then that the public perception of the ethics of business, government, and civil society is in reality the ethics of the individual organizational members; in other words the culmination of the morals, duties, values, goals, norms, and beliefs of those individuals who collectively comprise the organization. While many definitions exist for each of these terms the following definitions are instructive and provide the necessary context:

> *Morals* "...are ideals for behaviour"[6] or "...guidelines that set the boundaries of acceptable behaviour..."[7]

> *Duties* are "the attitudes and behaviours we feel that others have a right to expect of us because of their relationship to us, be it personal, professional, or societal."[8]

> *Values* are "clear and uncompromising statements about what is important to us...the abstract principles that we believe in and upon which we base our morals and ethics."[9]

---

6. Jane Ann McLachlan, *The Right Choice – Making ethical decisions on the job* (Toronto: Pearson Canada Inc., 2009), 8.
7. M. Minman Lawrence, *Ethics: A Pluralistic Approach to Moral Theory*, 4th edition (Belmont, California: Thomson-Wadsworth, 2008) p.4
8. Jane Ann McLachlan, *The Right Choice – Making ethical decisions on the job* (Toronto: Pearson Canada Inc., 2009), 8.
9. McLachlan, Jane Ann: *The Right Choice – Making ethical decisions on the job* (Toronto: Pearson Canada Inc., 2009), 9.

Goals are "the things we want out of life and the things we expect others probably want out of life as well."[10]

Norms "...are the ways we expect to act and the ways in which we expect others to act in given situations...Norms are expectations of behaviour [not] gauges of behaviour."[11]

Beliefs are "...the ways we expect to think, and the ways in which we expect others to think, about given situations."[12]

What influences the morals, duties, values, goals, norms, and beliefs of individuals? Some important influences include:

- Culture
- Parents, family, friends
- Religion
- Educators
- Government
- Media, and
- Organizational leaders.

Given the many influences on individual ethics it can be appreciated that organizational members may have different ideas of ethical conduct under certain situations and depending on one's reference point, can range from a perceived lack of ethics to a level of ethics that goes well beyond the legal requirements.

Descriptive vs. Normative Ethics

There are two main branches of ethics. *Descriptive* or *comparative* ethics is the study of people's moral beliefs. *Prescriptive* or *normative* ethics is the study of ethical theories that prescribe how people ought to act. In effect descriptive ethics concern what "is" and prescriptive ethics concern what "should be." Descriptive ethical theories include absolutism, relativism, enlightened self-interest, caring, and moral relativism.

Prescriptive or normative ethical theories include *deontology, teleology*, and *virtue*. The focus of this section will be on normative ethical theories, in particular deontology and teleology. Jane Ann McLachlan succinctly differentiates between principle-based deontological theories and consequence-based teleological theories:

---

10. LaRue Tone Hosmer, *The Ethics of Management*, Fifth Edition (Canada: McGraw-Hill Irwin, 2006), 6.
11. Ibid.
12. Ibid.

"*Deontological theories*…refer to all ethical theories that are based on the concept of duties or principles…and consider duties, rights, and principles as the correct measuring rods…for evaluating actions. This means that certain actions are intrinsically right, or morally good, even if they result in negative consequences…"[13]

"*Teleological theories*…refer to all ethical theories that focus on the end goals or consequences of our behavior…and are concerned with acting to achieve an outcome that is in keeping with the chosen goal, or that produces the best consequences overall."[14]

Teleology, also referred to as *consequentialism,* is exemplified by theories purporting that the consequences of an action should form the basis for deciding whether the action was moral. An action that is morally right produces good outcomes. Theories considered to represent consequentialism include *utilitarianism* - the best decision is the one that produces the best outcome for the greatest number, *ethical egoism* - the best decision produces the best consequences for the decision maker, and *ethical altruism* - the best decision produces the best consequences for everyone but the decision maker.

In contrast, *deontology* theories are based on guiding moral principles that do not consider the consequences of the decision but rather recognize that the decision is made on the basis of a sense of duty, and considerations other than the goodness or badness of its consequences that make the decision "right". Two approaches to deontological ethical reasoning are *Kantian deontology* and *contractarian deontology*. The former's focus is on duty and universal rules as determinants of the "right" decision or action; the latter, also known as the "social contract" approach, focuses on the general social principles upon which "rational persons in certain ideal situations would agree."[15] The foregoing brief descriptors of deontology do not do justice to its true complexity. Gerald Gaus has enumerated several ways in which deontology has been understood in the literature:

1. As an ethical theory
   a. in which the right does not maximize production of the good;
   b. admitting considerations of justice;
   c. in which duties and obligations are justified independently of the concept of good;

---

13. McLachlan, Jane Ann: *The Right Choice – Making ethical decisions on the job* (Toronto: Pearson Canada Inc., 2009), 68.
14. McLachlan, Jane Ann: *The Right Choice – Making ethical decisions on the job* (Toronto: Pearson Canada Inc., 2009), 77.
15. Al Gini, *Case Studies in Business Ethics*, Fifth Edition, (USA: Pearson Prentice Hall, 2005).

d. in which the concept of the right is not defined in terms of a substantive notion of the good;

e. according to which our values and conceptions of the good presuppose justified moral principles;

f. which would have us hold that we have reasons to respect as well as to promote value;

g. founded on, or giving a large role to, the concept of respect for persons;

h. which gives pride of place to moral rules;

i. that is imperatival; and

2. As a moral theory that advances absolute moral commands or prohibitions.[16]

Prescribing how people and organizations should act can provoke considerable debate. As with stakeholder theory it will be impossible for business, government, and civil society to always make decisions that are perceived by all stakeholders to be ethical. As well, the perception of the ethical acceptability of individual and organization actions is subject to a range of complicating factors including, for example, multiculturalism.

Against this brief theoretical construct it is appropriate to now ask three provocative questions:

1. What is an ethical business?

2. What is ethical government?

3. What is an ethical civil society organization?

The sections that follow will consider these important questions.

From Ethics to Business Ethics

Business ethics applies the study of ethics to business and is concerned with "the beliefs that determine what is acceptable (and what is not) in business."[17] Most if not all of the relatively recent spectacular governance failure fiascos have had, at their root, a perceived breach of trust associated with unethical practices. Enron used questionable accounting practices to bolster revenues that were not actually revenues, and to disguise liabilities. Arthur Andersen was accused of shredding important documents and ultimately convicted of obstructing justice in the Enron fiasco. WorldCom improperly allocated more than $7 billion in expenses matched

---

16. Gerald F Gaus, "What is Deontology? Part Two: Reasons to Act," *The Journal of Value Inquiry*, 35 (2001), 189-190.

17. Hunger and Wicks Wheelen, *Concepts in Strategic Management*, Canadian Edition (Canada: Pearson Prentice Hall, 2005).

to extend accounting reporting periods to falsely bolster earnings. Bre-X salted gold samples creating the perception of unheard-of gold yields from Busang in Indonesia where no gold actually existed. All these examples demonstrate unethical, and in most cases illegal, practices.

There are endless lists of ethical issues that can affect the business segment, some of the more common have been enumerated by Sexty and include:

- Fair financial disclosure to shareholders and treatment of minority shareholders
- Hiring and firing practices
- Wages, working conditions, and discrimination
- Labour relations practices
- Pricing policies
- Marketing tactics
- Exploitation of suppliers
- Lobbying activities
- Environmental responsibility[18]

From the list above it is obvious that business practices can have different ethical interpretations by different stakeholders. While in some cases interpreting and deciding "what is right" and "what is wrong" is obvious and straightforward, in other cases it is not quite as obvious. For example, using third world labour forces at a fraction of the cost of a Canadian worker in Canada seems unethical – however, if the competition is taking this approach, to remain competitive might require following suit. If the company decides not to take this approach, then profits will be lower and the return to shareholders will be reduced. The shareholders may elect to invest in a company that offers a higher rate of return, even though this new company may use third world labour. What seems ethically "right" to some stakeholders will inevitably seem ethically "wrong" to others. So what is the most ethical approach?

Complicating the terrain of the perception of organizational ethics is cross-cultural challenges exacerbated by globalization. At the level of culture, what is perceived as unethical by one culture can be perceived as ethical by another. Bribery provides an instructive example although nepotism, insider trading, misleading advertising, and untested products would be equally informative. Bribery in Canada is unethical and illegal; however, in some developing countries bribery (usually referred to as something different such as a "convenience payment") is a cost of doing business. A Canadian business publicly featured as paying bribes to officials in a developing country would be perceived by Canadians as operating unethically. So how might the management of a Canadian company operating in a culturally different

---

18. Robert W Sexty, *Canadian Business: Issues and Stakeholders*, (Canada: Prentice-Hall Canada, 1991), 534-535.

country decide whether an action would be ethical? Hamilton and Knouse of the University of Louisiana at Lafayette propose four ethical questions concerning a company in a host country adopting questionable practices of the host country:

1. Is the questionable practice in the host country less ethical than the [company's] usual practice or merely different?
2. Does the questionable practice violate the [company's] minimum [ethical] standards?
3. Does the [company] have enough leverage in the host country to follow its own ethical practices rather than the host country practices?
4. Do the host country's institutions have prospects for improvement?[19]

The decision tree that results from answering these questions can assist in determining whether the company should conduct business in the host country. For example if the questionable practice is less ethical than the company's usual practice and violates the company's minimum standards and the company does not have the necessary leverage to follow its own ethical practices then it should not do business in the country. If the questionable practice is not unethical but merely different this would not violate the company's minimum ethical standards, and "if the [company] has leverage in the host country, the [company] can decide whether to adopt the questionable practice or follow its own practices for non-ethical reasons such as efficiency, uniformity, or a desire to fit into the host's culture."

The perception of the ethical conduct of business is important, as is the perception of the country or countries in which the business conducts operations. Some countries are perceived to be more corrupt than others. The table below portrays the 2012 and 2018 corruption perceptions index.[20] Selected countries are listed in ascending order of corruption perception where a rank of 1 depicts a country that is perceived to be the least corruptive.

Rank in 2012	Rank in 2018	Country
1	1	Denmark
1	2	Finland
1	3	New Zealand
4	3	Sweden
5	3	Singapore
6	3	Switzerland
7	14	Austria

TABLE 11

2012 - 2018 Corruption Perceptions Index, Transparency International

19. J. Brooke III Hamilton, and Stephen B. Knouse, "Multinational Enterprise Decision Principles Dealing With Cross Cultural Ethical Conflicts," *Journal of Business Ethics* 31 (2001): 86.
20. Transparency International, "The 2018 Corruptions Perceptions Index," Transparency International, https://www.transparency.org/cpi2018, accessed July 17, 2019.

Rank in 2012	Rank in 2018	Country
7	4	Norway
9	9	Canada
9	8	Netherlands
11	14	Iceland
12	9	Luxembourg
13	11	Germany
15	25	Barbados
16	17	Belgium
17	18	Japan
17	11	United Kingdom
19	22	Unites States of America
20	27	Chile
20	23	Uruguay
37	31	Taiwan
43	51	Malta
43	56	Mauritius
72	53	Italy
72	89	Bosnia
94	99	Columbia
94	67	Greece
105	138	Mexico
118	105	Egypt
165	168	Venezuela
174	180	Somalia

Regardless of the approach taken, given the growing number of global stakeholders, the increasing and instant visibility of business decisions to these stakeholders (compliments of communications technology), and the increasing expectations of society as regards business's ethical activities, the realistic goal for business is to conduct business ethically in a way that creates the greatest perception of ethical conduct in the minds of its key stakeholders. This is not to suggest that operating ethically is optional. The ethical conduct of business is critical to a firm's survival as it forms the basis of trust in relationships with all stakeholders.

From Business Ethics to Managerial Ethics

As indicated earlier in this chapter organizations are made up of individuals and the ethical conduct of an inanimate organization then generally reflects the ethical standards of the individuals composing the organization. Major organizational decisions are made by its management team, and managers are found in all organizations: business, government, and civil society. Running an ethical organization will require ethical managers. *Managerial ethics* have been defined as "the standards of behaviour that guide individual managers and their work."[21] Managers are employees of the organizations for which they work, but they are also first and foremost *individuals* and this raises the issue of personal ethics and the many influences on the ethics of people both as individuals and as managers.

Far from being neutral and objective individuals bring with them their own cultural baggage, which constitutes determinants of moral standards at the level of the individual. LaRue Tone Hosmer proposes that an individual's moral behaviour is affected by four subjective standards that are in turn informed by religious and/or cultural traditions as well as economic/social conditions. These subjective standards include:

- *Personal goals* as expectations of outcomes - the things individuals want out of life,
- *Personal norms* as expectations of behaviour - the ways individuals expect to act and the ways individuals expect others to act in a situation,
- *Personal beliefs* as expectations of thought - the ways individuals expect to think, and the ways individuals expect others to think, about a situation, and
- *Personal values* as individual priorities among goals, norms, and beliefs the ways individuals exercise judgement.[22]

Every manager brings this ethical baggage to bear, whether directly or indirectly, on decisions made in his or her role as manager.

Not surprisingly this can lead to an ethical conflict between what a manager personally believes to be the most ethical action versus what the organization would believe to be the most ethical action. An individual agent would have fewer stakeholders than the organization resulting in a decision-maker perceived to be more ethical (or less ethical!) than the organization he or she represents.

---

21. Thomas Donaldson and Thomas W. Dundee, "Toward a Unified Conception of Business Ethics: An Integrative Social Contracts Theory," *Academy of Management Review* 19, No.2. (1994): 252-284.
22. LaRue Tone Hosmer, *The Ethics of Management*, Fifth Edition (Canada: McGraw-Hill Irwin, 2006), 6.

So what is an ethical company? For many years the international think-tank Ethisphere Institute, has developed annual lists of the world's most ethical companies. Ethisphere derives its proprietary *Ethics Quotient (EQ)* rating system based on five categories:

- Ethics and compliance program (35%);
- Leadership and Reputation (10%);
- Governance (15%);
- Corporate citizenship and responsibility (20%); and
- Culture of ethics (20%).[23]

The EQ score is derived from a complex analysis involving information verification, research, requests for additional documentation, and interviews with company representatives. In 2019 Ethisphere determined that the world's most ethical companies numbered 128, crossed 50 industries, and 21 countries; employed 6.75 million persons; and recognized $3.02 trillion in annual revenues.[24] The 2019 Canadian honorees included BMO, Capital Power and Covenant Health.[25] Drawing from Ethisphere's five categories, in simplified terms an ethical company is one that is ethically and socially responsible and accountable; a company that:

- has in place a formal ethics program complete with training, monitoring, enforcement and consequences of non-conformity;
- a strong ethical track record, public ethical leadership, and stakeholder engagement;
- strong corporate governance;
- formalized and measurable corporate social responsibility activities; and,
- an organizational culture anchored in ethical conduct.

Ethical Government

At first glance, the idea of ethical government seems obvious and conjures up ideas such as developing programs in the public's best interest – to paraphrase a famous alien - the good for the many being more important than the good for the one. For example, spending public tax dollars in a responsible manner so as to improve the quality of life for society and to ensure the voice of the people is appropriately

---

23. "World's Most Ethical Companies Methodology," Ethisphere, https://www.worldsmostethicalcompanies.com/, accessed July 17, 2019.
24. "World's Most Ethical Companies Methodology," Ethisphere, https://www.worldsmostethicalcompanies.com/, accessed July 17, 2019.
25. Ethisphere.com, "The 2019 World's Mosth Ethical Companies Honoree List", https://www.worldsmostethicalcompanies.com/honorees/?fwp_country=canada, accessed July 17, 2019.

reflected in activities, decisions, and practices. One would think that, while business has its ethical challenges, certainly government would always function in an ethical utilitarian way. However, governments around the world have had their ethical challenges, and Canada is no exception - as the chapter on the government segment indicated in its presentation of the top Canadian government scandals.

The government of Canada considers ethics to mean upholding the public interest through exercising principles and standards of right conduct. In its seminal work on ethics in government the Tait Task Force defined ethics as "enduring beliefs that influence our attitudes and actions as to what is right and wrong."[26] The relationship the government perceives between ethics and values is the former as a subset of the latter. Canada's government ethical history has progressed from a culture of partisanship (1840 - 1867); through efforts to transform the public service to a culture of non-partisanship (1867 – 1918); to the embedding of the values of efficiency, economy, and service (1919- 1964); through a focus on values (1965 – 1996) and continuously progressing to the current state of affairs in which public servants are to be guided by four sets of values – democratic, professional, ethical, and people.[27]

In 2003 the Government of Canada published its *Values and Ethics Code for the Public Service*, in which it defines the role of the Public Service as "to assist the Government of Canada to provide for peace, order and good government."[28] The code defines Public Service Values and the expectations attached to each as follows:

- Democratic values: Helping ministers, under law, to serve the public interest;
- Professional values: Serving with competence, excellence, efficiency, objectivity, and impartiality;
- Ethical values: Acting at all times in such a way as to uphold the public trust;
- People values: Demonstrating respect, fairness, and courtesy in their dealings with both citizens and fellow public servants"[29]

The code is explicit is defining ethical values and requires that public servants perform their duties and arrange their private affairs so as to preserve public confidence in integrity, objectivity, and impartiality; act in a manner that can withstand the closest public scrutiny; make decisions in the public interest; and place the public interest as first and foremost in any conflict that arises between official duties and private interests. The code's treatment of ethics exemplifies the Tait

---

26. Kenneth Kernaghan, "A Special Calling: Values, Ethics and Professional Public Service," *Public Service – Studies and Discoveries Series,* Canada Public Service Agency, accessed June 18, 2013, https://www.tbs-sct.gc.ca/psm-fpfm/ve/code/scv-eng.pdf, 20.

27. Ibid.

28. "Values and Ethics Code for the Public Service," Treasury Board of Canada Secretariat, date modified: 2012-04-12, https://www.tbs-sct.gc.ca/pol/doc-eng.aspx?id=25049, accessed July 17, 2019.

29. Ibid.

Task Force's assertion that "public service is a special calling…the rewards… not material. They are intangible…that proceed from the sense of devoting one's life to the service of the country, to the affairs of state, to public purposes…and to the public good."[30]

Several pieces of legislation contain provisions that relate to the application of values and ethics, some of which are: *Access to Information Act*[31]; *Financial Administration Act*[32]; *Official Languages Act*[33]; *Privacy Act*[34]; *Public Service Employment Act*[35]; and *Public Service Staff Relations Act.*[36]

As discussed in the chapter on the government segment, there are significant differences between government and business. Often these differences manifest in customary activities common to both, but that take on larger play in the government segment and raise questions concerning the ethics of following government protocol. Consider the following examples.

1. If a representative from a private sector company participates as a guest speaker at a private function and receives a gift as a gesture of thanks this generally would present no ethical concerns. However, if a politician or senior bureaucrat attended the same function and received a gift of appreciation the gift would be publicly scrutinized as regards its appropriateness so as to ensure no undue influence that could be perceived as a breach of ethical conduct.

2. The government's desire to have a civil service representative of Canadian society provides for simplified staffing of self-identified visible minority candidates by managers whose staffing plan demonstrates need and intention of such candidates to provide for a more representative organization. Is it ethical for a manager to hire visible minorities to meet imposed or implied quotas that might compromise access to employment opportunities for those equally qualified Canadians who are *not* visible minorities?

30. Kenneth Kernaghan, "A Special Calling: Values, Ethics and Professional Public Service," *Public Service – Studies and Discoveries Series*, Canada Public Service Agency, accessed June 18, 2013, https://www.tbs-sct.gc.ca/psm-fpfm/ve/code/scv-eng.pdf, 19.

31. "Access to Information Act (R.S.C., 1985, c.A-1)," Justice Laws Website, date modified 2019- 06-26, https://laws-lois.justice.gc.ca/eng/acts/a-1/FullText.html.

32. "Financial Administration Act (R.S.C., 1985, c.F-11)," Justice Laws Website, date modified 2019-06-26, https://laws-lois.justice.gc.ca/eng/acts/F-11/FullText.html.

33. "Official Language Act (R.S.C., 1985, c. 31 (4th Supp.))," Justice Laws Website, date modified 2019-06-26, https://laws-lois.justice.gc.ca/eng/acts/o-3.01/FullText.html.

34. "Privacy Act (R.S.C., 1985, c. P-21)," Justice Laws Website, date modified 2019-06-26, https://laws-lois.justice.gc.ca/ENG/ACTS/P-21/FullText.html.

35. "Public Service Employment Act (S.C. 2003, c.22, ss. 12,13)," Justice Laws Website, date modified 2019-06-26, https://laws.justice.gc.ca/eng/acts/P-33.01/FullText.html.

36. "Public Service Staff Relations Act (R.S.C., 1985, c. P-35)," Justice Laws Website, date modified 2019-06-26, https://laws-lois.justice.gc.ca/eng/acts/p-35/FullText.html.

3. The spirit and intent of the Official Languages Act requires that most senior positions in bilingual regions be staffed as bilingual imperative; that is, the occupant of the position must possess a prescribed level of bilingual capacity, as tested by the government, before officially starting in the position. Is it ethical to require all senior positions in bilingual regions to be bilingual? Is it ethical to hire only the best-qualified bilingual candidate and not better-qualified unilingual candidates? Is the government acting in the best public interest or in the best political interests and which one of these is the most ethical?

4. In the interests of transparency, the Access to Information legislation provides access to a range of government documents unless specifically severed on the basis of Cabinet confidence or national security, even though some of this information may be harmful to the government. If a public service manager, who is duty-bound to implement ministerial decisions, does not provide certain information because the content might create the perception that a minister made a wrong decision, is s/he acting unethically?

In Canada the politicians and the bureaucrats work for all Canadians. Their salaries and benefits are paid by Canadians through taxation (that is not optional). The equipment they use, the buildings in which they work, the furniture they use including the chairs they sit on, are all owned by Canadians. Decisions they make on program development or discontinuation are made on behalf of all Canadians. The money that is spent by government belongs to Canadian taxpayers and whatever is purchased is either for Canadians or to facilitate the development of a higher standard of living for all Canadians. While governments have very difficult challenges, there are certain areas in which doing right versus doing wrong is unambiguous. So what is ethical government?

An ethical government is one that develops policies, programs, and activities that will ultimately result in a better standard of living for all constituents. Such a government's work would be characterized by:

- transparency,
- honesty,
- respect,
- accessibility,
- consultation,
- timeliness,
- decisive action that reflects the wishes of the majority of constituents, and
- public corrective action with serious consequences for ethical compromises.

An Ethical Civil Society Organization

The very nature of the civil society segment centers on its sorting mechanisms of which trust emerges as arguably the most critical. More than any other segment ethical indiscretions of one group reflect poorly on the entire segment. Trust is essential to obtain funding from donors, government, and business. It is also essential as the mechanism through which partnering and collaboration occurs with government and business and through which this third segment frequently acts as the neutral broker between the other two segments. Within the third segment the existence of networks, collaboration, values, and norms are held together by trust, and as Andrew Brien, writing in the *Journal of Business Ethics*, so succinctly puts it: "…if you want compliance with norms then develop an atmosphere of trust; if you want to be trusted, then comply with norms."[37]

Charity emerges as another key theme in any discussion of the third segment and the expectation of donors is that the majority of the donation will have a direct effect on recipient constituents. Ethical questions arise when such civil society organizations pay their executives either any amount or excessive amounts, or when donations are used to fund travel expenses of volunteer board members.

Philanthropic foundations exist "for the love of mankind", true to the meaning of the Greek root word *philanthropos*. In the words of Carnegie Corporation of New York's president Vartan Gregorian, "foundations should stand for the best ideas and impulses of the … people, their idealism, altruism, and generosity…[and] their values, and how they conduct themselves, must be higher than the prevailing standards. We are accountable not only before the law and the court of public opinion, but before history as well."[38]

The third segment is not without its ethical challenges fuelled by the way in which community is changing. Third segment organizations are dealing with an ever-increasing cultural mosaic in which ethical behavior can mean different things to different people. Gobalization is transforming the third segment provoking new issues and providing a greater audience for many of its plights. Society is generating more complex problems that present more options, many with different outcomes that might test the limits of consequentialism. Changes in government funding models can contribute to mission drift whereby the organization is put in a position in which it must trade conviction for funding in order to stay operational.

---

37. Andrew Brien, "Professional Ethics and the Culture of Trust," *Journal of Business Ethics*, 17 (1998): 391-409.
38. V. Gregorian, "Philanthropy should have glass pockets," *The Chronicle of Philanthropy* Vol.16, Issue 12 (April 2004).

So what is an ethical civil society organization? One that:

- remains true to its vision and mission,
- works with the balanced interest of all its key stakeholders in mind,
- directs its resources to tangible and positive activities that directly support its vision and mission, and
- advocates for improved social well-being of its members.

Making and Defending Ethical Decisions

Faced with an ethical dilemma or a "problem perceived by the decision-maker as involving an ethical issue" managers need a basis from which they can arrive at a *defensible* ethical decision.[39] Simply put, in matters involving ethical decisions managers need a logical approach that can withstand public scrutiny. Recognizing that not everyone will agree with the decision or that the decision was the most ethical, using a logical, compelling approach that offers the perception of considered thought (as the decision and its possible outcomes were put through a series of tests) will greatly assist in making the decision and in how it is received by stakeholders. Several models exist ranging from the intuitively simple to the complex. For example, Michael Josephson proposes a "bell, book, candle approach" that consists of subjecting the impending action or decision to three tests:

1. "Listen for the bells warning you of an ethical decision (the 'bell');
2. Check to see if there are any laws, regulations or rules which restrict your choices (the 'book'); and,
3. How will your decision look in the light – could a reasonable, fair-minded person conclude you acted improperly? (the candle)."[40]

Another approach is offered by The Markkula Center for Applied Ethics at Santa Clara University:

1. Recognize an ethical issue
2. Get the facts
3. Evaluate alternative actions
4. Make a decision and test it
5. Act and reflect on the outcome.[41]

---

39. Scott J. Vitell, Saviour L. Nwachokwu and James H. Barnes, "The Effects of Culture on Ethical Decision-Making: An Application of Hofstede's Typology," *Journal of Business Ethics* 12 (1993): 753-760.
40. Andrew West, "Sartrean Existentialism and Ethical Decision-Making in Business," *Journal of Business Ethics*, Spring (2007).
41; "Making an Ethical Decision," Santa Clara University, The Markkula Center for Applied Ethics, https://www.scu.edu/ethics/ethics-resources/ethical-decision-making/, accessed July 17, 2019.

In comparison, Michael Rion's model asks six questions

1. Why is this bothering me?
2. Who else matters?
3. Is it my problem?
4. What is the ethical concern?
5. What do others think?
6. Am I being true to myself?[42]

And Anthony Pagano proposes six tests to provide ethical perspective on a considered action:

1. Is it legal?
2. Do the benefits exceed the costs?
3. Are you comfortable with your action becoming the universal standard in similar situations?
4. Are you comfortable with your action being featured publicly in the news?
5. Would you be comfortable if the impact of your decision was inflicted on you?
6. Get a second opinion from someone unaffected by the outcome of your decision.[43]

These approaches offer a good starting point and will catalyze a decision-maker to think through his or her decision against a legal, consequential, and transparent backdrop. However, in the author's opinion, while these models are intuitive and provide general guidance, an integrated ethical decision model would be more appealing to a manager. Such a model is suggested in the next section.

A Suggested Integrated Ethical Decision Model

Integrated ethical models provide a logical approach to performing reasonable due diligence in arriving at an ethical decision. The starting point is to generalize the decision you are making and then determine whether the decision to be made is actually a matter of ethics. To make this determination the decision could be subjected to the following two questions:

1. Does this decision involve doing what is right, just, and fair?
2. Does this decision cause you to reflect on your personal morals, duties, values, goals, norms, and beliefs?

---

42. Michael Rion, The Responsible Manager: Practical Strategies for Ethical Decision Making (San Francisco: Harper & Row, 1990), 13-14.
43. Anthony M. Pagano, "Criteria for ethical decision making in managerial situations," (proceedings of the National Academy of Management, New Orleans, 1-12, 1987).

If the answer to these two questions is "yes" then your decision to be made is a matter of ethics.

Once this has been established then it is necessary to bring as much precision as possible in framing your decision or decisions as there is seldom only one single course of action. At this point it is necessary to precisely articulate the decision(s) you must make. Unclear decisions to be made will only complicate the decision-making process and therefore you should strive to state your decision to be made as precisely as possible. Once the decision or decisions have been developed and made precise, the next step is to ask – is each decision legal? You can then identify the key stakeholders affected by the decision and, in the context of these stakeholders, determine the consistency of the possible decision outcomes with your own ethical beliefs by asking the two earlier questions once again – if I decide on X or Y or Z, for each of these:

*   Do I believe the decision is right, just, and fair?
*   Is the decision consistent with my ideals for behavior, the behavior others have a right to expect of me, and is this decision based on what I believe?

The final phase would involve a test of consequentialism:

*   Do I believe that this decision will produce the best outcome for the greatest number, or the worse outcome for the fewest number?

This proposed approach is summarized on the next page.

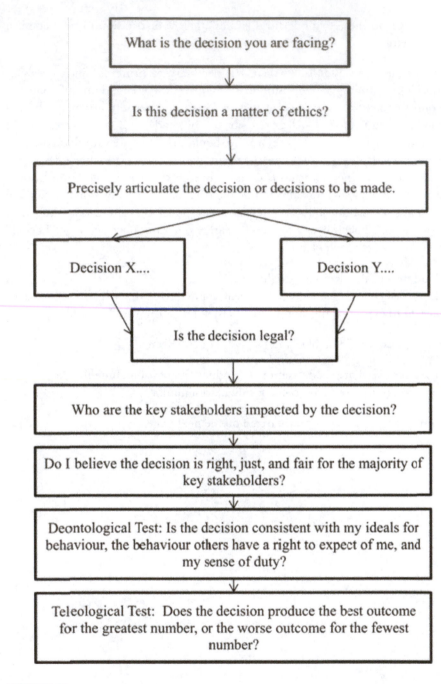

Source: David H.J. Delcorde

FIGURE 12

An Integrated Ethical Decision Model

Chapter Summary

Ethics is a complex but important subject that affects business, government, and civil society at many levels. Doing good and not doing bad; doing what is right, just, and fair; and acting in accordance with one's morals, duties, values, and beliefs are commonly found ways of describing ethics. Two main approaches to ethics concern "what is" and "what should be." Ethics is further complicated by cross-cultural influences exacerbated by globalization. At the heart of organizational ethics is the ethics of persons who collectively comprise the organization, and the influencers of personal ethics are numerous. An ethical business recognizes its responsibility to conduct operations in an ethical manner bolstered by ethical training and monitoring, strong governance, and formalized and measured corporate social responsibility activities, all anchored in a pervasive ethical organizational culture. Ethical government is one characterized by transparency, honesty, respect, accessibility, consultation, timeliness, decisiveness, and measureable and severe consequences for ethical compromises. An ethical civil society organization is one that remains true to its mission and vision, balances the interests of all its important stakeholders, and advocates improved social well-being.

Making and defending ethical decisions is a complex process. Notwithstanding every decision maker's desire to do the right thing, the many interests of diverse stakeholders, the complexities of running organizations, cross-cultural differences, and personal differences are but a few of the factors that collectively serve to complicate what is typically already complicated terrain. As such integrated ethical models provide the best approach to performing reasonable due diligence in arriving at an ethical decision.

End of Chapter Questions

1. Differentiate between descriptive and normative ethics.

2. Compare and contrast consequentialism theories with deontology theories.

3. Discuss some of the more important ethical issues faced by business and describe how the actions of business can affect its relationship with key stakeholders.

4. How do ethical issues in government differ from those faced by the business and civil society segments?

Application Question

Returning to the opening news article, discuss each of the following:

1. Using the Stakeholder Capacity Model presented in Chapter 6, identify, from the government's perspective, 10 stakeholders with "stakes" in Canada's appointment of its ombudsperson, and rank each stakeholder according to the model.

2. Using the Internet and other on-line resources, select an example of a Canadian company that has allegedly acting with questionable conduct and discuss:

    a. Which of the stakeholders identified in 1, above, would be impacted;

    b. Assess, in your view, the effectiveness of the ombudsperson's involvement in the matter

3. What are the ethical implications?

Research Question

1. Using the Internet and other external sources research the *Exxon Valdez* oil spill and discuss the ethical issues that arose. Use the Integrated Ethical Decision Model presented in this chapter to determine whether any of the decisions made by any party to the oil spill were ethical.

Team Discussion Project

Select a company of your choice that has been involved in an ethical scandal, as reported in the popular press. For this company:

1. Provide a description of the company and the scadall

2. To what extent did this "scandal" involve ethical conduct?

3. In your view, what was the root of the problem that led to this scandal – what decision was made that led to this problem?

4. After isolating the decision, use the Integrated Ethical Decision Model presented in this chapter to demonstrate how the decision was not ethical.

5. Which segment of the Canadian Macro-environment was most affected by this decision?

CHAPTER 8

Collaboration and Interaction

Sergey Nivens/Shutterstock.com

Collaboration in the News

Collaboration between industry and government key to enhancing the competitiveness of Alberta's oil and natural gas sector internationally: CAPP[1]

JULY 05, 2017 - CALGARY, ALBERTA

According to the report entitled *A Competitive Policy and Regulatory Framework for Alberta's Upstream Oil and Natural Gas Industry* and published by the Canadian Association of Petroleum Producers (CAPP), the energy industry was

1. The full article can be viewed at Collaboration between industry and government key to enhancing the competitiveness of Alberta's oil and natural gas sector internationally: CAPP.

expected to create more than 24,000 new jobs for Albertans and grow the province's economy by nearly $5 billion by 2020.

The article published in July 2017 discusses report in detail outlining how new competitiveness measures could be created to attract investment and create jobs in Alberta's oil and natural gas sector, while protecting the high standards already in place for health, safety and environmental regulation.

The Canadian Association of Petroleum Producers (CAPP) represents companies that explore for, develop and produce natural gas and crude oil throughout Canada. CAPP estimates the cumulative costs associated with the changes in provincial and federal government policies and regulations to conventional and unconventional development could range between $450 million and $760 million annually. Through collaboration with government on essential policy challenges the energy sector can attract new investment to Alberta and improve competitiveness.

Introduction

To this point readers have been introduced to the main segments of the Canadian domestic macro-environment: business, government, and civil society. Earlier chapters have presented overviews of each of these segments. With this basic understanding of what these segments are about, what is included in each, and how they function, discussion shifted to common issues faced by each: stakeholders, globalization and multiculturalism, and ethics. This final chapter focuses on the interaction between these segments – collaborative mechanisms in working together and how each segment influences the other two. An understanding of these important dynamics is essential for the manager.

This discussion will begin with a consideration of business and government working together in the form of public-private partnerships (P3s) and P3s in the civil society segment. In developing the discussion that follows on business influencing government and government influencing business, the differences between government and business will be discussed. The ways in which business influences government considered in this chapter will include direct lobbying as well as indirect lobbying in the form of advocacy advertising and think-tanks. Government's influence on business will include a discussion on government instruments, government regulation, tax policy, and government subsidies. This will be followed by a discussion on how civil society influences government and business.

A common denominator is the need for all segments to learn from each other with innovation and technological change the prime movers in a cognitive economy, that "implies a dynamic process of extracting information from the environment, and producing and sharing knowledge through communication," which is indeed necessary to add value to society.[2]

In this new paradigm governments must admit that answers to policy issues will not evolve without input from business and civil society, and businesses will need to recognize that success will be dependent on the extent to which they listen to stakeholders and uphold their responsibilities to society. Civil society will need to recognize more fully the way in which it can collaborate with government and business to achieve its objectives in representing the concerns of society on government and business agendas. Thus the greatest value-added to society will result from collaborative efforts between segments – "segments working together, especially in a joint intellectual effort."[3]

Public-Private Partnerships (P3s)

At the outset it is useful to consider partnering and partnerships in general. A *partner*, in this context, can be thought of as an associate who works with others toward a common action or endeavour.[4] More generally and more metaphorically a partner can also be thought of as "the person who agrees to be your prime collaborator through a given dance."[5] *Partnerships* are an association of one or more persons and are based on trust and reciprocity.

P3s Defined

A *public-private partnership (P3)* is "a long-term performance-based approach for procuring public infrastructure where the private sector assumes a major share of the responsibility in terms of risk and financing for the delivery and the performance of the infrastructure, from design and structural planning, to long-term maintenance."[6] This arrangement results in the pooling of resources and respective areas of expertise of both the public sector and the private sector through which the value-added to society is maximized. The P3 is differentiated from a "partnership" in two ways

---

2. Gilles Paquet and Jeffrey Roy, Governance in Canada – Competition, Cooperation and Co- evolution in Business-Government-Society Relations (Ottawa: Prime, 1997).
3. "collaborate," Dictionary.com, accessed June 19, 2013, https://www.dictionary.com/browse/collaborate
4. "partner," Dictionary.com, accessed June 19, 2013, https://www.dictionary.com/browse/partner?s=t
5. "Some Assorted Definitions," Contra Dance Terms, accessed June 19, 2013, http://users.fred.net/tds//contra-the-short.answer/glossary.htm
6. The Canadian Council for Public-Private Partnerships, "What are Public-Private Partnerships (P3s)?", https://www.pppcouncil.ca/web/Knowledge_Centre/What_are_P3s_/web/P3_Knowledge_Centre/What_are_P3s.aspx?hkey=2c6597c6-53bf-4a9d-adf0-86e108d003bb, accessed July 17, 2019.

– the delivery of a service that the government must provide under its constitutional obligations, and a transfer of risk from the government to the partner.[7]

Drivers

There are several drivers of public-private partnerships in Canada. The public sector is under pressure from stakeholders to utilize taxpayers' money with increased scrutiny and stewardship at a critical time when significant investment must be made to maintain and replace aging infrastructure and invest in new infrastructure. Changing demographics and lifestyles are resulting in community-based needs such as recreational facilities, also demanded by knowledge workers who require a greater balance between personal and work life. An aging population requires significant investment in health care-related support systems. These systems in turn require innovative approaches to program delivery involving a unique blend of private sector "know how" and government constitutional authority. The growing complexity of issues means that it is unrealistic to expect any one segment of the Canadian domestic macro-environment to resolve the issues. Advances in information technology are driving the need to innovate to sustain a competitive advantage and this requires collaboration between business and government that can be represented through P3 agreements.[8]

Types of P3s

Public-private partnerships come in many forms. The table below provides a list of some of the several possible forms of P3s.[9]

TABLE 12

Some Types of Public-Private Partnerships

Type of P3	Description
Operation & Maintenance Contract	A private operator, under contract, operates a publicly-owned asset (e.g. water/wastewater treatment plant) for a specified term. Ownership of the asset remains with the public entity.
Build-Finance	The private sector constructs an asset and finances the capital cost only during the construction period.
Design-Build-Finance-Maintain (DBFM)	The private sector designs, builds and finances an asset and provides hard facility management (hard fm) or maintenance services under a long-term agreement.
Design-Build-Finance-Maintain-Operate (DBFMO)	The private sector designs, builds, finances and provides hard fm or maintenance services under a long-term agreement. Operation of the asset is also included in projects such as bridges, roads and water treatment plants
Concession	A private sector concessionaire undertakes investments and operates the facility for a fixed period of time after which the ownership reverts back to the public sector.

7. Ibid.
8. David, H Jones-Delcorde and Jim Snaith, "The Impact of IT on Governance, Corporate Social Responsibility and Partnerships", *Optimum Online*, Vol. 36, Issue 1 (March 2006).
9. "Models of Public-Private Partnerships," The Canadian Council for Public-Private Partnerships, https://www.pppcouncil.ca/web/Knowledge_Centre/What_are_P3s_/Definitions_Models/web/P3_Knowledge_Centre/About_P3s/Definitions_Models.aspx?hkey=79b9874d-4498-46b1-929f-37cc461ab-4bc, accessed July 17, 2019.

Advantages and Disadvantages of P3s

Public-private partnerships are commonly found in several areas, including environmental projects, education, real estate, water management projects, and transportation, and while there are subtle differences between types of P3s they are thought to offer a number of advantages:

- Mitigation of risk on the part of the public partner, with the private partner assuming many risks, such as financing and cash flow. In infrastructure P3s, some examples of risk commonly transferred to the private partner include design, construction, and lifecycle[10]
- Freeing up of taxpayers' money for investment in other social needs facilitated through a P3 arrangement requiring that the private partner provide all necessary funding, thus facilitating and promoting private sector investment in public sector high quality infrastructure and avoiding public sector capital debt
- More cost-effective private partner would operate on "industry time" unburdened by government bureaucracy and the political realities of the public sector
- Combination of skills including the constitutional authority of government with the business-savvy of the private partner
- Knowledge transfer as both the public partner and the private partner engage in both technical and social learning and benefit from the resulting networks of contacts in each sector
- Maximization of efficiencies and innovation since to be competitive the private sector must operate efficiently and maximize the use of enabling innovation with due attention paid to performance measurement. This represents enormous value- added to the public partner.

Of course P3s are not without certain disadvantages:

- The transfer of control from the public partner to the private partner of ownership, service levels, and prices can diminish the public partner's ability to influence
- A P3 can blur accountabilities since the private partner is not directly accountable to the public and is not influenced by votes
- Many P3s represent a long-term commitment and changes in managing partners to the P3 could result in diminishing collaboration over time.

Some examples of P3s

In Canada the construction of Highway 407[11] in Ontario, the world's first all-electronic, barrier-free toll highway stretching 108 kilometers from Burlington to Pick-

---

10. Catherine Peacock, "Public-Private Partnerships P3 Purpose and Policy Issues," *The Continuing Legal Education Society of British Columbia* (March 2006).
11. "History," 407 ETR, https://www.407etr.com/en/highway/corporate/background-information1. html, accessed July 17, 2019.

ering, and the Confederation Bridge[12] in Prince Edward Island, a $1 billion 12.9 kilometre structure that connects Prince Edward Island to the mainland, represent two examples of large-scale P3s.

The City of Ottawa features some noteworthy P3 examples on a less grand scale than those mentioned above. One such example is the City of Ottawa Paramedic Service Headquarters, a 100,000-square foot state-of-the-art facility providing a central location from which to train and deploy paramedics.[13] This facility was created through a public- private partnership between the City of Ottawa and Forum Leasehold Partners Inc., a Toronto-based company that acquires and develops single-tenant properties. Forum Leasehold Partners Inc. used existing city land through a 30-year ground lease, and constructed the $19.9 million facility through a design-build-agreement with Westeinde Construction. Forum will be exempted from property taxes and other fees, and the City of Ottawa will sub-lease the facility from Forum and cover operating costs. At the expiration of the ground lease in 30 years the land and facility will transfer to the City of Ottawa for one dollar.

A second example in Ottawa is the $26 million Bell Sensplex sports facility that was created as a result of a public-private partnership agreement between the City of Ottawa and Ottawa Community Ice Partners whose members include the Ottawa Senators Hockey Club, Ottawa Senators Alumni, and Morley Hoppner Group.[14] Private sector- funded, the debt was guaranteed by the City of Ottawa who also waived property taxes and purchases 2400 hours of ice time annually that it resells to users at profit. At the end of the 30-year agreement, the City of Ottawa will purchase the facility and land for the sum of one dollar.

A more recent example is Ottawa's Light Rail Transit (OLRT) project. The project is a "design, build, finance and maintain" P3 endeavour.[15] The project is to be delivered in multiple stage, and involves international partnerships with firms such as SNC-Lavalin, US-based Kiewit Corp and the French firm Vinci.[16] The OLRT will be publicly owned and integrated into the City of Ottawa's existing transit service, and features a 12.5 km transit line, a tunnel through the downtown core, and

12. "Confederation Bridge," Take The High Road, https://www.confederationbridge.com/site/about, accessed July 17, 2019.
13. "Ottawa Paramedic Service Headquarters," City of Ottawa, accessed June 19, 2013, https://ottawa.ca/en/business/doing-business-city/public-private-partnerships-p3s/ottawa-paramedic-service-headquarters.
14. "Bell Sensplex," City of Ottawa, accessed June 19, 2013, https://ottawa.ca/en/business/doing-business-city/public-private-partnerships-p3s/bell-sensplex-west.
15. Infrastructure Ontario, " Ottawa Light Rail Transit - Confederation Line and Highway 417 Widening Project", https://www.infrastructureontario.ca/Ottawa-Light-Rail-Transit/, accessed July 22, 2019.
16. Global News, "City of Ottawa taps SNC-Lavalin, international consortium to build LRT extensions; price tag rises by $1.2B", https://globalnews.ca/news/4987939/snc-lavalin-east-west-connectors-announced-as-city-of-ottawas-top-picks-for-stage-2-lrt/, accessed July 22, 2019.

13 stations including three underground stations. [17] The project is due to be delivered by mid-August 2019 in spite of the many issues experienced along the way.[18]

P3s and the Civil Society Segment

To this point discussion has focussed on government and business partnering with each other. Some writers suggest that the requirement to invest money and absorb a significant share of the risk in delivering the product or service diminishes the role that civil society organizations can have in a P3. Others indicate that to build up the necessary expertise to be on equal footing is difficult for many non-profits as is developing the expertise to write and manage the P3 contract. An opposing view suggests that partnerships between non-government organizations (NGO) and business are in fact evolving. Recognizing that NGOs bring many assets to the corporate table including, for example, influence, innovation, reputation and trust, and networks, among others, the Canadian Business for Social Responsibility (CBSR) suggests that NGO- business partnerships can be categorized as philanthropic partnerships in which a company makes a cash or in-kind donation to the NGO partner, or an innovation partnership in which the goal is to improve how a company conducts its core business.[19] As with government, companies are increasingly challenged to develop responses to complex social responsibility-related problems for which they have limited expertise. Innovative partnerships involving all three segments can represent a melding of the segment sorting mechanisms that combine to add value to society.

For a business, a public-private partnership can increase the demand for its service and result in an increased supply of output. For government, working together with business in a partnership arrangement can mitigate political risk and work to appease stakeholders diminishing the need for government to coerce through regulation. For the third segment, as a neutral broker between government and business, the bonds of trust and cooperation can permeate both government and business and act to reduce the intensity of the normal sorting mechanisms dominant in those segments.

Business's Influence on Government

Most popular press coverage of "government-industry relations" tends to focus on how the actions and decisions of government affect business as this tends to carry

17. Infrastructure Ontario, " Ottawa Light Rail Transit - Confederation Line and Highway 417 Widening Project", https://www.infrastructureontario.ca/Ottawa-Light-Rail-Transit/, accessed July 22, 2019.
18. CBC News, "Finishing LRT trains by Sunday entirely achievable, rail director say", https://www.cbc.ca/news/canada/ottawa/finishing-lrt-sunday-achievable-1.5199690, accessed July 22, 2019.
19. Canadian Business for Social Responsibility, *Partnering for Innovation – Driving Change Through Business/NGO Partnerships*, (Toronto, Canada: Canadian Business for Social Responsibility, 2005).

more salience with business stakeholders. It is sometimes easier to use the government as a scapegoat to explain away the need for higher consumer prices, plant closures, rising operating and capital costs, the lack of subsidies, market failure, as well as a range of other issues. To be fair government policy decisions rarely please all stakeholders but whether these decisions are responsible for all business woes is debatable.

In Chapter 3 a number of differences between government and business were noted. The discussion also emphasized the need for business managers to understand fully these realities of government in order to become more effective managers. However, very few managers have had the opportunity to work in government and therefore their perceptions of government and how it works are rarely informed from a practical experience perspective.

Paradigms of Business-Government Relations

Jane Jacobs

Notwithstanding the frequently depicted view of business being subservient to government the relationship between the two has frequently been portrayed as adversarial. This relationship is perhaps better understood through a consideration of the different philosophies that prevail in both segments. The government segment upholds a *collectivist approach* – what is in the best interests of all stakeholders manifest in the people of Canada; an approach immediately at odds with the individualist approach taken by business that is concerned about what is in the best interests of business, or to be kinder – its key stakeholders. The government segment views itself as protectors of the public interest whereas business's interests are inherently private. The government segment is risk-averse as it uses taxpayers' money, the return on which is frequently nebulous at best, whereas to be innovative businesses are risk-takers: profit being seen as a reward for assuming a risk. Jane Jacobs described this difference in the form of two syndromes: the *Guardian Syndrome* and the *Commercial Syndrome*.[20] The Commercial Syndrome (a.k.a. the business segment) is characterized by "the shunning of force in favour of voluntary agreements, collaborating easily with strangers and aliens, using initiative and enterprise, respecting contracts, being open to inventiveness and novelty, efficiency, investment for productive purposes, industrious, thrifty, optimistic."[21] The Guardian Syndrome (a.k.a. the government segment) is characterized by "the shunning of trading, external prowess, being obedient and disciplined, adhering to tradition, respecting hierarchy and loyalty, and a willingness to take vengeance."[22]

---

20. Jane Jacobs, *Systems of Survival* (New York: Random House, 1992).
21. Ibid.
22. Ibid.

Notwithstanding the adversarial picture that results from the guardian versus the commercial paradigm, some writers perceive that Jacob's two syndromes are somewhat overdone and reflect "much misunderstanding about the paradoxical realities of modern society."[23]

W. T. Stanbury

Another paradigm of business-government relations has been advanced by W.T. Stanbury.[24] Stanbury examines the factors that prescribe the activities that occur in the public policy arena; he identifies five factors that affect business and eight factors that affect government. Those factors that significantly affect business include the nature of relations among business and its direct or primary stakeholders, the extent of government intervention in the sector, the degree to which government actions determine success or failure, the characteristics of members in the business interest group, and the perceptions of the public. Factors that affect how government conducts itself in the policy arena include the size of the government's majority; the regional distribution of seats in the legislature held by the government and the opposition; actions of other governments; the prevailing extent of government intervention instruments; the behaviour of the media; the legal and constitutional allocation of powers among the various levels of government; actions of the opposition parties; and public opinions, attitudes, and perceptions.[25] The Stanbury paradigm presents a portrait of industry-government relations which is similar to Jacob's two syndromes and which suggests that both parties are influenced by different factors and the influence of these factors will affect the ability of government and business to interact with one another. The result is public policy that results from a series of processes and influences.

Perhaps resulting from experience in the policy forum, industry and government frequently have differing perceptions of how they see themselves and how they are perceived. In a survey conducted by the Public Policy Forum involving government respondents and corporate respondents, government respondents saw themselves as open and responsive with industry representatives having impact on policies, but saw industry as lacking an understanding of government evidenced by submitting policy proposals that were anchored primarily in self-interest.[26] Corporate respondents, on the other hand, perceived their proposals were balanced and believed

---

23. Gilles Paquet and Jeffrey Roy, Governance in Canada – Competition, Cooperation and Co- evolution in Business-Government-Society Relations (Ottawa: Prime, 1997), 160.
24. W.T. Stanbury, *Business-Government Relations in Canada* (Toronto: Nelson, 1993).
25. Gilles Paquet and Jeffrey Roy, Governance in Canada – Competition, Cooperation and Co- evolution in Business-Government-Society Relations (Ottawa: Prime, 1997), 163.
26. *"Bridging Two Solitudes – A Discussion Paper on Federal Government-Industry Relations,"* Public Policy Forum, accessed June 19, 2013, https://www.toronto.ca/ext/digital_comm/inquiry/inquiry_site/cd/gg/add_pdf/77/Lobbyist_Registration/Electronic_Documents/Canada-Other_Provinces/Bridging_Two_Solitudes_report.pdf.

they understood how government works, but did not perceive they were adequately consulted by government nor did their interventions have any significant effect on government decisions.

It is therefore no surprise that the viewpoints of industry can be at odds with government, so how can business exert influence on government? What is the best way for business to deal with government?

Business Dealing With Government – Seven Fundamental Errors

This first step in business dealing with government is to avoid the seven fundamental errors that business typically makes.[27]

1. *Dealing always at the political level*. More often than not bureaucrats are the people who can help you, not politicians. Cabinet Ministers are very busy individuals with agendas typically filled for months in advance so the prospect of getting an appointment quickly is not promising. Cabinet Ministers are briefed by their departmental bureaucrats who frequently recommend whether the Minister should take the meeting or not and ultimately recommend the course of action on the issue to the Minister. If the issue is technical, parochial, anchored in existing policy requiring a policy interpretation, concerns only one business, and otherwise is not a strategic issue or an issue that would impact political issues, then meeting with a Minister is not even necessary or advised.

2. *Approaching the government at the wrong time*. On September 12th, 2001 the only issue of interest on the minds of politicians was national security. Regardless of how important a company's burning issue may have been on September 9th, the government's focus and agenda changed. While this is an extreme example, it demonstrates the importance of timing and this in turn requires knowing when the time is best. This requires knowledge and understanding of the government's agenda and priorities.

3. *Providing tome-like reports to politicians*. Politicians are on "information overload" just to keep up with legislative developments, Cabinet committee activities, and their responsibility to the government, their constituents and their political party – understanding all the details of an industry proposal is the responsibility of bureaucrats.

4. *Wading in on an issue after a policy is released to the public*. The best time to influence government is as soon as possible in the policy process. This argues for a very proactive approach to dealing with government. Once the issue is out in the public forum the government has made a commitment to its implementation.

---

27. D. Wayne Taylor, Allan A. Warrack, and Marck Baetz, *Business and Government in Canada Partners for the Future* (Canada: Prentice-Hall Canada, 1999).

5. *Assuming that influence is directly proportional to the size of the company.* While unquestionably a major corporate player would garner the interest of politicians more quickly than a small economic player, the pluralistic nature of the Canadian macro-environment means that the government must balance the interests of a large number of stakeholders, not just the interests of the largest.

6. *Using a disorganized, uncoordinated, and unprepared approach to dealing with government.* Going to the government and asking politicians or bureaucrats to do something is a bit like a student who requests that his or her professor re-grade his or her examination on the basis that "I deserve more marks." In dealing with government, business must offer options and informed solutions to its problem that government might consider, with full recognition that government must seek policy decisions that are good for stakeholders other than the business presenting the proposed policy or policy change. Such informed proposed solutions should be clearly anchored in government priorities and take a balanced approach: what is in it for the business *and* the sector *and* Canadians *and* the government?

7. *Reacting to government on an issue-by-issue basis.* Business must take a proactive approach to its relations with government, becoming well versed in government priorities and related policy directions, developing contacts, and making the time commitment to work with government on issues that may not be directly related to a company's immediate concerns. In this way a goodwill bank can be developed, and an understanding of government direction and priorities as well as the knowledge of which politicians and which bureaucrats are leading what policy initiatives can combine to form a very useful package of knowledge that can be used to increase government awareness of company issues. This also assists business in making operating decisions that will not be compromised due to being blindsided by a government policy.

Dealing with government or attempting to influence policy outcomes can be undertaken by business in a number of ways, direct lobbying being the most obvious and most frequent. Indirect lobbying activities such as advocacy advertising and funding think tanks, as well as using the media are three other activities that business could use to influence government.

Lobbying

"Ten people who speak make more noise than ten thousand who are silent."
(Napoleon, 1769-1821)

"The right to be heard does not automatically include the right to be taken seriously."
(Hubert Humphrey, 1911-1978)

From these quotes can be discerned two realities: 1) you must speak to be heard, and 2) that you speak does not necessarily mean you will be heard. Such is the practice of lobbying. Generally *lobbying* the government is exerting influence with a view to getting the government to do something your way, or not to do something someone else's way. Lobbying is typically directed at those who make policy decisions in an attempt to influence public policy. The policy issues and associated rules are increasingly complicated and a good lobbyist will assist his or her client in navigating through this terrain. What are the typical "asks" for which lobbyists lobby the government?

Joe Jordan of the BlueSky Strategies Group cites three types of asks of government through the lobbying process:

- Procurement (in excess of $13 billion per year on goods and services);
- Freebies (grants and contributions); and,
- Policy (most common and most complicated).

Regarding policy Jordan proposes there are four types of "rules," each having its own challenge.[28]

Policy Rule	Context	Key Challenge
Good Rules	The rule is acceptable but the interpretation is not.	Getting the government to interpret the rule differently.
Bad Rules	The existing rule is not acceptable.	Getting the government to drop the rule.
New Rules	You are proposing a new rule.	Getting the government to adopt the new rule.
Sad Rules	The current rule is obsolete and must be changed.	Getting the government to change the rule.

As a demonstration of the increasing complexity of government policy, Jordan cites the following example:

Document	Number of Words
Pythagorean Theorem	24
Gettysburg Address	286
Declaration of Independence	1,300
Charter of Rights and Freedoms	2,609
Regulations on the Sale of Cabbage	26,911

---

28. Joe Jordan, Senior Associate, interview with author, July 2019.

The author recently interviewed Joe Jordan to provide perspective on his work as a lobbyist. Here is a portion of the interview – a practitioner's perspective.[29]

A Practitioner's Perspective: An Interview with the Hon. Joe Jordan, The BlueSky Strategy Group

The Hon. Joe Jordan is a Senior Associate with the BlueSky Strategy Group where he develops and implements government-relations strategies at the provincial, federal, and international level. He has been a Member of Parliament (Leeds Grenville) for seven years, served as Parliamentary Secretary to a Prime Minister as well as to the President of the Treasury Board, and has served as the Director of Parliamentary Affairs with the Treasury Board Secretariat.

Canadian Business and Society: *How would you describe lobbying?*

Joe Jordan: I use a legal analogy. The legal system is complicated, confusing and the implications of getting it wrong can be significant. If they come in contact with this system, business will generally engage the services of a lawyer. A lobbyist performs much the same function, when a business has issues with government rules or regulations.

Canadian Business and Society: *How important is lobbying in influencing government?*

Joe Jordan: I think we need to dispel the notion that lobbyist have the capacity to get government to act in a manner that is opposed to its interests. From my experience, the most important function that the lobby sector performs is the identification of unintended consequences to proposed government action. Globalization and technology have fundamentally changed the nature of business and governments need to be sensitive to the implications that domestic action have on competitiveness. The relationship between business and government is one of the principal determining factors in the performance of our economy and the quality of our society. Politicians, bureaucrats, entrepreneurs and citizens all have a vested interest in this relationship functioning at as high a level as possible.

Canadian Business and Society: *Would you agree that the business-government relationship is adversarial?*

---

29. Joe Jordan, Senior Associate, interview with author, July 2019.

Contributed by Joe Jordan. © Kendall Hunt Publishing Company

Joe Jordan: It really shouldn't be, but the problem is that we only hear about the disagreements. The vast majority of decisions are made in a timely and cooperative way. Governing is about balancing interests and there is no clear right or wrong in these grey areas. The business community likes predictability and consistency and governments constantly struggle with this.

Canadian Business and Society: *Has the Lobbying Act strengthened or weakened the business-government relationship?*

Joe Jordan: I would say that it has weakened the relationship. There is a common thread of negativity that runs through the regulations, in addition to a significant paper burden. The danger is that government decision-makers will avoid contact with industry and that kind of vacuum is not good news for Canadians.

Canadian Business and Society: *Could you describe the most successful lobbying effort you have been responsible for and what made it successful?*

Joe Jordan: My biggest success to date was the lobbying effort that I prevented! I was contacted by an American association that was ready to launch a Canadian initiative.

They were operating under the false assumption that their messaging and techniques were seamlessly transferable and after much effort I managed to convince them to re-visit their basic assumptions and they pulled their campaign.

Canadian Business and Society: *What makes a successful advocacy advertising campaign?*

Joe Jordan: The most effective ones have a clear and consistent message, are based on facts, move the bar, and everyone thinks that they won.

Canadian Business and Society: *How effective are think-tanks in influencing public policy?*

Joe Jordan: The can be extremely influential. It really depends on the leadership style of the government. The real value is in supporting government as it makes decisions involving complex issues that are devoid of political interests. As soon as we mix any politics into the equation empirical analysis and facts get pushed to the back burner in a hurry.

Canadian Business and Society: *How does lobbying in Canada differ from lobbying in the United States?*

Joe Jordan: It certainly costs a lot less up here! The basic difference is that every elected official is potentially a legislator in the American system. There are infinite ways into the machine but there is also a bigger monitoring component. In the Canadian system we can focus on the governments, as the opposition role is generally restricted to a challenge function

Canadian Business and Society: *In your view how could lobbying in Canada be improved?*

Joe Jordan: We certainly don't need any more rules, as Canada currently has the toughest regulations anywhere in the world. I think that greater clarity around what constitutes registerable activity and removing the requirement for compensation would help simplify the application of the Lobby Act. The industry could also do a better job of defining the role of the sector.

The Federal Accountability Act and the Lobbying Act

The Federal Accountability Act has recently re-defined lobbying as "any oral or written communication made to a public office holder," and defines a public office holder as:

(a) "a minister of the Crown or a minister of state and any person in his or her office who is appointed under subsection 128(1) of the Public Service Employment Act,
(b) any other public office holder who, in a department within the meaning of paragraph (a), (a.1) or (d) of the definition of "department" in Section 2 of the Financial Administration Act,
  (i) occupies the senior executive position, whether by title of deputy minister, chief executive officer or by some other title, or
  (ii) is an associate deputy minister or an assistant deputy minister or occupies a position of comparable rank, and
(c) any individual who occupies a position that has been designated by regulation under paragraph 12(c.1)."[30]

The Federal Accountability Act included important changes to the *Lobbyist Registration Act*. In addition to changing the name to *The Lobbying Act*, other changes included the establishment of a New Commissioner on Lobbying as an independent agent of parliament, the concept of a Designated Public Office Holder (DPOH), requiring the monthly disclosure by lobbyists of certain lobbying activities, prohibiting a DPOH from registering and lobbying the Government of Canada for five years after leaving office, banning any payment or other benefit contingent upon

---

30. "The Lobbying Act (R.S.C., 1985, c. 44 (4ᵗʰ Supp.))," Justice Laws Website, date modified: 2019- 06-26, https://laws-lois.justice.gc.ca/eng/acts/l-12.4/FullText.html, accessed July 17, 2019.

the outcome of any activity performed by a consultant lobbyist, and doubling the monetary penalties for lobbyists found guilty of breaching the requirements of *The Lobbying Act*.[31] The need for lobbyists to register is intended to ensure transparency, the logic being that if citizens, lobby groups, and public office holders are aware of who is lobbying whom then everyone will know who is trying to influence public policy outcomes.[32]

TABLE 13

Some Current Lobbying Statistics

New registrations, by fiscal year							
Fiscal year	2012-13	2013-14	2014-15	2015-16	2016-17	2017-18	2018-19
New registrations	996	1,162	1,229	1,279	2,091	2,050	2,143
New registrations	996	1,162	1,229	1,279	2,091	2,050	2,143
Change year-on-year	-11.5%	16.7%	5.8%	4.1%	63.5%	60.3%	2.5%
Change compared to 2012-13	n/a	16.7%	23.4%	28.4%	109.9%	105.8%	115.2%
Change compared to 2009-10	-36.1%	-25.5%	-21.2%	-18.0%	34.1%	31.5%	37.5%

TABLE 14

Some Current Lobbying Statistics

Type of Lobbyist	Active Lobbyists (2013)	Active Lobbyists (2018)
Consultant lobbyists	783	1,408
In-house lobbyists (Corporations)	1,861	2,167
In-house lobbyists (Organizations)	2,612	3,244
Totals	5,256	6,819

As is evident from the tables above, *The Lobbying Act* identifies three types of lobbyists. *Consultant lobbyists* are consultants who are paid to lobby on behalf of clients. They may be consultants in public relations or in marketing or lawyers, notaries, engineers, or accountants whose functions include lobbying. *In-house lobbyists (corporations)* and *in- house lobbyists (organizations)* are salaried employees of either corporations or non- profit organizations who lobby on behalf of their employer.

The Office of the Commissioner of Lobbying of Canada cites Ten Things You Should Know about Lobbying – a Practical Guide for Federal Public Office Holders:

1. Lobbying is Legitimate
2. The Lobbying Act

---

31. "The Lobbyists' Code of Conduct," Office of the Commissioner of Lobbying of Canada, date modified: 2019-04-08, https://lobbycanada.gc.ca/eic/site/012.nsf/eng/h_01185.html.
32. Annual Reports, Office of the Commissioner of Lobbying of Canada, date modified: 2017-06-07, https://lobbycanada.gc.ca/eic/site/012.nsf/eng/h_00019.html, accessed July 17, 2019.

3. The Lobbyists' Code of Conduct
4. What is Lobbying?
5. Two Types of Lobbyists – Consultants and In-House Lobbyists
6. Public Office Holders (POHs) and Designated Public Office Holders (DPOHs)
7. Designated Public Office Holders and the Five-Year Prohibition on Lobbying
8. The Role of the Commissioner on Lobbying
9. The Registry of Lobbyists
10. Compliance Does Not Always Require Registration[33]

Lobbying Approaches

In its simplest form lobbying can be direct or indirect. *Direct lobbying* occurs through formal and informal meetings, submission of briefs and policy papers, appearances before parliamentary committees, telephone calls, written mail, e-mail, petitions, alliance and coalition building, organization of protests and demonstration, and litigation.[34] *Indirect lobbying* occurs when the intention is to shape policy ideas as differentiated from attempting to influence decision-makers directly. Indirect lobbying can involve such techniques as advocacy advertising and funding think-tanks. These approaches will be discussed later in the chapter.

Classifying Lobbying Issues - Strategic vs. Operational

The simplest approach to categorize lobbying issues is to differentiate between strategic issues and operational issues. Paquet and Roy differentiate these issues as follows:

Strategic Issues	Operational Issues
Offer broad policy direction	Offer detailed application
Affect corporate existence	Affect part of a corporation
Reflect attitudes, values	Mainly technical issues
Public	Private
Invite media attention	Exclude media
Top-down decisions	Bottom-up decisions
Legislative/parliament	Regulatory/bureaucracy
Proactive	Reactive

TABLE 15

Strategic Issues versus Operational Issues

Strategic issues involve the public resolution of broad policy issues requiring the incorporation of public opinion and generally involving a change in public policy

---

33. "Ten Things You Should Know About Lobbying, A Practical Guide for Federal Public Office Holders," Office of the Commissioner of Lobbying of Canada, date modified: 2012-11-30, https://lobbycanada.gc.ca/eic/site/012.nsf/eng/00403.html.
34. W.T. Stanbury, *Business-Government Relations in Canada* (Nelson: Toronto, 1993).

through legislation, whereas *operational issues* are comparatively technical and generally can be resolved without the need for public input.

Bartha's Issue Selection Paradigm

Another approach to classifying public policy issues has been advanced by Peter F. Bartha, who suggests that issues can be of four types:

- *universal issues* are broadly-felt issues characterized by a visible problem having a direct impact and for which the government needs a solution;

- *advocacy issues* are issues of potential concern that might have an indirect and/or future impact and that require a complex solution;
- *selective issues* affect a specific group and have generalized implications; and
- *technical issues* are characterized as somewhat abstract and remote, and of which the public is largely unaware.[35]

What Do Lobbyists Do?

The best lobbyists take a proactive approach in dealing with government on behalf of their clients or their organization in order to prepare their clients to lobby the government. This approach requires that the lobbyist:

1. Be informed of emerging and evolving legislation affecting their client(s);
2. Be aware of the positions of all key players in the issue (other businesses, other sectors, civil society) as well as public opinion;
3. Be credible and well connected with government contacts at the appropriate levels;
4. Understand the issue from the perspective of the client and the government, be able to position the client's issue on the government's agenda, and be able to provide strategic advice on developing possible alternate solutions that reflect the pluralistic reality of the macro-environment such that the solution the client prefers demonstrates salience for the government as well as the client;
5. Understand the public policy process and the lobbying process; and
6. Prepare the client to lobby, not lobby on behalf of the client.

How Lobbyists Lobby – Developing a Lobbying Strategy

Any attempt to influence public policy requires the development of a strategy and strict observation of the mantra, "prepare, prepare, prepare." There is no substitute for being fully prepared! There are several steps in developing a lobbying strategy.

---

35. P. F. Bartha, *"Managing corporate external relationships,"* in *Business Can Succeed!*, ed. J.D. Fleck and I.A. Litvak, (Toronto: Gage, 1984).

Framing the issue – Strategic or operational or a combination of both. This requires a comprehensive understanding of the issue from the perspective of the organization and the government. It is at this point that the lobbyist must be able to clearly position the issue on the government's policy agenda and clearly articulate how following the course of action suggested by the organization will provide benefits to the organization, the government, and many of the government's stakeholders. The lobbyist must also be cognizant of where the issue would fit in the legislative cycle and the political cycle. Issues will have different salience if the government is in a majority or minority situation.

The issue's salience in the industry sector – Is this issue important only to your firm or does it resonate well with other key players in your industry sector? Have others lobbied for this cause in the past (with whom, what approach, what was the outcome)? Could you collaborate with competitors, suppliers and other primary stakeholders to enhance the "clout" of your influence?

Whom to lobby? – Politicians, bureaucrats, the media, agencies and associations, special interest groups or some combination of all of these potential targets. The decision would be driven by the nature of the issue – strategic vs. operational; universal-advocacy- selective-technical.

Which lobbying approach? – Direct or indirect? Quiet diplomacy or a more "public" approach?

How long will your lobby run? – Timing is key in lobbying and it is essential to bring the right information to the right people at the right time. Timing the lobby properly will take time, and of course your perception of time may not be the same as the government's!

What resources will you need? – Resources can take many forms – people, organizations/collaborators, and financial. The more complex the issue, the more time and resources that will be needed.

Develop a contingency plan – As with resources, contingency has many constituents. A change in government, a sudden change in policy direction, a change in ministers (i.e. a Cabinet shuffle), a change in bureaucrats – all combine to cause risk and uncertainty for which the lobby must be prepared. Another important "what if" scenario includes the outcome of an unsuccessful lobby – if you are unsuccessful, then what?

Advocacy Advertising

A type of indirect lobbying, *advocacy advertising* involves selling an idea as opposed to a product or service. Stanbury defines advocacy advertising as "any kind of paid public communication or message, from an identified source and in a conventional medium of public advertising, which represents information or a point of view bearing on a publicly recognized controversial issue."[36] The ultimate objective of advocacy advertising is to influence public opinion and public policy on an issue of importance to the advertiser. Stanbury identifies five main target audiences of advocacy advertising:

- Stakeholders
- Politicians and public servant advisors
- Media influencers
- Influential intellectual leaders
- The politically aware with influence.[37]

Advocacy advertising may occur through a number of print and visual conduits such as, for example, newspaper, radio, and television. Most carriers will have standards that dictate the acceptability of advocacy advertisements. For example the Canadian Code of Advertising Standards includes strict advertising standards in which advocacy advertising is clearly defined: "any message that advocates a point of view or particular course of action on issues of public interest or concern," and are subject to restrictions noted in its published advertising standards and programming policies.[38]

Some examples of advocacy advertising campaigns include Ontario Chiropractors' Extended Health Care Patient Advocacy campaign, Health Canada's Heather Crowe story[39], and the Quebec "Buckle Up" campaign[40].

Think Tanks

A *think-tank* has been defined as "an organization or group of experts researching and advising on issues of society, science, technology, industry, or business."[41] Referred to by some writers as "policy institutes" or "think factories", a think-tank has also been contextualized as an "institute, corporation, or group organized for interdisciplinary research, usually conducted for governmental and commercial

---

36. W.T. Stanbury, in Readings and Canadian Cases in Business, Government and Society, ed. M.C.Baetz (Canada: Nelson, 1993).
37. W.T. Stanbury, in Readings and Canadian Cases in Business, Government and Society, ed. M.C. Baetz (Canada: Nelson, 1993).
38. AdStandards, "The Canadian Code of Advertising Standards", https://adstandards.ca/wp-content/uploads/2018/11/Canadian-Code-of-Advertising-Standards.pdf, accessed July 17, 2019.
39. "The Power of One Tragedy: The Heather Crowe Story," Smoke-free.ca, accessed June 20, 2013, https://www.cpha.ca/fighting-good-fight-heather-crowe
40. Société de l'assurance automobile Quebec, " Awareness Campaigns 2018 Seat Belt Campaign", https://saaq.gouv.qc.ca/en/saaq/awareness-campaigns/2018-seats-belt-campaign/, accessed July 17, 2019.
41. Merriam-Webster, "think tank", https://www.merriam-webster.com/dictionary/think%20tank, accessed July 17, 2019.

clients. Projects for government clients often involve social policy planning and national defense.

Think tanks are not-for-profit and non-partisan institutions which focus on policy, intellectual and ideological missions, striving to:

- Complement mainstream media coverage,
- Conduct independent research and produce technical reports
- Advocate on public policy with evidence-based argument, and
- Advise government, business and political parties.[42]

Commercial projects include developing and testing new technologies and new products. Funding sources include endowments, contracts, private donations, and sales of reports." Extracting the basic themes from these and other definitions proposed, Elliot, Hicks, and Finsel have found that think-tanks display commonalities in that they are typically independent, non-profit, and designed to affect the policy process through the creation and dissemination of scholarly research.[43]

The output of think-tanks is frequently used by government in informing public policy and as such think-tank participants have an important opportunity to indirectly lobby government using persuasive academic collaborations to have their views on issues of public policy recognized by government, such views perhaps otherwise not achieving the same degree of policy-maker scrutiny if advanced as an individual or as a company's platform.

In the United States, the Brookings Institution was considered to be the "Think Tank of the Year" in 2018.[44] The top twenty Think Tanks worldwide as rated by the University of Pennsylvania are:

Ranking	Think Tank	Country
1	French Institute of International Relations	France
2	Bruegel	Belgium
3	Chatham House	United Kingdom
4	International Institute for Strategic Studies	United Kingdom
5	Korea Development Institute	Republic of Korea

---

42. Carleton University, Macodrum Library, " Think Tanks", https://library.carleton.ca/find/news/think-tanks, accessed July 18, 2019.

43. William Elliot, Sarah Hicks and Christy Finsel, "Think Tank Typologies: Which Typology Best Fits with the Mission and Core Values of NCAI Policy Research Center", National Congress of American Indians (November 2005).

44. University of Pennsylvania Scholarly Commons, "TTCSP 2018 Global Go To Think Tank Index Report", https://repository.upenn.edu/cgi/viewcontent.cgi?article=1017&context=think_tanks, accessed July 18, 2019.

Ranking	Think Tank	Country
6	Danish Institute for International Studies	Denmark
7	Fundação Getulio Vargas	Brazil
8	Centre for European Policy Studies	Belgium
9	China Institutes of Contemporary International Relations	China
10	Japan Institute of International Affairs	Japan
11	Konrad Adenauer Foundation	Germany
12	Friedrich Ebert Foundation	Germany
13	Carnegie Endowment for International Peace Middle East Center	Lebanon
14	Clingendael, Netherlands Institute of International Relations	Netherlands
15	Asian Development Bank Institute	Japan
16	Fraser Institute	Canada
17	Amnesty International	United Kingdom
18	Stockholm International Peace Research Institute	Sweden
19	Stiftung Wissenschaft und Politik	Germany
20	Transparency International	Germany

Three types of think-tanks have been distinguished – *academic, contract, and advocacy* and their distinguishing characteristics are given in the table below.[45]

TABLE 16

Distinguishing Characteristics of Think Tanks

TYPE OF THINK TANK	FUNDING PARADIGM	HOW AGENDA IS SET	NATURE OF RESEARCH
Academic	Endowments, grants, organizations, private individuals	Researchers play a large role	Idea-driven; long-term, future oriented. Disinterested. Distribute social science research findings to serve all humanity
Contract	Primarily government contracts	Government needs	Driven by government contractor needs; long-term future-oriented but findings distributed primarily to contract authority
Advocacy	Constituents play a significant role	Driven by ideology	Short-term focus; ideologically driven research with findings distributed to constituents

While think-tanks represent a relatively recent concept their increasing use in public policy is due to several factors. First, policy issues are increasing in complexity due to globalization, cross-cultural demographic changes, and information technology advances, among other things. Secondly, in order to derive the most

45. William Elliot, Sarah Hicks and Christy Finsel, "Think Tank Typologies: Which Typology Best Fits with the Mission and Core Values of NCAI Policy Research Center", National Congress of American Indians (November 2005): 15.

palatable public policy that appeases the interests and wants of most stakeholders, all segments of the Canadian domestic macro-environment must make a full knowledge contribution. Third, think-tanks do not represent a threat to media and policy suggestions put forward by think-tanks can be relayed by the media as non-partisan and non-political, offering a greater perception of inclusion and objectivity. Fourth, think-tanks result in the development of networks for leaders with cross-disciplinary interests and responsibilities.

Business's Influence on Civil Society

Business influences civil society in a number of ways. First, as with government, business provides considerable financial resources in the form of donations, and non- financial resources in the form of equipment and software that would otherwise be unaffordable by the third sector. Second, business often encourages its employees to participate with civil society both formally and informally, offering paid volunteer days – a source of workers. Third, through interacting with civil society, business transfers knowledge and know-how to those third sector persons and organizations with which it works. Fourth, business can assist in developing networking opportunities for the third sector as senior business executives can open doors not always available to volunteers and other members of this segment.

It is also important to note that influence can be positive and negative. While business can provide several opportunities for members of the third sector, it is likely also to contribute to a number of the challenges including, for example, mission drift to follow the resources as well as reporting requirements.

Government's Influence on Business

In Chapter 3, it was noted that Senator Forsey has demonstrated through his writings how involved the government is with almost every aspect of life. There are those who would prefer that government not be involved with the affairs of business and citizens, arguing that market forces will ultimately optimize everything from price to social responsibility. Others perceive the government is not sufficiently involved in areas where more government influence would improve quality of life. One thing that has become obvious over the years is that whenever a catastrophic failure has occurred (Enron, Bre-X, WorldCom, Exxon Valdez, BP oil spill) it is the government that ultimately gets blamed for not exercising sufficient control through its public policy to protect the public interest.

Government Instruments

Notwithstanding where one falls on the issue of the appropriate level of government intervention it is not surprising that the government has several instruments at its disposal with which to influence public policy outcomes. This section will consider a number of the more important government instruments.

Government instruments are tools government can use to influence business and society in order to advance public policy. Some include:

- Developing laws and regulations
- Implementing taxes, subsidies, user fees, loans, and public expenditures
- Public ownership through crown corporations and other corporate interests
- Self-regulation of industries and professions
- Encouraging voluntary action and the development of standards
- Performance-based regulation
- Contracts and procurement
- Insurance schemes
- Encouraging formalized partnerships and informal networks.[46]

As the above list demonstrates, while laws and regulation remain important instruments, other options are possible and often preferred. In Canada the *Cabinet Directive on Law-Making* states that statutes and regulations should only be used when they are deemed to be the most appropriate instrument. Government increasingly favours an approach that combines instruments to improve Canadian industrial competitiveness and quality of life for Canadians. Treasury Board Secretariat, in its 2007 publication, *Assessing, Selecting, and Implementing Instruments for Government Action* directs government officials to consider how different instruments can be used together to achieve public policy outcomes that are risk-based, balanced, consultative, and in the public's best interest.

The several instruments available to government also demonstrate varying degrees of coercion in the sense of government involvement. Self-regulation would be the least intrusive whereas public ownership would demonstrate the greatest degree of government influence. In Canada the government is increasingly changing the focus of government instruments to be results-based, favouring a movement away from force-fitting any existing approach and incorporating new approaches to stimulate innovation in achieving policy outcomes. Stimulating innovation in the government can be difficult for a number of reasons. First, to innovate requires taking risks and the institution of government, while making strides toward taking

---

46. "Assessing, Selecting, and Implementing Instruments for Government Action," Treasury Board of Canada Secretariat (2007), https://www.tbs-sct.gc.ca/rtrap-parfa/asses-eval/asses-eval-eng.pdf, 3, accessed July 18, 2019.

measured and sensible risks is nonetheless a comparatively risk-adverse institution due in part to the political consequences of taking correct risks with taxpayers' money that yield less than optimal results. Secondly, the nature and complexity of the problems that government would need to resolve could involve significant risks with consequences that affect entire groups of key stakeholders. Nonetheless it is sensible to anchor the selection of a policy instrument in a thorough risk analysis that is part of a broader decision framework. Treasury Board Secretariat encourages the use of an analytical framework in their selection.

The selection of government instruments is a complex process. The use of a framework leads to better policy outcomes because, in addition to risk analysis, instrument selection is a result of increased transparency, stakeholder engagement, and the selection of performance indicators.

The starting point for this analytical framework is framing the problem for which a policy solution is sought. This means clearly understanding, defining and articulating the problem in its correct policy and political context. The problems that governments are required to solve are very complex and typically do not lend themselves to a quick solution, nor a solution that will please every stakeholder. As well, a government solution to a problem is future-focused: it is unlikely that any government instrument can change what has already happened. It is therefore necessary to fully understand what has caused the problem, as well as the major issues and the risks. If the problem cannot be framed correctly, any resulting policy supported by any range of government instruments will be ineffective and perhaps cause more harm than good.

With the problem defined and properly framed it is necessary to determine the goals and desired outcomes of the policy. A desired outcome could be viewed as the "benefit" to be achieved for Canadians. Policy goals are much broader than outcomes. For example a policy goal might be to decrease unemployment and a corresponding outcome might be to reduce the number of persons on unemployment insurance by twelve percent over the next three years. Note that there can be several outcomes associated with each policy goal.

The next step in the framework is concerned with when the government intervention would occur to maximize its effectiveness. Recognizing that government would typically take a longer-term perspective, certain government instruments can be put into play relatively quickly (such as tax reductions through a federal budget) while others would take longer (such as public ownership and laws). Often the choice of instrument will depend on perceived urgency and the risk associated with a longer time frame. For example the financial meltdown in late 2008 provoked many governments around the world to make quick and unprecedented direct financial investments in their economies to bolster economic strength and consumer confidence in the face of a recession. These actions ranged from significant financial bailouts of key industries such as the automotive sector, to purchasing and/or guaranteeing higher risk mortgages from banks, and in some cases, government taking ownership of the bank. In these cases the government's assessment of risk was such that its actions to use taxpayers' funds to bolster the economy were risk-justified to mitigate the threat of a complete economic failure that would adversely impact everyone.

Identifying key stakeholders is frequently difficult for the government because everyone is a government stakeholder at some level. Nonetheless it is possible and necessary to identify those stakeholders who should be involved in addressing the issue that the policy is intended to resolve. These key stakeholders would come from business, other levels of government, and civil society who can offer an informed perspective based on their respective areas of expertise. Note carefully that this stage implies consultation with groups closest to the issue; however, this does not imply that this would be the only level of consultation. Key stakeholders would include those who would be either directly or indirectly affected by the policy, as well as those who could collaborate in delivering the solution as a partner with government.

The following step involves assessing and selecting the instruments to use in the achievement of the policy objectives. Treasury Board Secretariat suggests that there are several considerations in assessing and selecting government instruments. First, the selected instrument must be effective in achieving the policy objective. Second, the instrument must be legal and within the government's authority to put in place. Next, the instrument must ensure behavioural change on the part of those constituents whom it is intended to influence, although coercion is not necessarily the preferred approach depending upon whether continued action would result in permanent and/or critical harm to Canadians or the environment. Fourth, the instrument must be expected to produce net social benefits. Fifth, the consequence of implementing the instrument must be perceived as fair insofar as its effect on the constituents affected across the country. Next, the instrument must lend itself to transparency and the ability of the government to show clearly how it has worked to resolve the issue in the best interests of Canadians.

Performance indicators are essential for the government to know that the policy and the instruments used in support of the policy are working as intended and resolving the problem. Performance indicators allow the government to evaluate the efficiency and effectiveness of its solution to the problem and can be qualitative, quantitative or a combination of both. A good performance indicator will offer an accurate representation of the result, provide a credible, independent view, and will be reliable, valid, complete, and cost-effective.

After the government instruments have been put in place and sufficient time has elapsed, it is necessary to evaluate the effectiveness of the government's solution to the problem. Does the problem still exist or has it changed? Is the policy still relevant? Do the instruments still work? Answers to these questions and others can lead to a refinement of the original problem or the definition of a new problem that would start the cycle again.

Government deals with an ever-changing, fluid environment where difficult issues arise frequently and nothing stays the same for very long. This calls for ongoing environmental scanning and continuous validation of policies and the government instruments used to bring about good policy outcomes for all Canadians.

Government Regulation

In terms of government's influence on business and society, regulation is the most frequently encountered and intuitive. *Regulation* is defined by Treasury Board Secretariat of Canada as "government intervention through a set of rules identifying permissible and impermissible activity on the part of individuals, firms, or government departments and agencies, along with accompanying sanctions and rewards."[47] Put differently, regulations are a form of law made by Cabinet, a minister or an administrative agency that typically set out rules that apply generally, as opposed to specific groups or individuals, and are intended to change behaviour. The Government of Canada's regulatory activities are intended to result in "the greatest overall benefit to current and future generations of Canadians."[48] In regulating the federal government seeks to:

- Protect and advance the public interest
- Promote a fair and competitive market economy
- Make decisions based on hard evidence and the best available knowledge
- Create regulation that is accessible, understandable and responsive
- Advance the efficiency and effectiveness of regulation
- Require timeliness, policy coherence, and minimal duplication.[49]

An example of regulation is in the area of genetically modified (GM) food – foods derived from biotechnology, considered to be 'novel foods' and regulated by Health Canada. Seven to ten years is necessary to research, develop, test, and assess the safety of a new GM food. Any manufacturer wishing to advertise or sell GM food in Canada must submit data to Health Canada who will assess and provide assur-

47. "Assessing, Selecting, and Implementing Instruments for Government Action," Treasury Board of Canada Secretariat (2007), https://www.tbs-sct.gc.ca/rtrap-parfa/asses-eval/asses-eval-eng.pdf, 4, accessed July 18, 2019.
48. "*Cabinet Directive on Streamlining Regulation*", Treasury Board of Canada Secretariat, (2007): 1, accessed June 20, 2013, http://publications.gc.ca/site/eng/309288/publication.html
49. "*Cabinet Directive on Streamlining Regulation*", Treasury Board of Canada Secretariat, (2007): 1, accessed June 20, 2013, http://publications.gc.ca/site/eng/309288/publication.html

ance of its safety. Key federal departments and agencies involved in the regulatory process include the Treasury Board of Canada Secretariat, the Department of Justice Canada, and the Privy Council Office. Government regulation is an area in which there is considerable debate in terms of whether it is good or bad, how much regulation is necessary, and how any type of government regulation in the marketplace can be positive in a market economy.

In addition to economic regulation the government is also involved in social and cultural regulation. These parameters of regulation will now be considered.

Pros and Cons of Government Economic Regulation

Whether government economic regulation is positive or negative generally depends on perspective. Whereas the government's perspective is one of collectivism in that its interest is to maximize benefits for the greatest number of constituents, business's perspective is more one of self-interest anchored to the profit motive and the need to maximize the wealth of its shareholders to ensure a stable capital investment base.

Several arguments have been advanced in support of economic regulation. Proponents would argue that such regulation has controlled monopolies, price discrimination, and other "market failures," prevented the exploitation of renewable resources, reduced the speed of economic change, and protected individuals from making bad economic decisions. Opponents would argue that economic regulation creates obstacles to growth, prosperity and innovation; increases costs to business in complying with regulations that are ultimately borne by consumers and not commensurate with the associated benefits; increases the costs to taxpayers in the form of the administrative burden associated with funding and operating the regulatory agencies; causes the loss of businesses that are unable to function economically within the tangled web of regulations; and acts as a disincentive for foreign firms interested in locating in Canada.

Social and Cultural Regulation

Social and cultural regulation is intended to achieve non-economic public policy outcomes that are in the best interests of the public, and typically concerns product or service attributes and/or information disclosure. Social and cultural regulation would be found in such areas as environmental conservation, the protection of human rights, health and safety, cultural content, and language. Among other things proponents of such regulation would argue that it has improved the quality of life for minorities and the elderly, provided a safer working environment by reducing the number of industrial accidents, provoked a more environmentally-conscious industrial sector, and protected civil liberties. While these claims cannot be denied, as with economic regulation, social and cultural regulation comes at a cost that is typically borne by companies as well as taxpayers.

Deregulation

A discussion on government regulation is not complete without considering *deregulation* a deliberate decision of government to reduce its regulatory regime in certain industries. The intent of deregulation is to improve profitability, encourage competition, and stimulate innovation by removing government influence; in other words, to counter many of the arguments against regulation. While this move undoubtedly pleases those who argue against regulation some writers suggest that deregulation is nothing more than the government bowing to the pressure of business who, in the pursuit of profit, has the most to gain at the expense of ordinary citizens who will inherit a more risky product, service, and social environment, and who will not necessarily benefit from reductions in the prices of products and services.

Other Forms of Government Influence on Business

Regulation is one way in which government directly influences business. There are, however, several other ways through which the government can directly or indirectly exert influence on the business segment. Three such ways are procurement, taxation, and government ownership.

Government Procurement

The government is a major customer of business. Federal government procurement means the acquisition of goods and services by contract. The goods and services may be off-the-shelf, an adaptation of an existing product/solution, or a unique government development.[50] Public Services and Procurement Canada is generally the government buyer on behalf of the federal government, although departments frequently procure their supplies and services directly. The Government of Canada purchases more than $18 billion of goods and services annually.[51] Therefore government has enormous potential to influence business through its procurement activities. Supplying the government with items such as office supplies and stationary, means filling massive orders: governments do not buy pens one at a time, but rather by the trailer load. This opportunity, however, also holds some risks for companies that become overly dependent on the government as the major or sole supplier of revenue in the purchase of a company's goods or services. Changes in government procurement policy can have disastrous effects on a company for whom the government is its largest or sole customer.

50. "Contracting Policy," Treasury Board of Canada Secretariat, date modified: 2012-08-16, http://www.tbs-sct.gc.ca/pol/doc-eng.aspx?id=14494&section=text

51. "2016 Purchasing Activity Report," Treasury Board of Canada Secretariat, date modified: 2018-05-16, https://www.canada.ca/en/treasury-board-secretariat/corporate/reports/contracting-data/2016-purchasing-activity-report.html, accessed July 18, 2019.

Supplying the government also requires time and patience. The contracting process is complicated and technical, and many firms employ specialists to deal with these complexities. Nonetheless once a government contract has been secured, the contractor does not have to be concerned with the contractee's ability to pay. In addition to the volume of purchases the government can influence product and service quality requirements and even create new markets for the supply of technical components.

Tax Policy and Subsidies

The government can influence business through changes in *tax policy*. For example modifications to income tax regulation can encourage investment in some activities and discourage investment in others. Decisions to make certain costs tax deductible from income can have a profound impact on the activities of the business segment. Allowing certain costs relating to research and development to be deductible from income but disallowing the costs of the overhead and administration relating to the research and development may detrimentally affect the amount of research and development undertaken. The deductibility of operating expenses is one aspect of tax policy; others include capital cost allowance policy and policies on tax credits.

A *subsidy* can be thought of as either the direct transfer of cash to a recipient or the indirect transfer of benefits. Subsidies can increase either the supply of a product or service, or the demand for the product or service, with the appropriate effect on product or service pricing and as such will affect competition. Subsidies are frequently made available to agriculture, fishing, housing and transportation industries. According to the Fraser Institute Canadians has paid out almost $684 billion in subsidies to private sector business, government business enterprises, and consumers since 1981.[52] The annual per-taxpayer cost of these subsidies has ranged from an annual high of $3,268 in 1984 to a low of $797 in 1998.[53]

Government Ownership

The most intrusive form of government influence is through direct or indirect government ownership of organizations that provide goods and services that arguably could also be provided by privately owned firms. The Government of Canada encompasses 159 Federal Organizations and 99 additional Corporate Interests.[54] Apart from the 21 Ministerial Government Departments there are several forms of federal government institutions including:

- 50 Departmental Agencies (e.g. Canada Space Agency);

---

52. Fraser Institute, "Government subsidies in Canadian: A $684 Bill Price Tag", published June 2014, https://www.fraserinstitute.org/sites/default/files/government-subsidies-in-canada-a-684-billion-price-tag(1).pdf, accessed July 18, 2019.
53. Ibid.
54. Government of Canada, "The Government at a Glance", https://www.tbs-sct.gc.ca/ems-sgd/edb-

- 45 Crown Corporations (e.g. Canada Post Corporation);
- 15 Departmental Corporations, including Canada Border Services Agency;
- 12 Special Operating Agencies, including the Canadian Coast Guard;
- 7 Parliamentary Entities, including the House of Commons;
- 6 Agents of Parliament, including the Office of the Auditor General; and
- 3 Service Agencies.[55]

Outside the federal government structure, the federal government has an interest in and/or participates in the oversight of other institutions referred to as Other Corporate Interests of Canada.[56] The table below shows the nature of these other interests.

TABLE 17

Other Corporate
Interests of
Canada

Other Corporate Interests	Description	Number in 2018
Mixed Enterprises	Corporate entities with shared ownership split between the Government of Canada and private sector	0
Joint Enterprises	Corporate entities with shared ownership split between the Government of Canada and another level of government e.g., The Lower Churchill Development Corporation Limited	2
International Organizations	Corporate entities created pursuant to international agreements in which the Government of Canada either owns shares or has the right to appoint members to the governing body e.g., International Monetary Fund	15
Shared Governance Corporations	Corporate entities without share capital in which the Government of Canada has the right to appoint members to the governing body and includes airport and port authorities	82

Crown Corporations

The dominant form of government ownership is the *crown corporation* defined by Treasury Board Canada Secretariat as "government organizations that operate following a private sector model but usually have a mixture of commercial and public policy objectives."[57] They are created through either an Act of Parliament or through articles of incorporation filed under the *Canada Business Corporations Act*. Crown cor-

bdd/index-eng.html#partition/org_info_by_ministry/org_info, accessed July 18, 2019.

55. Government of Canada, "The Government at a Glance", https://www.tbs-sct.gc.ca/ems-sgd/edb-bdd/index-eng.html#partition/org_info_by_ministry/org_info, accessed July 18, 2019.

56. "Overview of Institutional Forms and Definitions," Treasury Board of Canada Secretariat, date modified: 2013-03-05, https://www.canada.ca/en/treasury-board-secretariat/services/reporting-government-spending/inventory-government-organizations/overview-institutional-forms-definitions.html, accessed July 18, 2019.

57. Government of Canada, "Overview of federal organization and interests", https://www.canada.ca/en/treasury-board-secretariat/services/reporting-government-spending/inventory-government-organizations/overview-institutional-forms-definitions.html, accessed July 18, 2019.

porations typically operate at arm's length from the government with government exerting control through financing and appointing boards of directors. In Canada, crown corporations are operated both by provincial and federal governments and are involved in a range of product and service delivery.

In some instances services provided by crown corporations can compete directly with private sector enterprises as in the case of automobile insurance in some provinces.

Clearly the ownership by government of organizations that produce similar goods or services also on offer by the private sector can have an adverse effect on free market prices and could also discourage private sector firms from entering into the market. In recent years government has dissolved several government owned enterprises and turned them back to the private sector. The privatization of Air Canada, the Canadian National Railway, Teleglobe, Telus, and PetroCanada provide some relatively recent examples.

Civil Society's Influence

There is a certain amount of intuition regarding industry-government relations and how each segment influences and is influenced by the other. What is not so immediately obvious is that the civil society segment can also exert influence. Earlier in this book the 'currency' of the third segment has been described as 'goodwill' and the sorting mechanisms or the forces at play that describe how the segment operates are the imprecise mechanisms of networks, norms, trust, collaboration, and reciprocity. Given these vague sorting mechanisms it might be easier at first blush to perceive members of this third segment to be more 'takers' on the agendas of government and business. Yet this segment wields tremendous power in its ability to influence both government and business.

The Role of Civil Society

In their working paper on how civil society organizations use evidence to influence policy processes, Pollard and Court (2005) propose that Civil Society Organizations have three main objectives: to inspire, to inform, and to improve.[58] Regardless of the size and complexity of civil society organizations it is fair to extrapolate these objectives to all of civil society. These objectives dovetail well with Najam's proposed key roles for civil society organizations.[59]

---

58. Amy Pollard and Julius Court, "How Civil Society Organizations Use Evidence to Influence Policy Processes: A Literature Review," (working Paper 249 for the Overseas Development Institute, London, UK , July 2005). 59. A. Najam, "Citizen organizations as policy entrepreneurs," in *International perspectives in voluntary action: reshaping the third sector*, ed. D. Lewis, (London: Earthscan, 1999).

- Monitoring through which policy is kept "honest"
- Advocacy through which policy options can be supported or not supported
- Innovator through which different ways of doing things are developed and demonstrated
- Service provider through which a particular need is fulfilled
- Capacity builder through which support is provided to other civil society organizations

While meeting its objectives and assuming its roles are not small feats for civil society there are a number of drivers in the socio-economy that legitimize key policy roles for this important segment of the Canadian macro-environment. First, an increasingly culturally diverse Canadian population introduces new demands on civil society organizations, both domestically and internationally. Domestically in the type of issues to be supported, and internationally in that the plight and interest of other countries and cultures are made more visible. Secondly, information communication technologies enable civil society to bring attention to its causes almost instantaneously. Thirdly business stakeholders expect business to be involved with civil society in the same way that government stakeholders expect government to engage with civil society in matters of public policy. Finally and most importantly the issues faced by business, government, and civil society today are sufficiently complex to require a full knowledge contribution by all three segments of the Canadian macro-environment. Given these changes civil society has become essential to the effective operation of business and government and is positioned to influence both segments in many ways.

Civil Society's Tool Chest

Civil society can influence business and government both in supportive ways as well as in ways that provoke greater responsibility from each of these segments in their operations. Whether civil society is influencing business or government it has a number of tools at its disposal.

Publishing in print or on-line media, or social networks

Civil society organizations can undertake the writing of reports, research studies, and policy critiques with the intention of inspiring interest in the issue, informing citizens of an issue and business or government's position on the issue, and improving the instrument, whether a government policy or a proposed course of action to be undertaken by a firm or an industry.

Lobbying

Civil society can publicly lobby a government, industry, or individual business for changes in a proposed course of action whether through direct or indirect lobbying, or through advocacy advertising as a means of increasing public interest in the matter.

Media campaigns

When launching a media campaign through which to increase public interest, either through print media, television media, or on-line media, the media has a special responsibility in society – "serving the people's right to know about issues important to the fabric of society" and the amount of media coverage afforded an issue should be directly proportional to the significance to society of the issue.[60] Given civil society's role as the voice of society and the generator of trust and collaboration, a third sector unsympathetic to a public policy position or a strategic business decision can wreak public havoc. For example, on June 24, 2010, Greenpeace's website featured a story entitled "Greenpeace calls on the G8 and G20 to keep their promise to end fossil fuel subsidies" citing $100 billion annually that G-8 and G-20 leaders give to "polluting oil giants like BP and tar sands producers."

Demonstrations and protests

Civil society can organize demonstrations and peaceful (or not so peaceful) protests that serve to bring public attention to the issue at hand.

Apart from the more obvious ways that civil society can influence business and government that tend to suggest a combative approach to relations, there are numerous positive influences. For example, the adversarial relationship that tends to prevail between business and government relations frequently requires the use of a trusted *neutral broker* and civil society serves this need very well. Partnerships between industry and government can often be facilitated when a third segment organization is asked to deliver a service or program of strategic interest to both industry and government.

Volunteering and Canvassing

Civil society as a segment includes people and organizations with important knowledge and skills that may not always be available in sufficient quantity in government and business organizations. Volunteering and canvassing for financial and in-kind support requires the ability to work in cross-cultural and multidisciplinary teams without the expectation of personal financial reward. These highly developed interpersonal and empathetic skills can be knowledge transferred from civil society and can be invaluable to both government and business segments in their efforts to connect with key stakeholders.

---

60. David P. Baron, *Business and Its Environment,* Fifth Edition (New Jersey: Pearson Prentice Hall, USA, 2006), 71.

People

Third sector organizations make use of individuals with professional skills and can represent a source of workers for business and government.

Notwithstanding government and business's efforts to involve their stakeholders strategically in operations and policy matters it is often difficult to reach the right stakeholders at the right time for the right reasons. Members of the third segment, by the nature of their work and sorting mechanisms, are much closer to stakeholders, possess an intimate knowledge of the community, and can often provide a more reliable view of stakeholder interests in matters of strategic importance to both government and business.

Volunteerism

Civil society also assists business and government through its volunteer activities that can often bolster program delivery and stakeholder engagement. As well civil society organizations present a venue through which citizens can get involved and work to shape society and to improve social and community well-being – essential for the effective operation of business and government.

Networks

Readers will recall from the discussion of the output of the civil society segment that social capital – the networks, norms and understandings that facilitate cooperative activities within and among groups of individuals - is essential for the effective operation of business and government.[61] Civil society both generates and uses social capital and brokering bonds of trust between organizations and individuals engaged in different manners of philanthropy through social capital facilitates improvement in literacy and learning, recreation programs, assistance to immigrant families, and protection of the natural environment, all of which combine to improve the quality of life in communities.

Social Media and Community

Most Canadians are sympathetic toward civil society organizations as the purpose of these organizations is generally to improve society and quality of life as opposed to generating profits or votes. One of the influences civil society has on business and government is its ability to assist both segments in building their image as well as buffering the media.

Given the increasing complexity and emerging trends of Canada's civil society, meeting the needs of civil society is increasingly becoming part of the responsi-

---

61. John F Helliwell, "Social Capital, the Economy and Well-Being," *The Review of Economic Performance and Social Capital Progress* (2001).

bilities of both business and government. To engage in an increasingly diverse community, to navigate through previously uncharted social territory, and to ensure value for money for taxpayers and shareholders requires new models of community engagement and these models will emerge from the third segment offering alternative service delivery methods.

Advertising

Cause-related marketing refers to a style of marketing in which a profit seeking entity cooperates with a civil society organization in providing a specific donation each time its product or service is used. An example is the American Express Company's donation of a penny toward the restoration of the Statue of Liberty in New York each time the American Express Card was used. Civil society can avail themselves of cause-related marketing opportunities to generate funds but also to influence a firm's philanthropic investments through the positive publicity that can be generated for the firm in working with third segment organizations.

Awareness

Civil society can also help business and government to build awareness of issues that the other segments need to put in the public arena. Civil society has the opportunity to help form and position the issue if it is ultimately to support it.

Another important way in which civil society can influence government and business is in their approach to implementing the ultimate policy decisions of government and industry. In policy matters that directly affect society it is frequently civil society organizations that make the policy real and tangible, And in helping the "rubber hit the road" on policy issues, civil society can exert an important influence on the meaning of the policy and the way in which it will be implemented. In civil society's implementation of policy the segment can also provide important feedback on where improvements are needed and as a result can provoke subsequent changes to policies.

Information Dissemination

Civil society is also the distributor of information through information and communication technology means such as, for example, the Internet. As such third segment organizations can represent important points of entry for citizens to engage in policy debates and through which information from other third segment groups can be packaged. This affords the third segment with another way of influencing business and government – to the extent that business and government wishes to have its policy and practices presented as supported by key stakeholders both the policy and the messaging can be influenced by the third segment.

Chapter Summary

Collaboration is essential in the creation of economic and social value that is driven by the development and application of knowledge. The increasing complexity of both economic and social issues means that no one entity can "go it alone" and full knowledge contributions must be made from each domestic macro-environment segment. An important example of collaboration is the public-private partnership. A public-private partnership involves the bringing together of the skills and assets of each segment – a melding of the business economic acumen of the private sector with the constitutional authority of the public sector. There are many different styles of P3s that generally involve the delivery of service or infrastructure that government must provide under its constitutional obligations and a transfer of risk to the private sector.

Business working together with government has most frequently been described as an adversarial relationship. Business is seen as taking a self-interested individualistic approach on public policy issues while government must take a collectivist approach and adopt public policy that is in the best interests of a much broader range of stakeholders. There are differences in how business perceives government and how government perceives business and these differences contribute to errors business can make in dealing with government. Lobbying has been defined by the *Lobbying Act* as any oral or written communication made to a public office holder. Lobbying represents an approach available to business through which to influence public policy. There are three types of lobbyists in Canada – consultant, in-house (corporations), and in-house (organizations) and all must be registered with the Government of Canada. Lobbying can be undertaken directly or indirectly and lobbying issues can be strategic or operational. An effective lobbyist takes a pro-active approach in dealing with government and typically prepares, coaches, and advises his or her clients, developing a clear lobbying strategy anchored around the lobbyist's understanding of the government's policy agenda, among other things. Advocacy advertising is a form of indirect lobbying that involves selling an idea as opposed to a product or service. Think-tanks are organizations that engage in the creation and dissemination of non-partisan, objective, and disinterested scholarly research that can inform public process. The funding of think-tanks is another example of indirect lobbying. Think-tanks can be considered as being of three types: academic, contract, and advocacy differentiated by how they are funded, governance, and the nature of research undertaken. Business has a significant effect on the third sector through the provision of funds, knowledge transfer, and network development.

The government wields considerable influence over business and society through a range of government instruments intended to bring about public policy outcomes thought to be in the best interest of society. Government instruments can be portrayed as representing a continuum over which the degree of government influence varies from very little influence, as in the case of self-regulation, to total influence as in the case of direct public ownership in the form of crown corporations. In determining which government instruments are most appropriate to deal with public policy issues, the government employs an analytical framework that encourages the selection of instruments that are risk-based, balanced, consultative, and in the public's best interest. Among the better known forms of government influence is regulation which can take the form of economic or social and cultural regulation. There are many arguments for and against regulation. In recent years there has been a move toward de-regulation – a conscious move by government to reduce its regulatory regime in certain industries, thought to result in greater competition, price reductions, and greater innovation. The government also influences business through procurement and contracting as well as with tax policy.

Mixed and joint enterprises, international organizations, and shared governance corporations comprise other corporate interests of the Government of Canada.

Any action by the government to influence the activities of business and civil society is of utmost importance. The range of government instruments available can affect business markets, competition, operations, and profitability. Moreover, actions by the government to influence business behaviour can have an impact for years into the future hence it is essential for business and civil society to take a pro-active approach to monitoring government actions to influence and to engage in all public policy debate forums where the issue will have a measurable effect on operations. This engagement and involvement is what the government prefers in order to develop more effective public policy that will be reflective of stakeholders' points of views.

Civil society is an important segment in the Canadian domestic macro-environment. While frequently perceived as a passive taker on the margins of government and business strategy, as society and its issues increase in complexity the third segment has taken on a renewed importance and its involvement in business and government is now critical to successful outcomes in both of the other segments. It is important to note that civil society can represent a source of new ideas, intellectual capital, and a conduit through which favourable public opinion on business and government can emerge. However, at the same time this segment can bring unwanted public profile to issues it feels adversely affect civil society. As such the third segment is a critical stakeholder for both business and government.

End of Chapter Questions

1. Explain how collaboration generates economic and social value added.

2. What are the key drivers of public-private partnerships?

3. What are the advantages and disadvantages of public-private partnerships?

4. How does Jane Jacobs view business-government relations? Would you agree?

5. Which of Stanbury's factors affecting government would have the greatest impact on business-government relations in a minority government situation? Support your answer.

6. Discuss the errors frequently made by business dealing with government and indicate why these errors could be fatal with respect to business's desired outcome.

7. What is lobbying? How has the *Federal Accountability Act* changed the lobbying activity in Canada?

8. Compare and contrast a strategic lobbying issue from an operational lobbying issue. Give two examples of each type of issue and clearly indicate why they are strategic or operational.

9. What is advocacy advertising and why is it considered a form of indirect lobbying? Why do media organizations have standards for advocacy advertising?

10. What is a think-tank? Differentiate between three types of think tanks. In your view, which type of think-tank provides the best public policy advice? Support your position.

11. Discuss how business can influence civil society.

12. Give an example of a government instrument and indicate how it could be used by government to achieve a public policy outcome.

13. What are the arguments for and against regulation? In your view is regulation good or bad for Canada?

14. Give a brief description of "mixed enterprises," "joint enterprises," "international organizations," and "shared governance corporations." In your view is it acceptable that the government holds ownership in these types of enterprises?

15. What is a crown corporation? Why does the government establish crown corporations?

16. Explain the ways in which civil society can influence business and government.

Application Questions

Referring to the opening news article, discuss the following:

1. What is the nature of the collaboration suggested by CAPP?

2. Who are the key stakeholders?

3. Explain the influence and role(s) played by CAPP.

4. Suppose CAPP wishes to lobby the provincial government to work together with the energy industry in implementing CAPP's Competitive Policy and Regulatory Framework. Develop a lobbying strategy that would meet CAPP's objective.

5. What government instruments could be used by the government of Alberta in encouraging the energy industry to collaborate?

Research Questions

1. Select any Canadian think-tank of your choice and using the Internet and other sources, determine whether this think-tank would most closely resemble either an academic, contract, or advocacy think-tank. Fully support your answer.

2. Using the Internet and other sources compare and contrast Jane Jacob's two syndromes paradigm with W.T. Stanbury's paradigm of business-government relations.

3. Using the Internet and other sources select an advocacy advertising campaign and identify:

    a. why this would be classified as an advocacy advertising campaign;

    b. who were the key targets;

    c. who were the key stakeholders;

    d. what was the outcome; and

    e. how it could have been improved.

4. Using the Lobbyist Register on the Internet, select any lobbyist or lobbying firm of your choice and prepare a description of their lobbying activities. Be certain to identify the type of lobbyist you have selected.

Team Discussion Questions

1. Using the Internet and other sources of information comment on any regulatory reform initiatives the current government has underway or is planning. How will these reforms affect business-government relations in Canada?

2. Using the Internet and other sources of information compare and contrast any two crown corporations in Canada, and discuss why the government would establish the two enterprises you have selected, instead of leaving the provision of the goods or services provided by these corporation to private sector interests.

CHAPTER 9

Business, Government, and Civil Society: In the Beginning

beeboys/Shutterstock.com

Written and researched by Cindi J. Delcorde, MBA

In the Beginning

Time for a look back... throughout this text we've considered many theories and notions regarding the three elements of Boulding's triangle - business, government and civil society. But where did this complex relationship begin?

Canada as a chunk of earth is very old – thousands upon thousands of years. No one can be entirely certain as to when this vast landscape was first populated by human beings. The aboriginal or First Nations people who probably first populated what is now Canada arrived perhaps as long as thirty thousand years ago via the land bridge connecting Asia to North America's most northerly point. These First Nations people occupied the Plains and the Boreal Forest regions, living in small groups as hunter/gatherers. Perhaps they would meet periodically to share or trade items amongst themselves. But the existence or concepts of what we consider "business" today probably didn't exist at that time. These groups of people would have governed themselves and recognized a power structure within their society and respective groups. But much of life would have been centered on that which was required to survive.

The Norse or Vikings left clear signs of a settlement at L'Anse aux Meadows located in what is today Newfoundland. This historic site has been a UNESCO World Heritage site since 1978 and is thought to be the earliest European settlement in the New World.[1] These Norsemen, and women, would have come seeking riches, and would have found an abundance of timber, wild game and fish. All of which are commodities that Canada would be exploiting for many years to come. The Norse too would have functioned with a form of government and their business at home was primarily agricultural, and largely trade-oriented abroad.

Europeans stumbled on Canada's land-mass while seeking a passage to the Orient and the many riches that were believed to held there. The Portuguese and Spaniards traveled to the New World landing south of what is now Canada. John Cabot, an Italian explorer, arrived in Newfoundland in the late 1400s. And some years later, the French arrived to establish an outpost. The arrival of Samuel de Champlain in the early 1600s was indicative of the French outreach as explorers who came with a view to bring home goods to trade, and to acquire land for the French monarchy. The British had established themselves further south in New England and the French brought business, government, and the church to the more northerly parts of North America. Later the British would show an interest in the resources of Canada, particularly in the fish stocks, and well the rest of that story is history.

Business - Small Business, the Workforce, and Business Owners

In the beginning how was business defined? When did business start? What was the first business? A business transaction can be defined as an activity involving the voluntary exchange between parties where the objective is to realize a profit, or an increase in wealth.

---

1. "L'Anse aux Meadows National Historic Site of Canada," Parks Canada, date modified: 2011- 11-15, https://www.pc.gc.ca/en/lhn-nhs/nl/meadows/index

Five thousand years ago ancient Middle Eastern markets would have centred primarily on agricultural goods and livestock, later expanding to include mined products such as tin and copper, and some manufactured products such as basketry, jewelry and clothing. Keith Roberts in his book, *The Origins of Business, Money and Markets*, notes that business itself has been around for thousands of years. Probably first beginning with the trade of slaves as tribal leaders recognized that they could make a profit in the trade of human beings.[2] This concept of trading goods or services to make a profit took hold and has persisted throughout the history of western civilization.

Of course it is quite likely that slaves made up a substantial part of the workforce for other going concerns, particularly farming and the planting of crops. Women and children would have made up a large part of the labour force, as men were often needed for defense. Feudalism, prominent in northern Europe during the late Middle Ages, would recognize slave workers and serfdom, a condition that would tie an individual to the land and thus obligated the serf to work for the land owner, gender notwithstanding. Other members of the workforce might have been wage earners, perhaps skilled artisans for instance. Members of religious houses were active contributors to the labour force as the church played a significant role as a manufacture of goods, particularly agricultural products and cloth.

It's also likely that the original business owners were the governing leaders of the community at the time. Thus the interrelationship between government and business would not have existed in the same sense that we see today. Often power and wealth were concentrated in the hands of a few individuals. And it was those powerful citizens that led communities, villages or towns, and owned the land that was the primary source of goods. Over time this would alter as the configuration of governing would evolve.

Government – Structure, Challenges, and Issues

Chieftains and tribal councils were probably the first ways that people governed themselves. Great leaders throughout history often had military backgrounds or military support for their leadership. Many Roman emperors were military leaders first. The Roman Empire governed most of the European landscape before 400 CE and experienced many challenges, including a shift in the role of the military, and the legitimacy of the emperorship, as there was no provision for orderly succession. Additionally, the Roman Empire was faced with many economic challenges, including an imbalance in trade, shortage of currency, and inflation. Infrastructure presented challenges where the provision of clean water and func-

2. Keith Roberts, *Origins of Business, Money and Markets* (New York: Columbia University Press, 2011), 5.

tional roadways became difficult to maintain.[3] Any or all of these issues may have contributed to the ultimate fall of the Roman Empire itself.

Early kings were originally "elected" by community members. Often they were those individuals with some higher standing amongst the local population. Over time, kingship became hereditary, and governments functioned under the leadership of the monarch. Formal legal systems evolved and were integrated with governance structures creating administrations to support monarchs in the governing of their kingdoms. Parliament has its origins in revolution. A concept with its origins embedded in the Magna Carta of 1215, it was the actions of the English Barons in the 13th century that created a permanent council that evolved to be called "parliament". Not quite what we are accustomed to as our modern day parliament, this council served the purpose of initiating administrative methodologies for how laws and government would function, and it was this English parliament that would evolve into our familiar institution of representative government.

Civil Society - Form and Function

Earlier in the text we defined organizations in civil society as "…as any organizations that are independent of business and government and that cannot be classified as part of the business or government segments… voluntary and civic organizations, non-profits, and philanthropic organizations, unions, academia, hospitals, and human rights organizations just to suggest a few."

The methods employed by individuals and communities for the provision of education have taken many forms throughout history. Universities, as we know them, emerged from the Catholic schools of the Middle Ages, and were largely driven by the demand of the new merchant class who wanted to educate their children. Education, particularly in the field of law, was seen by many as a way of rising in society. As merchants acquired wealth, they wanted to provide an education for their sons in particular to facilitate a better future for them and to ensure a legacy for the family.

During the Crusades, the Hospitalers and Knights Templar established orders that took vows of poverty and chastity and cared for the sick and injured and provided protection for travellers. The first hospital in Canada was established by Jeanne Mance, a French woman who was successful in persuading the wealthy to finance this philanthropic endeavour.

Social reform in Canada was active and somewhat extreme by our modern standards in the pre-confederation days. Poverty was a very real issue in the mid- 1800s, while the

3. John M. Riddle, *A History of the Middle Ages* (Lanham: Rowman & Littlefield Publishers Inc., 2008), 29.

country struggled with the consequences of the Industrial Revolution and the many changes it wrought in the colonial economy. Social policy was a mix of private and public initiatives, and included almshouses, hospitals, poor or "work" houses, and asylums. Privately, the church and ethnic organizations provided assistance to the poor.

The union movement began in earnest with the Industrial Revolution, introducing a significant stakeholder and a key player in the balance of power between business and government. The Winnipeg General Strike of 1919, which resulted from social tensions and conditions in post-WWI Canada, is an example of how the union movement influenced Canadian history.

Commonalities

The three segments presented in this book share certain aspects, as discussed throughout the text. Historically, these commonalities have persisted.

Stakeholders, globalization, multiculturalism, lobbying, concepts of social responsibility and ethical behaviour existed in the past and presented some of the same challenges as they do today.

Stakeholders

Stakeholders of business, governments, and organizations within civil society are represented by the people who interact with these bodies. The European population of Canada in 1605 was 44 persons living at Port Royal.[4] By the mid 1800s, that population had grown to over 2,000,000, and it was beginning in this time period that we see the modern categories of business, government and civil society, in the form of charities, interacting in Canada.

Prior to this time period in Europe, the people, not just the wealthy, but also the poor and working classes, wanted to have a say in how leaders governed. The Peasants' Revolt in the 1300s demonstrated this boldly as the peasant classes in Flanders and subsequently in England demonstrated violently against the burdens of taxation.[5] The rise of a "middle class" and the business-man during the 14th and 15th centuries created a new group of stakeholders that would continue to exist and influence governments, business, and charitable organizations.

---

4. "Estimated population of Canada, 1605 to present," Statistics Canada, date modified: 2013-03- 20, https://www150.statcan.gc.ca/n1/pub/98-187-x/4151287-eng.htm
5. Riddle, 413.

Globalization

Migration and transportation involving the distribution of people and things, first by water or land, have been undertaken by groups since the first individual began to explore the lands outside of the Fertile Crescent. Roads were built by the Roman armies to move supplies and men. The Vikings were master shipbuilders, using shallow hulled boats to transverse the many rivers of northern and central Europe to explore and establish trade routes.

Prior to the invention of the steam engine, oxen and then horses were used to move goods to markets over land. Shipping of goods and movement of people were further facilitated as bigger boats and ships, and nautical and navigational advances evolved.

In Chapter 6 we defined globalization as a multinational collaboration in the creation of business, political, and social wealth by maximizing the unique knowledge contributions of nations and cultures worldwide in developing a better living standard for all nations. What prompts effort towards globalization? Historically, people have sought collaboration (although perhaps they didn't call it that at the time) in search of wealth in the form of goods or land. Another reason to seek the assistance of another group is the need to flee a bad situation, perhaps as the result of disease or tyranny.

Culture and Multiculturalism

The Roman Empire spanned much of the known world in the 4th century. Roman soldiers would have intermingled with many ethnic groups and assimilated many as Roman communities and "villas" were established throughout Europe and Northern Africa.

The Vikings likewise transferred their Nordic culture and belief systems during their own travels, initially travelling east through Eastern Europe and into Russia, and then moving westward into England. "Rus" is thought to be an old Norse word meaning "men who row"- perhaps a reference to the seafaring Scandinavians who arrived the medieval Russia.

First contact doesn't always end well. The Portuguese and Spanish were responsible for the demise of many North American tribes, inadvertently introducing disease, or in some instances simply taking advantage of a gentle people who practiced a very different way of life. The French were responsible for the near extinction of the Huron people of Canada. Subjected to smallpox and measles their population was diminished significantly in the 1600s. Further, as the survivors became more closely allied with the French fur traders, the aboriginal people became more dependent on their would-be benefactors.

Irish world immigration prompted by famines of the 1800s in Europe would change the Canadian landscape forever. Between 1825 and 1845, at least 450,000 Irish landed in Canada.[6] The population of Upper Canada, Lower Canada, New Brunswick, Nova Scotia, and Newfoundland in 1851 was approximately 2.4 million people.[7] We can surmise that 1 in 5 were Irish who brought with them culture, religion, language, and other aspects of their uniqueness.

Corporate Social Responsibility

The concept of corporate social responsibility was first coined in William J. Bowen's 1953 publication *Social Responsibilities of the Businessman*.[8] Earlier theories were developed by J.M. Clark in 1916, Theodore Kreps in 1930 and Peter Drucker in 1942. All these ideas centred on the ideal that businessmen should be aware of their actions and the consequences of their business engagements. The concept that there is a linkage between the power that a business holds and the social obligations of the business's owners or leaders apparently is not new, but perhaps has become more widely known and accepted with the advent of media and the use of technology and social media formats.

Ethics

Determination of what is ethical behaviour is largely culturally defined. Proper behaviour is often defined by the time period itself. What was considered acceptable in pre-Christian Rome, 12th century England or 17th century British-North America will vary widely.

The birth of the Protestant church could be considered the beginning of a change in how people saw their position in the world in relation to God as well as other people. Before the Reformation, morality was largely governed by the Catholic Church. Popular religious movements dictating proper and acceptable behaviour of men, women, and children were prominent in the 1800s, and how business was conducted or government policy was formed would have been influenced by the common views professed by such practitioners.

Lobbying

The intent of lobbying activities is to influence those in power. Early governments based in kingship invited lobbying as cases were presented for decision in halls of

6. Riddle, 266.
7. "Estimated population of Canada, 1605 to present," Statistics Canada, date modified: 2013-03- 20, https://www150.statcan.gc.ca/n1/pub/98-187-x/4151287-eng.htm.
8. "Corporate Social Responsibility (CSR) - the society responsibility of companies," Reset For A Better World, accessed June 26, 2013, http://in.reset.org/knowledge/corporate-social-responsibility-csr-%E2%80%93-societal-responsibility-companies

justice regularly held for this purpose. These are the bases for our modern day court system. Royal courtiers actively vied for positions at the royal court to gain employment in the royal retinue, but also to be close to the reigning monarch in order to be better positioned to influence decisions.

In pre-confederation Canada, newspapers and journalists often fulfilled this role, expressing the views of the public and providing an educational role in support of responsible and representative government.

Early Interactions of the Three Segments

Recognizing that business, government and civil society organizations evolved at different times and under varying circumstances, when did government, business and civil society first come together?

The devastating effect of the black plague that struck Europe in mid-1300s decimated the population and reduced the available labour force to perhaps less than half of what it had been. The consequences of this singular event were to change how business was conducted, how governments reacted to economic crises and the need for law and order, and prompted religious houses to offer solace and refuge to those in need on a scale never before required.

Feudalism would collapse. Manorial land-owners could no longer demand that labourers remain bound to the land. Serfdom could not continue as individuals, who had previously been legally tied to the land, could now demand wages in return for their labour. Land owners were forced to change their business models, and in many cases adopted new farming methods or shifted from crops to animal husbandry.

Government was required to respond to economic crises, including inflation, and issues with trade. Civil security and maintenance of law and order were a priority and also a challenge, as soldiers were also in short supply.

Interrelationships of the "sorting mechanisms" introduced in Chapter 1 can be seen in this initial "collision" of the three segments. Shifts in the supply and demand of goods and services, government efforts to re-establish a stable economy and a balance of trade to compensate for losses in domestic markets, and the church offering solace through monasteries and nunneries all came together after the plague. Unfortunately, many of those who died were those who offered care to the sick and dying.

In part, the plague was a catalyst for change in the societal structure and a transition from one era to another. Altered class definitions prompted a desire for greater education and shift in labour markets. The subsequent movement away from a highly agrarian dependent society to an industrialized society was followed by a shift to democratic governing bodies where educated commoners served as administrators taking the place of hereditary aristocratic ruling class members - a legacy that continues to be visible today in Canadian business in its social context.

Last Thoughts

Let us consider for a moment what event or occurrences throughout our collective history have had the greatest impact on the relationship between the three sectors – business, government and civil society.

Perhaps it could be argued that the invention of the printing press had the greatest influence on our society in general, as it was with this 'invention' the general population gained the ability to understand and disseminate information more readily. While direct economic benefit is difficult to measure, it has been suggested that the growth of cities can be directly attributed to the advent of the printing press.[9] Dittmar notes that "cities that adopted print media benefitted from positive spillovers in human capital accumulation and technological change…"[10] The ability to share information on such a wide scale had never before been experienced. The ability to disseminate information over shorter distances with greater speed, as well as the new requirement for greater face-to-face communication among those who benefited from that shared information would create a synergistic effect that blossomed and multiplied.

Shared information began to cross demographic and cultural divides. The transmission of ideas would now infiltrate minds of the many. The Renaissance was born, and along with it a whole new segment of the population – the merchant class. Education would become more widely accessible and with it questioning minds would challenge old ideas. Universities would produce greater numbers of graduates who would become the doctors, lawyers, and administrators. Politics would become the realm of the 'everyman'. Religion would be debated – and challenged.

The printing press represented a revolution in information technology that would only be seconded by the advent of the Internet and social media.

9. Jeremiah Dittmar, "Information technology and economic change: The impact of the printing press", VOX, 11 February 2011, https://voxeu.org/article/information-technology-and-economic-change-impact-printing-press, accessed July 22, 2019.
10. Jeremiah Dittmar, "Information technology and economic change: The impact of the printing press", VOX, 11 February 2011, https://voxeu.org/article/information-technology-and-economic-change-impact-printing-press, accessed July 22, 2019.

Social media

Facebook, Twitter, Instagram, Snapchat surrounds us and have become integral to our functioning. The BBC conducted a survey which found that three billion people (approx. 40% of the world's population) use social media, spending approximately two hours every day online.[11] While social media may affect our overall well-being having been linked by some researchers to anxiety, stress, depression, and disturbing our sleep patterns, just think for a minute what has social media done to our world. [12]

What business can survive without considering the use of social media as part of its marketing campaign? What 3rd sector organization could risk not using social media as part of their campaign to get out their message? Consider the use of social media by governments today – and what the impact is on privacy, confidentiality and reliability of the information published.

The Government of Canada has multiple Facebook pages. Provincial and Municipal governments as well rely on social media to communicate with their constituents. Political parties use social media as campaign tools.

Businesses must have a Facebook presence to complement their web pages, and they must have a team of communications support specialists to respond *quickly* to customer inquiries.

Charities must also be able and willing to compete for the news byte. This is a promotional platform and opportunity that cannot be ignored.

But what does this mean for the citizen, the consumer or the supporter. It means that we are swamped with information. Information that is moving so fast and in such quantity that is it hard to keep up with the pace. But it also means that we as consumers of information have choices – many choices; as well as responsibilities.

Virtually anyone can be a reporter, a publisher, an author or a commentator. As responsible citizens, consumers, supporters it is our responsibility to be diligent and considerate in confirming sources of information, and to use the data wisely.

This is a historical revolution of huge proportion – perhaps greater than that precipitated by the invention of the printing press. Only time will tell.

---

11. BBC, "Is social media bad for you? The evidence and the unknowns", http://www.bbc.com/future/story/20180104-is-social-media-bad-for-you-the-evidence-and-the-unknowns, accessed July 22, 2019.
12. BBC, "Is social media bad for you? The evidence and the unknowns", http://www.bbc.com/future/story/20180104-is-social-media-bad-for-you-the-evidence-and-the-unknowns, accessed July 22, 2019.

Team Discussion Question

Compare and contrast the impact of the invention of the printing press on the relationship between business, government and civil society, with the impact of the recent explosion of the use of social media on this relationship.

In your response address which event, in your view, has presented the greatest opportunity, threat, and/or risk to the relationship between the three segments?

CPSIA information can be obtained
at www.ICGtesting.com
Printed in the USA
BVHW011413150820
586366BV00001B/2

9 781792 400957